Sociological Thinking:
An Introduction

ANDOVER COLLEGE

John T. Pullinger

Sociological Thinking:
An Introduction

ISBN 1-903-499-44-5
978-1-903499-44-3

Printed and bound in the United Kingdom by
4edge Ltd, 7a Eldon Way Industrial Estate, Hockley, Essex, SS5 4AD.

Contents

Chapter 6   Research Methods   **125**

Chapter 7   Power and Politics   **157**

To my wife Suzanne, who was always there during hard times.

In memory of my uncle, Dr J D Marshall, who was an inspiration to us all.

Sociological Thinking - An Introduction

Preface

The author has approached this work with the aim of providing a manageable length and accessible introduction to sociology. This text concentrates more heavily than conventional texts on developing the psychological and intellectual qualities that are necessary to effectively approach the subject. It is pitched at GCE A Level and is aimed at the sociology student or general reader who is looking for an alternative to the standard texts.

The text is different to the latter in that, as the title suggests, it focuses more on guiding the reader into thinking sociologically than providing a comprehensive grounding in the academic content of the subject. The idea for this type of text originated from a perceived need for such an alternative in teaching Access to Higher Education students and is modelled on an approach that has been applied successfully in working with such groups.

The approach adopted by the author guides the reader to develop a critical and open-minded outlook on society. With this aim in mind, readers are led to examine and deconstruct their preconceptions about society and reconstruct an understanding through the reflective use of sociological concepts and theories.

Based on this approach, the text caters for the following needs of sociology students and the general reader. It:

offers an inroad into the subject at an introductory level which makes no assumptions about prior knowledge in the subject;

guides students / the reader through the process of breaking down preconceptions on the way that they view society and their own lives;

leads the reader into appreciating the challenges that sociological thinking poses;

provides a clear introduction to sociological concepts and theories and offers a challenging learning curve in constructing sociological approaches and insights.

This volume concentrates on guiding the reader to raise essential questions about society and use sociology to develop reflective insights. It does not aim to be comprehensive in terms of academic content or breadth within the topic areas covered.

Instead, the work focuses more on the task of guiding the reader in the development of intellectual qualities necessary to think sociologically. To assist this process, the approach adopted in the text:

introduces the terrain of the subject and alerts the reader to a range of challenges that it offers (Chapter 1);

prefaces each chapter with an abstract to orientate the reader to the forthcoming chapter content;

starts chapters by highlighting typical preconceptions that need to be confronted in making a successful transition from layperson to sociologist;

guides this transition by developing sociological understanding of social phenomena.

Definitions of key terms are integrated into the text to help the reader acquire a sound conceptual grounding in the subject. A historical chronology is built into each of the chapters two to eight to assist the reader in acquiring a feel for historical developments in the subject. Each chapter can be approached independently but the text also takes the form of a building process. For example, contemporary theory is briefly introduced toward the end of chapter two. It is then built on at the end of each topic chapter three to eight and taken to a more detailed level in chapter nine.

Although the theories considered in the text are broadly, sometimes even globally, applicable, the main geographical target audience is a British one and the data and research included reflects this. Audiences who would benefit from the text include:

those looking for a text which can help them make the transition from GCSE to GCE A Level thinking in the subject;

A Level students who are looking for a reflective alternative which can be used to complement the standard texts;

mature students who are looking for an unintimidating text which can nevertheless guide them to a challenging level of study;

students in higher education who are new to the subject area and are looking for an introductory text in sociology which has less the feel of an A Level textbook than the more traditional ones;

the general reader who is interested in contemporary issues such as those surrounding globalisation and who is looking for an approachable text.

Finally, the author hopes that in this work he has been able to make a contribution to a rewarding intellectual venture for the reader.

1: Sociology – The Terrain and the Challenge

Abstract

This chapter introduces a small number of key sociological concepts. It emphasises the complexity of the subject, goes on to chart some of its key dimensions, and alerts the reader to a number of difficulties that a newcomer to the subject is likely to experience. The complexity and difficulties necessitate the development of certain intellectual qualities to successfully tackle this area of study. The chapter also attempts to allay and reverse some of the negative preconceptions that commonly abound regarding the subject.

A psychological perquisite for the sociologist is a state of open-mindedness regarding the way that society is viewed. The sociologist needs to be able to question their everyday knowledge and assumptions about society. This requires a certain distancing of oneself from society and a heightening of critical awareness of unquestioning preconceptions regarding it that we are socialised into.

The nature and nurture debate is touched on and the reader is alerted to being on guard against the master justification that is sometimes used to accept certain ways of behaving - 'it is human nature'.

An essential quality required of the sociologist is to be able to develop an understanding of the social and global picture as the broader context of our personal experiences. This is initially illustrated by reviewing what C. Wright Mills once referred to as 'The Sociological Imagination'.

Finally, the issue of sociology providing an academic basis for enlightened social intervention is briefly raised.

Sociology – not a pushover

Sociology has often faced image problems. There are those who doubt the academic credentials of the subject and others who dismiss it as merely subversive. It is hoped that in following this and other sociology texts, the reader will agree with the author that sociology is not an academically lightweight discipline. Indeed, sociologists face problems of great complexity. As for the subversion criticism, if this amounts to a distorted expression of 'encourages critical awareness', then the author would argue that the rephrasing should be taken as a compliment to the capacity of the subject.

To the newcomer, sociology is likely to appear to be a bewildering subject. Students often initially experience confusion and frustration. Why is this so? Firstly, it is a discipline of great magnitude and complexity with a broad range of technical concepts that require understanding and careful application. This takes time and requires patience. Secondly, there is no single indisputably correct theory, but rather rival perspectives that require rigorous evaluation. Developing the ability to move between and compare alternative theories and explanations will therefore be necessary. Thirdly, to pursue the subject effectively, requires that the sociology student be prepared to suspend and re-examine much that may have been taken for granted about society. This requires the development of mental flexibility and a predisposition of open-mindedness to unexpected findings.

The aim of this short chapter is to indicate the scope and nature of sociology, introduce a small number of the defining concepts, raise some important implications regarding the subject, and alert the reader to key difficulties and challenges which lay ahead.

The meaning of concepts

All subjects have their own concepts. The purpose of concepts is to offer ways of conceiving reality. They help us to make sense of reality, structure our observations, communicate our understanding with others and assist our analysis. A small number of sociological concepts such as socialisation, culture and role will shortly be introduced. We should be aware, however, and will see later, that as sociological concepts need to correspond as closely as possible to reality, new ones may need to be devised as society changes. Indeed, some of the concepts and theoretical foundations upon which the subject was developed have increasingly come into question as being inadequate for the task of understanding contemporary times.

The scope, nature and key concepts of sociology

An important starting point in sociology is the realisation that instinctive pre-programming is an extremely small element of human behaviour compared to that of animals and that our capacity for learning is much superior. This is indicated by the diversity of social and cultural environments which have existed and our capacity to develop new institutions, ways and beliefs in response to problems encountered. But if individual behaviour is not largely predisposed by instinct, something else must be responsible for a level of collaborative behaviour and mutual understanding necessary for co-existence to be possible. This realm is the subject matter for sociology in the understanding of human behaviour – it is 'society'.

As individuals, we are born into society. As we awaken to society, we encounter an environment which we tune into through our senses and adjust to through experience. In so doing, we learn and internalise features of this environment and respond to it. The extent to which the individual engages in a relatively active or passive relationship with the social environment has been much debated within sociology. However, sociologists emphasise that **socialisation** – the influence on individual consciousness and identity of culture, social values, norms, social roles, moral pressures and laws - will be profound during our early years and accompany us throughout our lives. Let us briefly define some established sociological concepts which comprise the mainstays of the social environment.

The term **culture** in sociology refers to the beliefs and values that make up a common way of life. It becomes internalised through our capacity to learn the meaning of sounds, gestures and symbols in the form of language. Culture also includes commonly recognised ceremonies, dress, rituals, traditions and artefacts which may substantially pre-date any contemporary society. Whilst socialisation into culture is a universal feature of human life, the cultures of different societies (and arguably increasingly across and within societies) are highly diverse. However, through socialisation, individuals tend to take their culture as their universal reference point.

Social **values** are a part of culture. They are belief systems which offer general guidelines by which behaviour is judged as desirable or undesirable. Societies and cultures tend to have dominant value systems. For example, modern western societies value highly opportunities for individual achievement based on individual merit. A society which operates in such a way is referred to as a meritocracy. Evidence, however, may indicate that behaviour which departs from dominant values is quite widespread. Regarding meritocratic values, some sociologists point to significant disparities between these values and what happens 'on the ground', particularly in the spheres of educational and occupational opportunity and achievement. In sociology, social values which systematically distort reality are referred to as **ideology**.

Norms relate to values but provide more clearly defined expectations of behaviour. They specify what is deemed to be normal and acceptable in society. Thus, norms regarding family life in Britain in the 1950s emphasised a uniform model of a married male and female partnership for the upbringing of children, with primary financial support provided by the male breadwinner and domestic chores and childrearing the responsibility of the housewife. These norms were powerfully supported by **moral pressures** upholding segregated male and female roles and stigma against cohabitation, illegitimacy and divorce. Norms of contemporary family life indicate the acceptability of much greater diversity of lifestyle and arguably reflect a liberalisation of social and moral values.

Social **roles** are social niches which specify to individuals who occupy them standard expectations of behaviour *vis-à-vis* the occupants of other roles. The relationships between people in different roles are accompanied by mutual expectations. Task orientated roles may be highly formalised niches within organisational power structures, whereas leisure roles may be more informal. Individuals occupy many roles, which engage them in social relationships of reciprocal expectations. Key roles, such as those linked to domestic life and careers, were once relatively fixed for individuals. Now, arguably, society is more fluid and people have to navigate their way through many role changes throughout their lives.

The **law** formalises sanctions and imposes controls which tend to reflect dominant social and moral values and norms in codified form. As norms and values change, we tend to find parallel changes in the law. For example, a liberalisation of norms and values regarding family life has been accompanied by a liberalisation of divorce laws and more liberal sexual morals has led to changes in the law whereby homosexuality ceased to be a crime and, more recently, same sex civil partnerships have become possible.

The above mainstays structure society and impose a degree of order. We have now reached the position where the problem is not that of explaining social order but explaining levels of conflict and disorder encountered in modern societies. We will later see that emphasising order or conflict in society was a fundamental dimension of dispute between different founding theoretical perspectives.

Some important implications

A number of implications follow on from our brief introduction to the subject:

1 The scope and complexity of sociology is massive, ranging from the study of the smallest social environments of friends, families and partners, right up to the societal and global level. No single all embracing theory holds a monopoly, but a number of theories compete for plausibility and demonstrate strengths and weaknesses in different areas. In this text, a number of theoretical perspectives will be reviewed, from those of the founding fathers through to more contemporary thinkers.

2 Sociologists challenge the view that human behaviour is largely the outcome of innate and fixed capacities in individuals – the 'nature' argument. Rather, it is

primarily viewed in terms of socialisation and the restrictions and opportunities that derive from the social environment – the 'nurture' argument. Consider, for example, evidence which may suggest that levels of intelligence run in families. A simple nature interpretation, once emphasised by psychologists of the eugenics movement, is that the evidence is proof that intelligence is genetically inherited. Sociologists, in emphasising nurture explanations, do not deny that people are born with different intellectual capacities and potential. However, the same evidence would be studied more in terms of the influence of social environment on the development of intellectual potential. Interest would focus on the inheritance of different life chances that people are born into, affording varying opportunities for intellectual success rather than explanations emphasising fixed and genetically transmitted genetic qualities.

3 We should beware of explanations of behaviour couched in terms of 'human nature'. This term can be, and has been, used as a largely vacuous justification for almost any type of behaviour. As a single example, to say that it is human nature to be materialistic and individually competitive is to: a) ignore the evidence of cultural diversity – many cultures have held more communal based values, b) apply a fatalistic attitude to possible alternatives, and c) ignore the key message of sociology that human nature is malleable through socialisation within different social environments. To say that materialism and individual competition are fundamental values of contemporary western society that we are socialised into is much nearer to the mark. To put this more provocatively, when peoples' minds become the receptacles of the trash of contemporary advertising and celebrity culture, the sociological question is not what is human nature but what have we become by the type of society that we (and who are the we here?) have created.

4 Our everyday worlds are a product of the influences and experiences that we have been exposed to. However, given the diversity of societies and cultures, as well as groups within society, it is clear that our world view is only one of many. Difficult as the previous section implies that it may be, we must make every effort to suspend what we take for granted if we are to attempt to understand this diversity and become effective sociologists.

The purpose of this text is to encourage the reader to make a transition in thinking about society from that of the layperson to that of a sociologist. This may not be a simple task. It is not uncommon for newcomers to the subject to find the early stages of their studies disorientating. The subject seems to click for different people at different stages. In anticipation of these early difficulties, the reader is alerted to the need for patient commitment to this subject.

The sociological challenge:

1 Developing your sociological imagination

People often individualise experiences and problems. As such, they tend to look to themselves and others, and examine experiences in terms of individual abilities or shortcomings. This may sometimes be an appropriate level of analysis for tackling problems. However, it may also sometimes be misplaced and indicate a lack of what C Wright Mills once referred to as the 'sociological imagination'. Just what Mills meant by this term is indicated in the following section which is abridged and paraphrased from 'The Sociological Imagination' (1959), pp.14 – 17. For purposes of authenticity, the author of this text has retained the male dominant language which was characteristic of the time that Mills was writing.

Perhaps the most fruitful distinction with which the sociological imagination works is between that of 'personal troubles' and 'public issues of social structure'. This distinction is an essential tool of the sociological imagination.

Personal troubles occur within the character of the individual and within the range of his or her immediate relations with others. They relate to the self and to those limited areas of social life of which the individual is directly and personally aware. Therefore, the statement and resolution of personal troubles lies within the individual and within the scope of his immediate environment – the social setting that is directly open to personal experience and to some extent the wilful activity of the individual.

Public issues of social structure transcend the local environments of the individual and the range of his inner life. They are to do with the organisation of many immediate environments into the institutions of society as a whole which has structure and historical life. An issue is a public matter which relates to cherished values which may be felt to be threatened – a matter open to debate. But issues, unlike personal troubles, can often not be easily defined in terms of the immediate environment of the individual. An issue often involves a crisis in institutional arrangements.

In these terms, consider unemployment. When, in a city of 100,000, only one man is unemployed, that is a personal trouble. For its relief, we may look at the character of the individual, his skills and his immediate opportunities. But when in a nation of 50 million employees, 15 million are unemployed, that is an issue. We may not hope to find its solution within the range of opportunities open to any one individual. The very structure of opportunities has collapsed. Both the correct statement of the problem and the range of possible solutions requires us to consider the economic and political institutions of society, not merely the personal situation and character of a large scattering of individuals. Yet, in such situations, blame is sometimes focussed on individual shortcomings.

Consider marriage. Within a marriage, partners may experience personal troubles. But when the divorce rate during the first four years of marriage is 250 per 1,000 marriages, this is an indication of a broader structural issue having to do with the institutions of marriage and the family and other institutions that bear upon them.

In so far as an economy is so arranged that slumps occur, the problem of unemployment becomes incapable of personal solution. In so far as the family as an institution turns women into darling little slaves and men into their chief providers, the problem of a satisfactory marriage remains incapable of purely private solution.

What we experience in immediate environments is often the product of the broader structural features of society. Accordingly, to understand personal experiences and troubles we are required to look beyond them. As society modernises, it undergoes structural changes involving institutions that are intricately connected with one another. To be aware of the influence of the social structure and to develop the ability of tracing complex linkages between institutions and between the public and personal world is to possess the sociological imagination.

What was Mills' central message? Mills was emphasising that a preoccupation with explaining behaviour in terms of individual characteristics or the little picture of our immediate environment is likely to blind us to asking more searching questions. These only become evident when we develop the ability to relate the experiences of our immediate world to that of the broader social structure. This is not to deny individuals responsibility for their action, but to generate insight into the reasonable limits of that responsibility given the broader constraints operating on people and the options available to them.

Developing the sociological imagination arguably remains a process of creative sociological insight by which personal problems can be effectively analysed in terms of the social structure and posed as public issues. For example, a growing number of people in Britain in the early 1990s experienced the personal troubles of mortgage arrears, repossession and homelessness. Although many had originally made far from reckless decisions when taking out mortgages, an increase in these personal troubles can be related to the broader issue of social policy designed to expand the private housing market that left many individuals relatively powerless in the face of rising interest rates.

A more contemporary problem may be that of job insecurity. Although directly experienced as a personal trouble, analysing job insecurity and its consequences associated with the impact of a flexible labour market on peoples' lives may increasingly require the sociological imagination to take a more global focus. Adopting a global perspective is likely to raise issues regarding the nature of the global investment market and government policy responses as well as the conditions of employment in other parts of the world.

2 Making the transition from layperson to sociologist

What does making the transition from layperson to sociologist entail? It essentially requires a person to be prepared to examine their taken for granted assumptions about society and contemplate whole new social panoramas. To achieve this, it is necessary to adopt a mental position of standing outside of the very society that a person has been brought up in and feels so familiar with. For the sociologist, the layperson's familiarity with society through everyday life assumptions may be misleading. For the layperson, the experience of stepping outside of a taken for granted world may, at least at first, feel disconcerting. But to be an effective sociologist, this step needs to be made. A key aim of this text is to offer guidance in this process.

Why, then, is everyday knowledge likely to be inadequate for purposes of sociological analysis? There are many reasons. Perhaps the first question to ask is where does the lay observer of society obtain his or her working knowledge of society from? This knowledge is likely to come from a variety of sources including mass media information, the opinions and experiences of others that we converse with and our own personal experiences. It may often be adequate for everyday purposes, but would not stand up to the criteria of scrutiny required in academic sociology. Knowledge of society gained in the above ways is likely to be biased, unsystematic, and unrepresentative, and, in the light of sociological scrutiny, the self-evident may turn out to be misleading.

Consider, for example, how one may relate to the tabloid press. The everyday reader may be susceptible to such newspapers shaping what they believe to be important and influencing their opinions and common sense outlook. The tabloid press may also be of interest to the sociologist. However, the purpose will be a different one. By studying how the tabloids attempt to manipulate common sense through the use of stereotypes, emotional language, positioning of articles etcetera, the sociologist adopts a more detached and analytical posture.

One way of gaining analytic distance on society is through the vantage point of historical distance. This can help us to gain insights into society that may have eluded contemporaries. For example, think of the dominant values behind the American Declaration of Independence of 1776. The writers of this tract based their reasoning on the Enlightenment view that all men are created equal and that citizens have the right to throw off a tyrannical government. In this day and age, we may be astounded to learn that some of those who professed adherence to these values were also slave owners. From our outside vantage point, we can easily spot what appears to be a clear contradiction between professed values and social institutions. However, during their time, this incongruity did not seem so apparent to many.

Being encapsulated in everyday thinking may blind us to what may be seen by the outsider as logical inconsistencies. Unless we can gain a similar analytic distance from contemporary society, future others may look back at us with similar amazement that we failed in our everyday lives to recognise the contradictions of our own time. We must therefore find some way of distancing ourselves from our taken for granted world. The theories and concepts of sociology can assist us in making detached and critical evaluations. On the other hand, governments, not always great supporters of subjects like sociology, may have a vested interest in promoting that common layman activity of not engaging in joined up thinking on social issues.

Sociology is not just an academic exercise, but sociological analysis can be a prerequisite for intelligent intervention is society. However, it does not offer us solutions for the creation of a perfect society. If this was once the aim of some early social theorists, the disappointments of the twentieth century and the social complexity and relentless change of the contemporary world have curbed such expectations. For those who are dissatisfied with everyday knowledge of society, sociology offers a more exacting level of analysis to help us formulate a broadly considered and academically based view of society. This is the aim of the following chapters.

2: Sociological Perspectives

Abstract

This chapter will introduce the reader to key founding theoretical perspectives in sociology. It will not attempt a critical evaluation of these theories, but rather locate them as responses to the challenge of radical social transformation.

These theories form an underpinning to sociology as it emerged in the context of nineteenth century modernisation. The classical theories of modernisation - functionalism, Marxism and social action theory - attempted to gain a grip on understanding a much changed social environment to that of traditional society by offering rational and scientific explanations.

Although developed slightly later, the writer also includes symbolic interactionism in this section, as, like the above mentioned theories, it retains faith in the capacity to rationally understand society and deals with problems of identity in the modern world. An introduction to phenomenology and ethnomethodology is included. These perspectives are really intermediary to founding and contemporary theory.

The chapter concludes by reiterating that the main purpose of sociological theory is to act as a guide in the insightful understanding of society. It is therefore important to remember that developing sociological understanding should remain a live activity in which theories act as touchstones but not as fixed and final explanations. Indeed, the idea of the need to rejuvenate the subject as a result of far reaching changes in contemporary society is introduced, with postmodern and high modern perspectives identified as contemporary responses.

Introduction

Compared to the insights generated by sociological thinking, non sociologists may appear to be either in a state of sleepy acceptance or if critical of society ill equipped to develop penetrating insights and analyses of society and social issues. However, sociology does not offer a single infallible alternative viewpoint. Instead, it offers various theoretical perspectives. Theoretical perspectives are made up of logically interconnected concepts. A concept is an idea which stands for something in the real world. For example, in sociology, social status and political power are concepts which explain stratification and influence in the real world. Concepts are combined in sociological theories to act as interpretive and filtering devices through which to see society. The plurality of competing perspectives reflects the near infinite complexity of society which can be plausibly represented in many different ways. Theories are also likely to relate to the different values and vantage points of theorists themselves.

The process of utilising different theoretical perspectives can be likened to that of trying on different pairs of glasses, each of which equips the wearer with an alternative view of society. Each perspective, through its interconnected concepts, offers a filter through which the observer is equipped with a simplified view of society. Each simplified view offers its own patterned understanding. It is through working with a number of sociological perspectives that new windows of awakening on society can be developed and the transition from lay person to sociologist made. The aim of this chapter is essentially to delineate a number of sociological perspectives, whilst alerting the reader that they should ultimately be applied reflectively, selectively and critically.

Before reviewing the major founding perspectives of sociology, it is important to pause and consider the social context of their origin which made the quest for a new understanding of society so necessary.

Modernisation and founding social theory

The major perspectives comprising the early theoretical foundations of sociology were developed during the nineteenth and early twentieth centuries. The impulse for social theorising was rapid and far-reaching social, political and industrial change, which, based on the advance of rational and scientific thinking, was challenging an old social order and the religious outlooks upon which it was based.

In France, the dramatic events of the Revolution of 1789 and the associated values of liberty, equality and fraternity, brought the collapse of the old feudal order and promoted the idea of progress toward a new type of society based on reason rather than religion.

In England, from about the same time, new machinery and sources of power were introducing mass production, and, in concentrating workers in ever larger numbers in factories, were setting in motion large scale rural to urban migration and the unprecedented growth of towns and cities. England's revolution was an industrial one but the changes were also social. In promoting urbanisation and the factory system, it undermined the ways and traditions of rural life.

Throughout the nineteenth century, advances in science – especially geological - were increasingly throwing the literal interpretation of creation derived from the Bible into question. Fatalistic religious attitudes toward illness were being challenged as medical science grappled to eradicate contagious diseases which ravaged populations living in squalid urban environments.

The forces of modernisation were bringing about a new type of society in which the power and values of the old landed elite were being challenged by the growing power of industrialists. For the latter, power in the new order should be based on economic wealth derived from industriousness rather than inherited privilege. But the new society was also spawning a mass urban working class and generating problems of mass poverty, disease, social polarisation, economic destabilisation, and social unrest. How could these problems be addressed? As science and rational thinking were at the centre of progress, it was reasonable to believe that science and rational thinking should have the capacity to tackle the problems that progress had brought. In modernising societies, there had emerged a context of both need for and belief in the capacity of man to rationally understand and control the conditions of modernisation. The term 'modern' sociological theory is used to refer back to theory originating in this context. Modern should not therefore be confused with the term 'contemporary'.

Early functionalism and the science of social engineering

Functionalism was one of the earliest foundations of sociological thinking. It can be traced back to French social theorists who were writing against the backdrop of social revolution and looking to develop a theory of social order. Indeed, the aim of these theorists was to develop, in functionalism, a social science whose practical usefulness would be to help policy makers to rationally intervene in society so as to promote social order.

Originating in Auguste Comte's more philosophical writings, which dated from the 1820s, functionalism found its sociological formulation from the late nineteenth century in the works of Emile Durkheim. These early functionalists developed a view of society based on a biological or organic analogy. Analogy assists understanding through the process of comparison. Through analogy, the understanding of one area of knowledge can be enhanced by indicating similarities to another area which is better understood. The biological analogy did not mean that society was literally viewed as an organism, but that the understanding of society could best be advanced by comparing it to a living body. Sociology could advance as a science of society on this basis because biology was also a science of life but a more advanced one. Sociology could haul itself up by the insights derived from the biological analogy.

In what ways is it beneficial to view society as like an organism? The term function firstly requires definition. A function is a recurrent activity of a part of an integrated body which operates for the benefit of that body. For example, the beating of the heart is of crucial functional importance for the well being of the human body. In this sense, it is a 'functional prerequisite' – its operation is a pre-requirement for the very life of the body. Other organs play their own allocated functions. They are each interdependent, and the health and vitality of the entire human body relies on each organ performing its appropriate function.

The biological analogy can be suggestive of conditions of social good or ill health. Like the organs of a body, social institutions perform functions for the health and well being of the entire society. For example, the family rears the next generation and socialises them into the values and expectations of broader society. As well as instilling academic knowledge, the education system imposes on pupils the need to abide by institutional rules and regulations, the habit of regularity, and the acquisition of work related skills, all of which are functional for efficient participation of individuals in the workplace. The workplace enables resources to be provided for society, incomes for families, and taxation for public services such as education. At the extreme, without the routines of productive activity, modern society would soon cease.

The biological analogy would suggest that society should be viewed as a whole entity. By this, it is meant that the purpose of the parts of society – its various institutions which bring together individuals to structure and regularise behaviour – can only be understood through firstly obtaining an overview of society in its entirety. Just as it would be insufficient to try and understand the workings of an organ within a human body in isolation from the whole body, so it would be insufficient to attempt to understand the functioning of society by starting with an analysis of individual institutions. An overview of society must first be acquired to understand the functional workings of its different elements such as the family, educational institutions, the workplace, etcetera, and how they relate to each other. This emphasis is referred to in sociology as 'holism' and it makes functionalism a macro theory – one which focuses on the broad dimensions of society. Furthermore, functionalism equated society with nation as a discrete unit of analysis.

Like organisms, societies evolve. As they grow and advance, they develop more complex forms of organisation. Like primitive organisms, primitive societies are simple social structures - they exhibit little institutional specialisation. They also tend to be segmented into only loose associations of small groups. For these reasons, as in a primitive organism, damage to one part of society will have limited repercussions for the whole.

However, as societies evolve, they develop more specialised institutions which perform specialised functions. They become integrated on a larger scale as the whole of society becomes dependant on each specialised institution performing its necessary functions. Given the complex interdependency of institutions in modern society, it is more vulnerable to the widespread consequences of the malfunctioning of any of its institutions. Social conflict or factionalism can be highly damaging. A faction ridden society is one where order, consensus and integration have broken down and people put factional interests ahead of broader social needs. The possibility of widespread disruption to the social organism through, for example, high levels of strike activity, is, from a functionalist perspective, a sign of social ill health which needs to be remedied. At the extreme, revolutionary change would be a condition of chronic ill health. The natural and healthy state suggested by the organic analogy is that societies grow and evolve through a process of gradual change.

Functionalists maintain that social hierarchies are a natural and inevitable feature of all societies. Not all individuals have identical abilities and not all institutions are of equal functional importance. Although the principles around which social hierarchies are organised change over time, functionalists argue that in modern industrial societies, the functional importance of institutions provide the framework of the social hierarchy and ability is the main criteria for the allocation of individuals to roles in their occupational capacity. This enables the efficient utilisation of human ability for the general social benefit.

But it needs to be remembered that the biological analogy cannot be taken literally. For example, society does not have the physical boundary of a body form – people can migrate between societies. So what is it that holds a society together and maintains order and regularity? For functionalists, society is ordered and structured by institutions, roles, rules, regulations, and laws. It is integrated through shared values imparted through socialisation and education and by the pressures toward conformity imposed by moral constraints. Shared values promote broadly recognised norms of behaviour, social consensus and a degree of harmony which enables society to function smoothly. A smoothly operating and efficient society represents a condition of social good health from which all, as members of society, benefit. For the individual, conformity to the constraints of society, gives liberation, through the capacities of society, from the condition of necessity provided by nature.

Bound up with functionalism in sociology has been the development of positivism – the view that society could ultimately be understood in scientific terms. If this were to be the case, sociologists would be able to act as social engineers assisting policy makers in their reforms from a position of scientific neutrality as opposed to factional interest and bias. Policy interventions could then engineer institutions to promote social harmony, integration and consensus in a way analogous to a doctor or surgeon using scientific knowledge to promote the health of a patient.

Classical Marxism and the science of class conflict

Marxism, a theoretical perspective developed by Karl Marx and Frederick Engels at the height of nineteenth century free enterprise capitalism, provides both a materialist explanation of the causes of social change throughout history and radical critique of capitalism. Both aspects will be dealt with in this section.

Marx's materialist interpretation emphasises that social and historical change has as its driving force economic and material factors rather than ideas. From this perspective, ideas emerge mainly as a response to economic change and take the form of justifications benefiting the economically powerful and controlling a subject class.

Related to this materialist position, Marxism is often interpreted as a form of 'economic determinism'. This means that the economy is the determining force around which the rest of society is organised. The economy and the distribution of wealth and power 1) structure society into relationships between social classes, arrangements which 2) are justified through dominant ideas and controlling institutions.

For Marx, work is the most fundamental social activity, without which society could not exist. Within society, therefore, the essential social relationships revolve around productive activity, which Marx analyses through the following concepts:

All production requires 'forces of production' which comprises levels of technology and machinery, production techniques, raw materials and labour power. For production to take place, there must exist social relationships. The term 'relations of production' refers to the form, shaped by duties and obligations between the parties, by which social relationships necessary for production take place. For Marx, these relationships mark out social class divisions. Of the forces of production, the 'means of production' are those that can be legally owned. The fundamental feature of social class divisions is that one class will own the means of production and have at its disposal the only asset that the other class owns – its labour power. The utilisation of the labour power of this latter class of workers is necessary for the owners of the means of production to create value and wealth. The hiring out of labour power by the worker is necessary to provide an income. There is therefore inbuilt conflict between the classes over the allocation of value created by the productive process.

The term 'mode of production' specifies how production is organised and refers to levels of advancement by which societies are differentiated as, for example, feudal, capitalist or communist modes of production.

Private ownership of the means of production has been a feature of most of modern history. Indeed, when people were not free, for example under forms of slavery, the entire forces of production were privately owned. For Marx, private ownership of the means of production is the source of social power. Power is the capacity that some people have to exert control over others. From this perspective, it is a fundamental characteristic of the relations of production which exist between the social classes. It enables the owners of the means of production to extract an excessive appropriation of the value created in the productive process for themselves. This means that those who have provided their labour are short changed in relation to the value it creates in terms of the products produced. The relations of production therefore promote class based exploitation.

Why, then, is not open class conflict a common feature of this relationship? An understanding of this question requires a distinction to be made between the 'infrastructure' and the 'superstructure'.

Together, Marx refers to the means of production and the relations of production as the 'economic base' of society or the infrastructure. It is here where class relationships are based and tensions generated. The term superstructure in the Marxist perspective refers to society's dominant social values, beliefs, laws and institutions. These operate as controls of the relations of production and as broader social controls. Therefore, whilst class conflict is built into the economic infrastructure, the ideas and institutions of the superstructure operate to hide or suppress this conflict of interests and actual open conflict. Ideas and institutions reflect the distribution of power within society and primarily benefit the owners of the means of production. Thus, the laws of the land reflect the needs of the dominant class, for example, for efficient and profitable production and the protection of private property.

Power and control can take the form of coercion. Coercion refers to the use or threat of the use of force. Within the superstructure, institutions of coercion, such as the armed forces, police, judiciary and prisons, impose order and suppress discontent. But, for Marx, dominant social ideas also have a controlling effect. From this power model it follows that the prevailing ideas in society are the ideas conducive to the ruling economic class. They aim to give legitimacy to the existing social order by providing credible justifications for it and hiding or disguising the conflict of class interests. Such distortions of reality are referred to by Marx as 'ideology', and through the process of socialisation ideology induces a false consciousness into the subject class for the purpose of gaining its compliance.

Marx argued that these controls cannot persist in the long term. This is because 'contradictions' (a term which has various applications!) exist at the heart of systems based on exploitation. Class exploitation, and the potential for conflict that it generates, can be disguised or hidden by ideological distortions, such as the notion of a contract freely entered into and a fair wage, which enter and help govern the relations of production. However, for Marx, the reality of exploitation cannot always remain hidden. At times of great hardship during economic depression, contradictions between ideology (fair wage) and reality (exploitation) are very likely to become evident.

Contradictions can also emerge between the means of production and the corresponding relations of production. The emergence of new means of production, for example the rapid growth of urban based factory mass production and the decline of rural based agrarian production, will contradict old relations of production which were suited to old means of production. As more appropriate new relations of production emerge, new ideological justifications for them become necessary. In the process, revolutionary social transformation takes place from one system to another.

This process can be illustrated with reference to the transition from feudal to capitalist modes of production. Feudal society is pre-industrial and largely agricultural, typified by life in small rural communities. Religion and superstition are powerful sources of explanation and moral values. The means of production comprise land, agricultural buildings, machinery and implements of a low technological level (which may utilise wind and water power) and animals. Working the land is the main basis for the generation of wealth. Land ownership is concentrated largely in the hands of the nobility and the church, who therefore comprise the ruling class. Various grades of commoner below the nobility in the social hierarchy may own some property and land, but at the bottom of the social scale reside a large stratum of impoverished and landless agricultural labourers known as serfs. For Marx, the defining class relationship in this type of society is the exploitation of the labour of serfs by a landowning nobility and church. These relations of agrarian production, which are a potential point of fracture in the social hierarchy, are maintained by force where necessary and by an ideology which emphasises the importance of deference and loyalty of the lower orders toward their lords who claim for themselves the virtues of superior social breeding. This 'natural' order is sanctified by the church in its religious teachings.

However, within the feudal social order, new means of production were being developed by enterprising merchants and artisans. In time, as industrial technology and machinery develop, both the feudal relations of production of serf bonded to master, based around land ownership, and the supporting ideology of superior social breeding of the nobility and deference and loyalty expected from serfs, begin to look antiquated and outlive their purpose. A point is eventually reached where a capitalist class gains sufficient wealth and power to achieve social ascendancy. Around the new means of production, new relations of production emerge which are appropriate to a dynamic industrial economy. These are embodied in flexible wage labour contracts which benefit a new ruling class of capitalists employing and exploiting waged workers. This transformation from feudal to capitalist society requires correspondingly new ideological values to disguise exploitation and manage conflict. These values are essentially those derived from the writers of political economy - that the system is best left to self regulate by responding to forces of supply and demand and workers are free to engage in contracts of employment with whom they wish. Furthermore, position in society is apparently achievable by individual merit.

From the Marxist perspective, the emergence of capitalism from feudalism simply replaces one form of class exploitation by another. Although the system has changed, conflict and contradictions remain and must in the long term come to the surface again. The potential under capitalism is for that conflict to bring into opposition a minority exploiting capitalist class and a majority exploited working class, referred to as the proletariat. This is because the conditions of production under capitalism bring together workers into larger aggregates in both workplace and the urban environment. Free enterprise capitalism is essentially unstable. It is particularly at times when the system malfunctions, producing downward pressure on wages and rising unemployment, that workers facing a common plight will see through the ideological justifications of capitalism and develop a common class consciousness which recognises that capitalism and exploitation are the cause of their plight. Such class consciousness is a prerequisite for revolution. The mechanics of capitalism therefore virtually impel, in the form of laws of change, the proletarian working class toward revolution. As the revolutionary class will now be the majority class, a successful revolution will take the means of production into common ownership. The resulting communist society will therefore be the product of the final revolutionary transformation of society since it would resolve all class conflict and contradictions.

It is clear that functionalism and Marxism are diametrically opposed perspectives. However, they do have at least one characteristic in common. They are both macro perspectives which emphasise the downward impact of socialisation in moulding the consciousness and behaviour of individuals to the dominant values of society. As such, they offer little insight into the potential of individuals to act as free and purposive agents whose activities can have a feedback influence into society itself. Max Weber's social action theory was an attempt to correct this in-balance.

Social action theory – social science and contingency

Max Weber was a German theorist and contemporary of Durkheim, producing his major works between the late nineteenth and early twentieth centuries. Compared to both functionalist and Marxist perspectives, Weber's social action theory is more difficult to tie down because of its scope and relative openness. As a scholarly historian, Weber recognised that social phenomena and historical change are extremely complex. Contrary to the Marxist perspective, for Weber the course of social change is not seen to be closely pre-determined; the future cannot be anticipated in terms of causal laws. Chance events, inventions, and complex social interactions mean that the application of science and prediction to society must be approached through painstaking research and with caution. In emphasising the difference between causality in the physical realm of nature and conscious choice, freedom of action and contingency within social conditions, Weber's approach to understanding society is less positivistic than that of Durkheim or Marx, although he did identify powerful forces of social change.

Weber is classified as a conflict theorist and he emphasised the importance of both the macro and the micro social levels for obtaining a full understanding of social action. Viewing society at the macro level, Weber maintains that groups tend to compete for power and resources and that those who hold these assets will usually attempt to retain exclusive control through erecting barriers to access by others. However, whether and how this leads to conflict in particular societies at particular times is a matter for analysis. It is therefore not appropriate to refer to either consensus or conflict as natural to societies in the way that functionalists and Marxists respectively do. For Weber, it is also misleading of Marxists to reduce social conflict primarily to that between economic classes and to use economic class defined in terms of relation to the means of production as the single key with which to explain the social structure and motive force for social change.

In trying to explain social structure and change, focus should not be automatically placed on the determining effect of economic factors – there is no reason why they should always be of primary importance with belief systems simply emerging to justify economic relationships. For Weber, cultural values can sometimes be more important influences on social change than economic factors. They can be the motive forces behind peoples' actions which can have economic outcomes – a proposition which criticises Marx's economic determinism and historical materialism and gives cultural values a potentially more dynamic role to play in promoting social change. It is ultimately for the analysis of particular societies and specific periods of history to uncover the complex and contingent influences on conflict, consensus and social change.

For Weber, belief systems influence the motivations and actions of social actors. These systems form a social backdrop to action and can themselves change over time. The major change in values associated with capitalist modernisation in the west is referred to by Weber as the process of rationalisation. In pre-capitalist society, Weber argues that action was guided largely by custom and tradition. It was seen as legitimate that established ways were followed. By contrast, in modern capitalist societies, action is more efficiency orientated, providing dynamism and change. It is guided by rational and logical thinking whereby courses of action are decided through making projections into the future, calculations and comparing different means to achieve goals. As part of this process, efficient organisational structures increasingly take the form of large, impersonal power hierarchies which progressively formalise social relationships.

What has brought about this change from traditional to rational society if not primarily economic forces? Weber traces the emergence of rationalisation and with it the values and institutions of modern western capitalism back to particular religious belief systems in pre-capitalist societies. Calvinist religion formed a value system for believers whereby the prospects of entering heaven were related to living a life of strict rectitude in the form of sober application and sacrifice. Consequent worldly success in the form of wealth creation could be taken by the believer as evidence of leading a good life and a sign of god's favour. These religious beliefs, more prevalent in protestant England, gave a powerful motive for the believer to the type of action which would promote the accumulation of capital and, along with other fortuitous conditions, enhance the prospects of western style capitalist modernisation.

However, the analysis of action would be one-sided and incomplete if it were only seen as being determined by broad belief systems and social institutions. This emphasis tends to be a weakness of the functionalist approach which elevates society and its 'needs' to such a level that individuals seem to be just passing through it. For Weber, although society and its institutions precede and tower over people, it is also the case that institutions are consciously planned, created and changed, and that society is to some extent the product of purposive action by individual actors. Likewise, individuals have a degree of choice in adopting belief systems. Indeed, the real danger in the modern world is that the very processes of rationalisation and bureaucratisation (the latter referring to the spread of large formal and impersonal organisational structures which Weber argued were the most efficient means of achieving goals) may tend to constrain individual freedom and purposive action and reduce individuals to the position of operating like cogs within efficient social machinery. For Weber, the experience of this process would be one of dehumanisation and disenchantment (see Chapter 8 on Religion) and must be resisted.

The study of social action must also include a micro dimension of direct observation. To fully understand action, account must be taken of the meanings and motivations which reside behind it in the consciousness of social actors. Although individual meanings and motivations may relate to broader belief systems, the difficulty facing the analyst is that similar observed actions may be based on different subjective motives and vice versa. The observer must therefore attempt the challenging process of ascertaining the underlying subjective motives of social actors through engaging in empathy – a process which Weber refers to as *'verstehen'*. To practice social science therefore requires acknowledgement of the gulf that exists between the physical process of the natural sciences and the need to interpret subjective states in the social world.

For Weber, the ultimate project of sociology could only be complete when (if ever) the micro and subjective realm of action driven by the motives of individuals is related to an understanding of the changes in and impact of a contingent and complex mixture of conditions in the broader social structure.

The emergence of micro perspectives

Although variations on the founding perspectives have retained an influence in sociology for much of the twentieth century, new perspectives were developed which focussed wholly on the explaining social action at the micro level. They pursue the problem of subjectivity in social analysis and can be generally referred to under the heading of 'interpretive' sociology. Included under this category are symbolic interactionism, phenomenology and ethnomethodology.

1 Symbolic interactionism – from passive to active self

Symbolic interactionism was a perspective developed in the United States relatively independently of the influence of Weber around the turn of the twentieth century. The founding father of this perspective was G.H. Mead. It views social encounters as fluid processes of communication and negotiation mediated through a shared understanding of the symbols of language and gestures. Individuals negotiate with and influence each other through the exchange of meaning. As society is largely the outcome of these fluid interaction processes which take place at the micro level, it can best be analysed through a vast accumulation of small-scale research.

Interactionists emphasise that self-identity and behaviour are not biologically predetermined. Focussing on the social makeup of self-identity, Mead distinguishes between the 'me' and the 'I'. People are born into a pre-existing society with its language, values, laws etc. which come to impact upon them. In its immediate surrounding, the young child initially imitates 'significant others' in its sphere of experience. It then experiments with playing the roles of significant others. The internalisation of self-identity during this early stage is a relatively passive process. The child's self-appraisal largely reflects others' attitudes toward or treatment of it. This element of the self, largely moulded by environment, is referred to by Mead as the 'me'.

But neither are identity nor behaviour determined by social structures. For Mead, the 'I' is a growing element of the self which develops initiative toward others and social situations. It reacts back toward others who become the 'me' to this active and wilful self. The 'I' learns how to act in such a way as to manage the responses of others.

As individuals participate in more organised settings, they learn to take on the role of the 'generalized other'. This means that they learn what the setting requires in terms of the behaviour of each participant toward each other. For example, the child needs to develop this awareness when entering school. However, individuals also develop the capacity for working organisation's and society's rules. The mature self consists of the stabilised 'me' which is the product of social constraints and imposed identity, and the assertiveness and spontaneity of the 'I', the active self.

Although Mead formulated his perspective philosophically, there are liberating practical implications. Based on Mead's insights, C.H.Cooley developed the idea of the 'looking glass self'. This emphasises that our self-identity reflects the way that others view us. When we interact with others, they view us in a particular way through which they reflect back to us our identity (Mead's 'me'). If we have been negatively viewed by others and have low self-esteem, we may act in confirmation of these views and retain the identity imposed by others. However, as symbolic interactionism reveals, social interaction is not just a one-way process of passive acceptance. We can initiate a change of self-identity, but this is not just a private matter. By learning the changes necessary in our behaviour that would convince others that we are not as they see us, our 'I' can assert to others a new image which can become stabilised in us as it is reflected back to us from them. Individuals therefore have a degree of freedom and responsibility and an element of say in their own identity.

2 Phenomenology and ethnomethodology – getting back to the everyday world

Alfred Schutz is recognised as the founder of the phenomenological approach in sociology. Between the 1930s and the 1950s, he attempted to develop more exclusively Weber's micro and situational based sociology. In so doing, Schutz developed a perspective which focussed on explaining how, in their everyday life encounters, people engage in making their experiences meaningful.

For Schutz, people are able to attribute meaning to events through classifying and typifying experiences in terms of their similarity. As a result, based on a stock of knowledge and experience, they consciously create meaning contexts to interpret behaviour. This construction of meaning in everyday life is referred to as first order typifications.

The radical implication of this position is that behaviour is not the product of the constraints of external structures but is guided by the conscious interpretations placed upon situations by actors.

For phenomenologists, a problem of the macro and structural approaches to sociology is that sociologists are attempting to analyse behaviour through the rational constructs of a discipline one step removed from the experiences of social actors. By so doing, their theories and concepts create intellectualised and science based second order typifications which artificially distort the world of actors' meaning.

Ethnomethodology shares the same philosophical terrain as phenomenology. However, this approach, developed in the late 1960s, is more empirically based; it attempts to ground an understanding of social action in a study of the methods by which actors construct meaning in everyday life situations to enable them to make sense of the world.

Following the outlook developed by Schutz, Harold Garfinkle viewed behaviour as taking place in situations toward which individuals adopt a taken for granted stance. This is based on shared meanings and mutual expectations which provide a framework for the routines of everyday life. When shared meanings are undisturbed, we are often hardly aware of them.

However, sometimes situations confound our expectations and we need to actively engage in the process of reconstructing meaning. As a simple example, consider the following situation. Imagine that you have just moved into a neighbourhood and are getting to know local people. In the street, you acknowledge a person that you have come to recognise as a local, but find that your acknowledgment is sometimes returned and on other occasions you are completely ignored. How do you respond to this apparently random behaviour? You will probably try to attribute sense to it by considering plausible reasons for the behaviour: perhaps he didn't hear me? perhaps he didn't remember me? perhaps he was preoccupied in thoughts or worries? If this behaviour should persist, there is likely to come a time when you will attempt to impose a new interpretation on the situation – this is an ill mannered person that I can not be bothered to acknowledge any more. You have resolved the ambiguity by interpreting behaviour and imposing meaning on it to make it understandable.

To study this process of the construction of meaning in everyday life, ethnomethodologists set up natural experiments. These are sometimes referred to as 'breaching experiments' as the aim is to break rules and cause confusion for the purpose of studying the process of the reconstruction of meaning that is engaged in by actors to make sense of the situation. Examples of such experiments can be found in the research methods chapter of this text.

By such means, ethnomethodologists substantiate that people operate in worlds of taken for granted meaning structures but that they do not just do so passively. Situations also need to be made sense of and are therefore responded to 'reflexively'. Social order is thus actively produced from the micro level up in social situations through the construction of meaning. It is not imposed by a social structure and neither can it be understood in structural terms.

Sociological theory – the way ahead

Without the discipline of theory and evidence, the sociological imagination remains speculative and subjective. On the other hand, as mentioned at the beginning of this chapter, whilst theories equip the sociologist with the tools for perceiving and analysing society, being an effective sociologist is not just about uncritically applying theory to society. Instead, theory must be a living thing in the sense of being applied reflectively to society and modified whenever evidence suggests it necessary.

With this caution in mind, and without making the claim that the previous pages comprise a comprehensive history of sociological theory, this chapter will be concluded with brief reference to three main ways ahead for sociology. The first position refers to sociologists who still largely adhere to one or more of the founding perspectives, if in somewhat modified form. However, the viability of these perspectives to explain the social world at the beginning of the twenty first century has been increasingly called into question. How can functionalism adequately explain how societies function when through the processes of globalisation societies are no longer, if they ever were, clearly delineated functioning units? How can Marxist analysis, rooted in industrial capitalism and clear divisions between owners and non-owners of the forces of production, explain the workings of post-industrial societies which have undergone the reforms of popular capitalism?

A second and radical position is adopted by a range of theorists referred to as postmodernists, including writers such as Jean-Francois Lyotard and Jean Baudrillard. They define the 'modern' period as that emerging from the Enlightenment and now coming to an end. This period was dominated by the discourse of science and the aspiration to use science and rational thinking as the method to achieve absolute truth and assist progress. Sociology itself emerged during this period to analyse society in scientific terms, in, for example the writings of Durkheim and Marx.

Postmodernists argue that the brutal track record of dominant science and the creation of a world devoid of emotional intelligence are leading the abandonment of science as a single and absolute truth. In a society of competing belief systems, each of relative worth, it is becoming realised that neither founding social theory, nor, in more extreme postmodernist accounts, any social theory, are equipped to offer a single explanation of society which is superior to any other explanation. For postmodernists, 'truth' in the contemporary world of media created images is becoming illusive and with it sociology as a superior discipline for understanding and organising society is becoming redundant.

Thirdly, are those such as Ulrich Beck and Anthony Giddens, who view contemporary society as having reached a stage of second or high modernism. They maintain that major changes have taken place in contemporary society and that progress has brought new risks, but that it is still possible to guide practical intervention through sociological theory. Indeed, theoretical guidance is much needed, but new approaches and concepts are required to reconnect sociology with a rapidly changing and globalised world.

Postmodernist and high modernist approaches will be explored further at the end of the topic chapters three to eight and developed in the concluding chapter nine.

3: Sociology of the Family

Abstract

This chapter introduces the reader to some of the difficulties involved in attempting to adopt a relatively impartial stance when adopting a sociological approach to the family. At the outset, the reader is alerted to the importance of examining personal experiences and values regarding the family to enhance awareness of personal bias and encourage a broad overview of family diversity.

Following the introduction of some founding concepts, the sociological perspectives of functionalism and Marxism are utilised to provide broad theoretical starting points and contrasting interpretations of the role of the nuclear family in society. A broad social and historical context on changes in family life is also touched on. Some traditional sociological research into changes in nuclear family life is then reviewed and provided as a benchmark against which more contemporary patterns of family life can be later compared.

The reader is encouraged to appreciate that evidence can be assembled and looked at in different ways to give different messages. Some guidance on the interpretation of data is given.

Although also a founding perspective, it is suggested that interactionism offers greater flexibility and accommodation of analysis to more contemporary trends of growing diversity in family life. Evidence of such growing diversity is then introduced.

More contemporary theories emphasise that society has been undergoing fundamental changes which render the founding perspectives of functionalism and Marxism increasingly redundant for the purpose of explaining the diversity of family life in contemporary society. These perspectives include postmodernist and high modernist and explanations which raise issues of freedom, tolerance, lifestyle choice and risk and are reviewed in the last section of this chapter.

The sociological challenge

What guidance can be picked up from the previous chapters to prepare us to adopt a sociological approach to the family?

Firstly, it is important to pause and reflect on our personal experiences within the family and be vigilant regarding any personal bias that these experiences may predispose us toward. There may be emotive issues that we need to stand back from.

Secondly, we should also be aware that our personal experiences of family life may not be very representative of the experiences of others. Personal experiences can provide helpful insights, but will provide a too narrow and subjective base from which to generalise for sociological purposes.

Thirdly, as sociologists, we should be cautious of explanations that rely heavily on human instincts or human nature to justify particular forms of family organisation. If the precise form of the family were determined by human nature and instincts, we would expect to find a high level of uniformity in family life throughout the world and little scope for change. In fact, anthropologists have pointed to the diversity of family forms which have existed across the world and even in such a brief period of history as the last fifty years in Britain, there is evidence of both substantial change and growing diversity in family life. Whilst the very being of society is dependant on instincts to procreate and provide care for the vulnerable young, there is great diversity of family institutions through which this is possible.

Having raised the need for caution, how can we become armed with a more analytical approach to the study of the family? For a start, we can utilise and build on the sociological perspectives raised in the previous chapter to see what light they shed on our understanding of the family. Furthermore, we can use more concrete information obtained from research. Theory and research findings will give us access to a broader range of information on family life than that based on our personal experiences and may also help us to critically evaluate the perspectives.

It is particularly instructive in the study of the family to be aware that the moral values that provided a compass bearing for past generations were often experienced as prejudices by minorities in that generation. These prejudices have become more broadly recognised as such in generations since as society has moved on. It is important, but perhaps more difficult, to appreciate the likelihood that outlooks and ways regarding family life that are taken for granted today may be looked back on likewise as based on prejudices by future generations. Developing this awareness may help us question our taken for granted assumptions about family life.

Definition of main concepts

Sociologists need to be clear about the definitions that they use and the measurements they take. Some of the founding sociological concepts on the family will therefore be introduced and defined.

The term **monogamy** refers to the legal limitation of marriage to one partner, traditionally of the opposite sex, at any point in time. This constraint provides the broad framework for marital relationships in western societies, although legislation has allowed single sex monogamous marriage in a small number of countries and civil ceremonies in far more. However, monogamy itself is not a universal family form. Other cultures have developed polygamous (marriage to more than one spouse simultaneously) familial arrangements which seem perfectly natural to members of these societies.

The sociology of the family has changed along with changes in the family itself. Theory and research in the 1950s operated within the social context of a widespread standard family institution referred to as the **nuclear family**. This family type comprised married parents of opposing sexes and their children, living together under the same roof. There is evidence of relatively high levels of conformity toward this family type at the time. For example, in 1961, 38% of households in Britain conformed to the above definition. An immediate reaction may be that this is not a particularly high figure for the date in question. It needs to be born in mind, however, that once children have left home, the unit is no longer a nuclear family. Additionally, if the numbers of people living within nuclear family units were counted, the percentage for 1961 will be higher than that of households since on balance other household units were smaller than nuclear family ones. Most children were therefore raised within a nuclear family setting. Stigma was applied to control deviations from this norm. For example, the pejorative term 'illegitimate' was commonly applied to children born outside of marriage and strong moral pressures for a 'shotgun marriage' would often be applied on the partners in the case of pregnancy outside of marriage.

Roles are the patterned activities that people engage in which involve them in relationships with others. They are based on broadly recognised social guidelines but can also leave scope for negotiation. Role relationships generate reciprocal expectations regarding appropriate behaviour. Post war sociological research tended to take the nuclear family as given and focussed on studying changing role relationships within this institution. The term **conjugal roles** was used to refer to role relationships between partners within marriage and a distinction made between two different types of marital role relationship. **Segregated conjugal roles** referred to a clear distinction between the activities of husband and wife which followed traditional gender expectations: the husband was the sole or major wage earner, with the wife being responsible for the daily running of the household and care of the children. These distinctions were often themselves passed down the generations through socialisation and strongly maintained by social and moral pressures. By contrast, **joint conjugal roles** indicated a greater involvement of the husband in household chores and childcare and a degree of merging of domestic activities between husband and wife. This pattern of role allocation within the family has also been referred to as a **symmetrical** role relationship and was more likely to lead to wives entering employment. Although roles did not usually become indiscernible, evidence of growing symmetry has usually been viewed as change toward greater gender equality.

The **extended family**, whilst including the nuclear family, refers to a more extensive community of **kin** (relations established through marriage or blood relatives). Comprising a higher tier of generations and a broader span of relatives, it would potentially include kin relationships over three generations as well as uncles, aunts, nephews, nieces, and cousins. They would not necessarily all live in the same abode but traditionally resided in close proximity to allow ease of face-to-face contact and mutual help. There is evidence that extended family life was once abundant in many stable working class communities.

The term **reconstituted families** refers to family units which come together following the break up of previous family units. They include children from at least one of the previous marriages to whom new parents may become step-parents.

Founding sociological perspectives on the family

Two contrasting perspectives on the family will now be introduced – functionalism and Marxism. Both perspectives took the nuclear family encompassing segregated conjugal roles as the standard family type. This is understandable given the social and historical context of the development of these perspectives, but it should also be considered whether these theories are able to adequately explain subsequent changes in family life.

Functionalism – the functional fit of the nuclear family

American functionalism, represented in particular by the towering influence of Talcott Parsons, was a highly influential perspective within sociology during the 1950s. It explained the prevalence of the nuclear family based on segregated conjugal roles as a key institution of modern industrial society in terms of its relationship to the broader social structure and features of modernisation.

The term 'functions', applied to any social institution, refers to the positive contributions that it makes toward the broader social well being and consequently the lives of members of society. The family is a key social institution for functionalists because it transmits society's norms and values through successive generations, thereby promoting social consensus and continuity. To explain how this operates, Parsons places a heavy emphasis on environmental influences, especially primary socialisation. He maintains that at birth the mind of the baby starts as a relatively blank slate. The child's mind gradually awakens to society's values, rules and norms through experiences within the nuclear family. These values, rules and norms become internalised into the personality structure. This process of socialisation is relatively uniform across families and is functional because it equips the young to fit into society and provides the basis for social stability.

The family unit benefits from role specialisation. Parsons argues that in an increasingly competitive and impersonal social world external to the family, the male is best suited for the breadwinner role through which the family is financially supported, and the female is better equipped for childrearing and domestic responsibilities. Interestingly, despite Parson's emphasis on the impact of environmental influences and primary socialisation on the personality structure, natural predispositions also enter the analysis. Parsons backs up this complementary role specialisation by an emphasis on natural and inbuilt differences between the sexes in the form of male capacity for instrumental and rational thinking and female affective and emotional qualities.

Parsons attempts to locate changes in the family within the context of long-term broader social changes. Here it is important to recall that from the functionalist perspective, the family is viewed as a basic social unit whose changes synchronise with changes in the broader social structure. In terms of broad structure, pre-industrial society tends to be a relatively closed social hierarchy, offering few opportunities for social mobility – movement up or down the social structure between the generations. Peoples' status within the social structure is relatively ascribed, or fixed, at birth. There is also little geographical mobility or industrial dynamism. Life tends to follow tradition and agricultural routines. Within this broader context, it is argued that the extended family is a logical adaptation. Ascribed status within the family, usually based on age, was compatible with ascribed status within society, and nepotism – using one's position to place relatives in employment – was common and not dysfunctional within this context. Boundaries between family and community life were often quite limited, enabling the intrusion of the prying community into domestic life.

For functionalists, the transition from pre-industrial to modern industrial society involved a fundamental change in the broader social structure from that governed largely by inherited social status to a society of achieved status. In modern society, there are more opportunities for geographical and social mobility as an efficient social and economic system needs to effectively utilise its human resources. It does so by offering high levels of economic reward to those who have demonstrated their individual ability by competing successfully with others in a relatively open social structure.

What, according to Parsons, are the implications of these changes for the family? One is that the privatised or isolated nuclear family is a necessary adaptation to the needs of modern industrial societies. The privatised nuclear family refers to the tendency of the modern family to establish a clear sense of boundary between itself and broader society. If the extended family were to persist, there would be growing inconsistency between ascribed positions within the family and achieved occupational status. Nepotism would also be dysfunctional in a society where occupational standing needs to be allocated on individual merit. Also, the privatised nuclear family, in shearing its emotional and supportive bonds with the broader kinship network of the extended family, is able to allow the necessary geographical and social mobility that modern society requires of its workforce.

For Parsons, the privatised nuclear family is also functional because it offers adult members – especially the male breadwinner – the possibility of retreat and replenishment within a haven of emotional security. Additionally, it caters for the therapeutic needs of adults to act out childish residues – affective, childlike behaviour which would not be acceptable in the outside formal and competitive adult world.

Functionalists argue that as society modernises, new institutions emerge to take on increasingly specialised functions. Functional specialisation accompanies 'structural differentiation'. Through these changes, more efficient specialist institutions are engaging in exchange relationships in a functionally integrated society. The family loses some of its broader functions in this process. It is no longer a significant unit of economic production, of education, or of welfare as specialist institutions external to the family have largely taken over these functions. But for Parsons, this does not mean that the nuclear family is a less important institution. It has adjusted to the needs of modern society through conjugal role specialisation, privatisation, and focussing on the key functions of primary socialisation of children and the stabilisation of adult personalities.

Marxism – the nuclear family as a support mechanism for capitalism

Classical Marxism agrees with functionalism that the family, headed by the male breadwinner, is a key institution of socialisation and support for the social system, but fundamentally disagrees on the nature of this system. From a Marxist perspective, a society of achievement through individual merit – a meritocracy – is incompatible with capitalism. In reality, there remains a relatively closed class structure based on the inheritance of private property. Power especially derives from ownership of the means of production. The owners of business constitute a capitalist class who rely on the supply of exploitable and disciplined labour to enhance their profits. The profits of one class are therefore based on the exploitation of another. The worker cannot escape exploitation within this system, but with the pressing needs of subsistence and family responsibilities becomes tied to the workplace. As an instrument of his employer's profit, the labour of the worker is treated as a commodity and the worker controlled as an object in the productive process. The outcome is an experience of alienation – a feeling of powerlessness and meaninglessness. Within this broader context, the family acts as a safety valve against potential class conflict as other members of the family absorb aggression from the breadwinner which has been generated within the workplace.

Additionally, the family performs for employers the utility of the upbringing of the next generation of exploitable labour at maintenance cost to the worker. Within the home, the young are socialised into submission to the authority of the father figure. This relationship works as a form of preparation for acceptance of the authority of future employers over workers. And as a fallback position, women constitute what Marxists refer to as a 'reserve army of labour' which can be taken up when beneficial to employers and more readily disposed back to the family when not required.

Marx was confident that the class based stresses built into capitalism could not be soaked up indefinitely and that this system would eventually explode in class revolution. However, as capitalism has endured, other schools of Marxist thought have become less sure of this outcome. Neo-Marxist (modern revisionist) writers of the Frankfurt school, such as Herbert Marcuse, retain the basic Marxist analysis of class exploitation under capitalism, but recognise the growth in the seductive influence of the mass media. They argue that the mass media encourages heightened domestic consumption by associating it with the image of freedom. The housewife is thus free from heavy domestic drudgery if she has the latest domestic gadgetry. Acquiring a new fast car is also associated with the image of freedom. This demand for goods keeps capitalism buoyant. But, more than this, it locks workers further into un-free, repressive and exploitative relations within the workplace to afford these goods or keep up payments. From a Marxist perspective, the attractions of consumerism distract workers from recognising the need for genuine freedom which can only be achieved through replacing capitalism with a social system in which the means of production are commonly owned and labour not exploited for private profit. The 'freedom' often associated with conspicuous consumption is therefore a false consciousness that in fact binds workers to capitalism.

Clearly, functionalist and Marxist perspectives on the family are diametrically opposed. The former idealises the family as a haven of sanctuary within a competitive society whilst the latter views it as a prop for an exploitative social system. However, they both traditionally take the nuclear family and the male breadwinner as given. They both also strongly emphasise powerful moulding forces of socialisation working in uniform ways to mould individuals to society. Given evidence of growing diversity of family life, both perspectives now look dated and inadequate. This diversity will later be reviewed, along with the question of the decline of the family, and alternative theoretical perspectives will be considered. Firstly, a brief review will be made of changes in the family from a social historical context. This will be followed by an identification of areas of interest established in traditional sociological research into the family.

Family change from a broad social historical context

Life in pre-industrial societies was for most experienced in a rural and agrarian setting. Most people lived out much of their lives within local communities which were well established social hierarchies with little opportunity for social mobility. Research, for example by Shorter, has suggested that romantic attraction or expectations thereof played little part in marriage. Instead, for the wealthy, marriage was a means of consolidating wealth and power. In poorer households, it brought together members into an economic unit of production as the home was often also the workplace. Here, family members engaged in agricultural or handicraft activities with young children usually allocated the housework. In some cases, boys were apprenticed into other families to learn a trade. For landless agricultural workers (serfs), life was often brutal and harsh, limiting the possibility of the cultivation of romantic feeling. Furthermore, as bonded to their landlord, he effectively owned them and had legitimate control over most aspects of their lives, including a final say on whom they may marry.

For most, therefore, both modern conceptions of romantic attraction as the basis for marriage and the separation of home and work would have made little sense.

To what extent does historical research square with the functionalist model which suggests that the extended family was prevalent in pre-industrial society and then declined with the needs of more dynamic capitalism? Research by Laslett into family life in pre-industrial England suggests that only about 10% of families included kin beyond the nuclear. However, Anderson found that in industrial Preston in1851, 23% of families contained kin other than nuclear. Other research has suggested that the extended family has undergone significant decline in recent decades. Put together, this evidence seems to support a three stage model of the extended family rather than the two stages suggested by functionalist theory.

What accounts for the above findings? Firstly, in pre-industrial society, life expectancy was relatively short, so it is likely that any three generational families would also be relatively short lived. Secondly, the common practice of primogeniture (the maintenance of property intact through inheritance by the eldest son) meant that other family members would have to make their way in the world. Both the nuclear family and the work ethic therefore could be argued to precede and assist industrialisation rather than adaptively emerge from it.

What changes did industrialisation involve? Advances in science and technology, culminating in England in the late eighteenth century, brought about a revolution in the productive process. Workshops and factories were able to utilise powered machinery which could produce standardised goods more cheaply and efficiently than domestic workers who relied much on hand powered machinery were able to. Unable to compete, there was increasing pressure on domestic workers to seek employment in factories, bringing about massive population movements from the countryside to the towns.

The key changes that industrialisation promoted regarding the family were: 1) a redefinition of work as something external to the family where labour was sold for wages, 2) the emergence of the extended family and 3) the development of segregated conjugal roles with the male becoming the chief breadwinner and the female taking on domestic chores. Taking each of these in turn:

1) The factory system meant that labour had to be offered outside of the domestic setting to an employer who owned the new productive technology which required the concentration of waged workers in factories to maximise productivity.

2) When workers moved to the towns, their accommodation would invariably be rented. Sometimes one family member, usually the father, would make the first move and acquire employment and accommodation. Employers often relied on workers to put in a word for other family members (nepotism). These members would then follow and employers would come to take on whole families. This process allowed the intensive occupation of meagre accommodation and the greater dividing up of the cost of rent. In such circumstances, extended family life offered some safeguard of mutual support to cover for situations of adversity at a time when little welfare provision was available.

3) By the 1830s, protective legislation came to limit the employment of women and children in factories. The consequent tendency was of women to withdraw from the factory to the home, a location which was now viewed as a non-work environment. If women did work outside their own family, it was often as domestic workers, thus reinforcing their association with the domestic sphere.

Traditional sociological research: a focus on the nuclear and the extended family

The extended family proved to be a durable arrangement in working class communities well into the twentieth century. Whilst employment opportunities were stable and populations remained settled, the process of nepotism was able to continue. Men often put in a word at work for their sons and women provided the daily contacts of mutual support which comprised the extended family networks in the domestic setting. Indeed, Young and Willmott found such life still quite common in working class communities of Bethnal Green in the mid 1950s. However, broader forces of change were beginning to undermine the cohesion of the extended family in this and other localities. What were these changes?

One factor was the development of post war welfare state provision. This enabled people to fall back more on the impersonal help of the benefit and welfare system during times of need rather than feeling bound by the reciprocal obligations associated with extended family help. Another change related to housing in the context of post war reconstruction. From the mid 1950s, families were being re-housed as new housing estates were built further out from slum areas, such as in parts of the East End, which were demolished. Such re-housing usually led to the departure of the young nuclear family unit, attracted, as many interviewees in research conducted by Young and Willmott stated, by the prospects of a better environment for their children. Industrial change in the form of a decline in the availability of dock work meant that younger family members could place less reliance on nepotism for finding work. Consequently, they sometimes needed to work or even move outside their area of origin. And soon, the expansion of service sector employment and changing social attitudes enabled more women to find employment outside of the home, thus undermining their role at the hub of the extended family.

So, has the extended family fallen into further decline? Possibly, but evidence appears to be a little mixed. For example, Young and Willmott found that when the young nuclear family unit was re-housed further out from the East End, wives direct contact with extended family kin declined significantly and they often experienced loneliness and isolation. However, in some cases, husbands retained employment in the locality of extended family kin and through their visiting whilst working in the area were able to perform the role as the link person in an extended family to some extent.

More general research conducted by the British Social Attitudes Survey in 1995 has indicated that, when measured in terms of seeing a specified relative outside of the nuclear family at least once a week, the extended family is more a feature of working class life than middle class, that women are still the main participants in maintaining contact, and that contact is more likely if there is a dependent child. In working class families with dependent children, 65% of mothers had regular contact with a relative whereas only 33% of males in non-manual occupations and without children retained equivalent levels of contact.

Increased access to private transport has enhanced the opportunities for regular face-to-face contact with relatives over greater geographical distances. However, part of the reason for lower levels of contact between middle class relatives may be related to greater dispersal as their occupations and careers tend to require higher levels of geographical mobility. Despite this, research evidence from Colin Bell in Swansea and Young and Willmott from a North London suburb suggest that there existed similar levels of positive concern within middle class families to maintain contact, even though it may be by such means as telephone and letter. More recently, the growth of the internet is surely enhancing opportunities for maintaining instant contact with relatives over vast distances. Assessing the survival of the extended family into the present day may therefore require taking into account the extent to which these technological based forms of communication are comparable with or a substitute for the help and support which once came from face–to–face contact with relatives living locally.

We are now in a position to call into question the functionalist account of the extended family. Historical evidence suggests that it was not a common fabric of pre-industrial life, but became more prevalent with the process of industrialisation. And sociological research into post war society has shown that the extended family, along with the practice of nepotism, remained relatively vibrant in some communities. Even in contemporary society, it has shown some resilience, even if, as suggested above, in more superficial form. The functionalist argument that the extended family is not well suited to the needs of a modern dynamic economy should therefore alert us to the fact that if theoretical perspectives are to illuminate our understanding of society, we must apply them cautiously. We should not be blinded to alternative evidence just because it contradicts the self-contained logical consistency of a theory.

As in post war functionalist theory, so in traditional sociological research, the nuclear family was taken as given. The main focus of attention was on role relationships within this institution. The research of Elizabeth Bott and Young and Willmott bear this out well.

Bott's pioneering small scale study of families in London – 'The Family and Social Network', (1957) – generated some early insights into the influences behind whether partners engaged in segregated or joint conjugal roles. She found that a connection existed between type of conjugal role relationship and type of friendship network. Her evidence suggested that segregated conjugal roles were more likely to exist in cases where each partner had established a closely knit friendship network outside of marriage where many of the members knew each other. This also tended to be more common in working class families. Joint conjugal roles were more characteristic of middle class partners who had established dispersed friendship networks outside of the family in which few members knew each other.

Young and Willmotts's larger scale research entitled 'The Symmetrical Family' (1973) came to some similar conclusions to that of Bott's regarding middle class and traditional working class family roles. In their research, the term 'symmetrical' referred to joint conjugal roles whose advance was viewed as a sign of progress in the direction of more egalitarian domestic roles. However, this later study of working class nuclear families found evidence that contrasted to the traditional working class pattern of segregated conjugal roles within the broader context of vibrant extended family life. Evidence of a more symmetrical role relationship was associated with growing working class affluence and home centred consumerism. Husbands were spending more time on DIY household chores and more wives were taking on paid work. Convergence with the middle class prevalence of joint conjugal role relationships was related to sections of the working class gaining access to more middle class levels of affluence.

Evidence of trends toward joint conjugal role relationships is a departure from the family of the Parsonian functionalist model. However, such changes are not necessarily inconsistent with the functionalist perspective as they could be argued to represent adaptation of nuclear family roles to broader social changes. As pressures of consumerism and changes in the economy bring more work opportunities to and pressures on women, a more egalitarian role relationship within the family can be seen as a necessary adaptation. To what extent can changes in the direction of gender equality within the family be further substantiated?

One area to consider is that of the perception of equality or inequality by partners themselves. A British Social Attitudes Survey of 1987 suggested that there were differences in perception between men and women on the practice of gender equality within the family. 16% of men believed that household tasks were shared equally but only 9% on women thought so. These different gender perceptions may well relate to different starting points and expectations.

Sociologists themselves sometimes disagree on the interpretation of research evidence. This may relate to their own gender and sociological perspectives. Whilst Young and Willmott were confident that their research findings indicated the progress of joint conjugal roles, the feminist Ann Oakley (1974) was much more cautious about the findings. She suggested that their optimism was undue since their starting point was that of segregated conjugal roles and measurements were taken in such a way that even modest evidence of husband's involvement in household tasks was taken as a sign of joint conjugal roles. They had therefore over interpreted the data. By contrast, her study of 40 families in London found more symmetry in the role relations of middle class parents than that of working class, but that even in the former symmetry was found to be minimal.

Oakley's research, based on detailed interviewing, may have however included it's own in built bias. R. Pahl's research found that conjugal role relationships can be affected by the stage reached in the typical family life cycle. Joint conjugal roles may be a more workable option for couples without children. However, if couples have children, it was found that the wife was more likely to give up employment when they were young. More segregated conjugal roles are likely to be associated with this phase. Later, as parenting responsibilities decline, the wife may re-enter the workplace and domestic roles tend to become more jointly allocated again. The important point here is that Oakley's research may have been predisposed against finding evidence of joint conjugal roles, since all 40 housewives in the sample had young families.

It may be reasonable to expect evidence to show that joint conjugal role relationships are well advanced in dual career families. What does the evidence show? Summarising a range of research, J. Gershuny suggested that between 1974 and 1987, husbands of wives in full-time employment doubled their involvement in cooking and cleaning activities. However, wives still tended to retain primary responsibility for housework. The term 'dual burden' has been applied to women in this situation. Furthermore, research by Rapoport and Rapoport (1982) suggested that enhanced career opportunities have placed many women in a situation of double disadvantage. The pressure of traditional gender expectations requires them to retain major responsibility for domestic work whilst pay and career opportunities are still limited. Having a foot in both camps does not just lead to work overload but to a situation of 'double exploitation'. A key question here is whether or not these experiences are part of the painful process of transition for working wives toward more genuine equality of opportunity and reward.

Looking at conjugal roles alone may tend to overlook other areas of potential gender inequality within the family. Such areas can include that of decision making and control of family finances. These dimensions are more to do with power in a sociological use of the term – that is, the ability to exert one's will over others. Research conducted by Stephen Edgell (1980) found that although there was evidence of more joint conjugal role relationships in child rearing, males tended to predominate in making decisions which were defined by the couples as major and important, whilst females had responsibility for more routine and less important decisions. Interestingly, research carried out by Jan Pahl (1993) found that husbands still tended to have more control over family finances and that both partners experienced highest levels of marital unhappiness in situations where husband's control was strong.

Another area which has been researched covers a rather more subjective dimension – that of emotional input into relationships. Evidence from Duncombe and Marsden (1995) found that male partners were less likely to recognise the necessary extent of emotional input required to keep a relationship together and that women put in most of the work in this area and also took much of the strain.

In summary then, this section of the chapter has concentrated on the nuclear family and found that there is modest evidence of growing gender equality. The evaluation of this evidence can vary significantly. Those who use a position of segregated conjugal roles as a starting point may argue that substantial change has taken place, whereas many feminists are likely to maintain that the changes are modest and token. There is a broad range of research evidence which suggests caution regarding the extent of adaptation of nuclear family life to modern society's apparent requirement for far greater gender equality. However, we will shortly consider evidence of a growing diversity of family types which makes research based on the nuclear family itself look rather dated.

Symbolic interactionism - family as defined by participants

Although established in the founding tradition of sociological perspectives, interactionism may better equip the sociologist to approach the diversity of contemporary family life than functionalism or Marxism. Interactionists emphasise that individuals participate in social situations where roles are chosen, negotiated, constructed and redefined by purposive social actors. Rather than operating as a rigid and structured imposition on people's lives, broader society, as the product of their wilful action, can be dynamic and diverse.

This interpretive perspective also emphasises the importance of sociological researchers seeing society as through the eyes of social participants. Interactionists studying the family would therefore attempt to gain an understanding of any family life viewed as such by people themselves rather than working from preset definitions of what counts as a family. This approach enables the sociologist to adopt a neutral attitude toward family diversity. It emphasises, in contrast to positivist approaches, that sociologists should not base their knowledge entirely on the convenience of using social statistics derived from official definitions. Such number crunching loses sight of a broader diversity of relationships which are meaningful as families to participants. By adopting a micro approach, interactionists might certainly look at the experiences encountered by married couples as they negotiate married life and experience divorce (with marriage and divorce being the milestones provided in official data). However, they would also study those in other relationships which the participants define as a family which do not form the basis of official statistics on the family, but which are equally worthy of study. In other words, sociologists should be guided in their research to try and understand all social life in ways meaningful to individuals or groups rather than the blinding convenience of easy to acquire social statistics based on conventional definitions. The sociologist who limits him or herself to the latter task risks the bias of making themselves an instrument of convention.

The family – decline or change?

1 Increase in divorce

One area frequently associated with the question of the decline of the family is that of rising divorce rates. There are official statistics available on petitions filed and divorces granted which make it clear that throughout the twentieth century there has been a substantial rise in divorce. Depending on how one measures divorce, it could be argued that divorces peaked in England and Wales in 1993 and have fallen somewhat since then, or it could be argued that divorce has reached a plateau from 1991. This is because divorce can be looked at either in terms of whole numbers or rates. Whole numbers simply express the total number of divorces granted during a particular year. By contrast, divorce rates refer to the number of divorces per 1,000 married couples per annum. Aggregate numbers are useful if interest is primarily in the magnitude of divorce. Figures from Social Trends,1993, show, for example, that there were about 25,000 divorces granted in England and Wales in 1961 and that by 1986, the figure had reached approximately 154,000. If these figures were expressed in terms of rates, they would be 2.1 and 12.9 respectively – indicating a greater than six-fold increase, which is roughly commensurate with the proportionate increase in aggregate totals for this time period as indicated above. However, there is a sense in which rates may offer a more revealing gauge of change in divorce. As they relate to a standard gauge of divorces per 1,000 married couples, rates may not always exactly mirror changes in the aggregate totals. For example, compared to the 1986 aggregate figure given above, in 1996 there were approximately 155,000 divorces yet the divorce rate had increased significantly to 13.8. How is this possible? It is because if there are fewer people married, then the ratio of divorces to the numbers married can increase even if the total of divorces remains much the same - and of course the opposite is also true.

Understanding statistics

One way of understanding the logic of such figures in sociology is to invent a situation where the figures are much smaller. Imagine a small town in which there are 2,000 married couples. If in a given year there were 22 divorces, the rate would be 11 per 1,000 married couples. However, if in another year there were only 1,000 married couples, then the same aggregate of 22 divorces would represent a leap in the rate to 22. The same logic can be applied to the figures outlined further above, and, of course, this type of exercise is worth recalling to assist the understanding of statistical information in other areas of sociological study.

Figures for 2005 show a fall in divorces in England and Wales to approximately 142,000, but the divorce rate remains about the same as that of 1996 as the number of people married continues to decline. In 1971, over two thirds of the adult population were married. The figure has since fallen to about 50%.

2   Why an increase in divorce?

How can the relatively high divorce rates of recent decades be understood sociologically? Changes in divorce laws over the last 150 years have gradually made divorce more accessible. These changes are referred to as enabling legislation. However, this alone is insufficient to explain the large increase in the divorce rate. As the law changes, it usually reflects society's changing moral values which it codifies. Therefore, more liberal divorce legislation has accompanied a decline in social stigma against divorce – but it is not necessarily the case that there is a clear cause and effect relationship whereby changing moral values bring about corresponding legal changes. It could also be argued that the greater frequency of divorce which the legislation makes possible will have an impact on moral values.

But this still does not explain why more people decide to divorce. One explanation requires the application of historical understanding of the choices available to people, the expectations associated with marriage and the nature of marital bonds. Edward Shorter (1977) argued that in pre-industrial society, the family was a relatively uncaring environment, based around the perpetuation of property or the domestic work unit. The economic necessity of it remaining intact was often important. By contrast, high expectations of romantic attachment and emotional fulfilment are the mainstay of modern marriages. Such high expectations can be easily thwarted, leaving little else to hold the marriage together.

Secularisation is a further dimension of social change which may be relevant to the long term rise in divorce rates. Secularisation is the assertion that the significance of religion in peoples' lives declines with the process of modernisation. This assertion will be reviewed in greater detail in a later chapter – it is not a simple proven fact. However, from the point of view of this topic area, it can be argued that religion and the church may play a diminishing role in peoples' lives, as witnessed by the increase in marriages in registry offices and other licensed premises. The implications for divorce are that the sanctity of the church and the belief in making a promise before an all seeing god are more powerful sanctions making for a marriage to endure. A key issue here though is that one would need to know more about the reasons why people marry in church or a secular setting and whether the choice has been freely available to them. For example, as divorce has increased, if the church retains a traditional attitude of not remarrying divorcees, then more people may be pushed toward secular remarriage options.

Other social factors which coincide with the steep increase in divorce rates since the early 1960s include higher marital expectations and greater assertiveness of women which accompanied the women's liberation movement from the late 60s. From about this time, women have also gained more opportunities to become economically self supporting through an expansion in their employment opportunities accompanying economic modernisation. As we have seen, despite increasing expectations, these 'opportunities' have often involved them in the stress of a dual burden. Putting all this together, it should not be surprising that divorces filed by women rose to over 70% of those filed.

Despite historically high divorce rates, a majority of those who divorce will remarry and statistics show that their future marriage will also be more prone to divorce. Indeed, over a third of marriages are now a remarriage for at least one of the partners. In 1970, the American writer Alvin Toffler put such figures into the context of a society of accelerating pace of change and increasing human longevity in which the odds were increasing stacked against couples developing and remaining together for life. He argued that a trend toward 'serial monogamy' – an emerging pattern of temporary marriages - was already under way. Toffler predicted that the traditional expectation of lifelong marriage would give way to the anticipation of relatively short lived marriage and declining stigma against divorce. Couples would be increasingly confronted with key decisions as their paths diverged on whether they could find a more parallel path with another partner. Such issues will be touched on again in the last section of this chapter.

3 Growing diversity

As those who divorce often remarry, the result can be an increasing number of reconstituted families. Such families bring together children from different marriages into a single home which can lead to problems of mutual adjustment. These 'binuclear' or stepfamilies may also pose the problem of the relative authority over children of step and biological parents.

Statistics indicate that there has been a fall in the number of marriages in England and Wales in recent decades from an annual average of almost 400,000 between 1965 and 1975 to under 300,000 by the mid 1990s and, despite increases in the early years of the twenty first century, a fall again to 244,710 in 2005. If further allowance is made for the increasing divorce rates over this period, the tendency for divorcees to remarry, and the fact that the above figures include an increasing number of second marriages, there is evidence to suggest that the population has been dividing into a declining number of people who are marrying, more of whom are divorcing and many remarrying, and a significantly increasing number who are not marrying. So what is the evidence of alternatives to marriage that are emerging?

There is clear evidence of increased rates of cohabitation. From research conducted in the 1950s, approximately 5% of married women said that they had cohabited with their husband prior to marriage. Although not in strictly comparable form, the findings from General Household Surveys indicated that the percentage of women cohabiting doubled between 1981 and 1996 to 25% and that the time period of cohabitation was increasing. The figures also showed different cohabitation rates for different age groups and different rates for males and females within the same age group. The highest rate was for males in the age range of 30-34 where the figures exceeded 40%. It is, of course, possible that an element of this increase may be due to people feeling freer to volunteer this type of information than in the past when such arrangements were more heavily stigmatised. Also, the extent to which cohabitation is forming an alternative to marriage may be a little more questionable than the statistics suggest. This is because many cohabiting couples eventually marry and high rates of divorce mean that more new couples need to await the completion of a divorce before they are able to remarry and may cohabit during this time.

Nevertheless, figures show that there are currently over two million opposite sex couples in cohabiting relationships in England and Wales and although projections should always be treated with caution most predictions suggest that this figure will increase significantly in the coming decades. For example, according to Population Trends research, the figure is expected to rise to about 3.8 million couples by 2031.

Changing attitudes appear to correlate with these trends. A British Social Attitudes Survey of 2001 found that long term cohabitation was becoming accepted as relatively normal and that only just over 50% of those interviewed believed that people should marry before having a family, compared to almost 75% in 1989. Few, however, dismissed marriage which remained viewed as a viable lifestyle choice.

There is, of course, reason for some doubt over the precise accuracy of official figures on cohabitation. It raises issues of how officials on the one hand or the parties themselves define a relationship, and the extent to which there may be incentives, such as claiming benefit, which are likely to encourage some people to hide cohabiting relationships from prying officials and others.

Another aspect of family diversity relates to the ethnic diversity of British society. The term 'ethnicity' refers to shared national culture and traditions. Although different ethnic groups are often distinguished by such physical characteristics as skin colour, when the term ethnicity is used, ethnic differences are viewed as socially as opposed to biologically based. The cultural identity and ways of different ethnic groups are therefore acquired through socialisation and cultural traditions may persist or change in the cultural environment of the host population.

In Britain, a substantial proportion of the non white ethnic minority population is now second or third generation. A key question at this point is whether life in British society is narrowing the differences in family life between different ethnic minorities and white British or whether ethnic traditions are more resistant to change.

The complexity of differences between and within ethnic groups cannot be tackled here, only emphasised. As two quite contrasting examples, South Asian and Afro Caribbean family life will be briefly commented on. Generally, South Asian families have retained the highest marriage rates and low divorce rates, tend to partake in extended family life where possible (including contacts with and visits to relatives in their country of origin or ancestral origin), sometimes still exert pressure towards arranged marriage, and place a strong emphasis on traditional segregated conjugal roles. One important difference between Pakistani and Indian families, though, is that in the former, the influence of Islamic strictures is more likely to require a wife to stay at home. Although single parenthood in both Indian and Pakistani families has significantly increased, this is from a very low base, and reaching about 5% remains below that of the white British population.

By contrast, single parent families are much more common within West Indian communities, marriage rates are relatively low, divorce rates high and cohabitation, at about 10%, is not uncommon. However, research has shown there to exist a diversity of Afro Caribbean family life in both country of origin and in Britain. This is partly economic based. Economically successful West Indians are more likely to follow a model of family life similar to the conventional British nuclear family. By contrast, common law families are more common amongst the less economically successful. A third pattern identified is the female headed households in which males play only a peripheral role and the mother, usually working, relies on the help of female relatives or neighbours to run the family.

Overall, the data from surveys and more in depth research suggests both quite high levels of continuity in the different ethnic traditions and some diversity of family life within ethnic minority groups. This would tend to add to the overall diversity of family life in Britain.

According to official statistics, single parent headed households in Britain have increased from 8% of all families with children in 1972 to 15% in 1989-1990 and 24% in 1998-1999. Although revealing a massive increase in single parenthood, there is much that these statistics alone also hide. Firstly, they are just a snapshot measurement. Many single parents and their children will have lived or come to live in married or cohabiting households for part of their lives. Secondly, the distinction between married and single parent households may not always be as clear cut as definitions suggest. In some married households, the requirements of certain occupations may necessitate that a partner be frequently absent, or in other cases the partners may be separated, whereas some single parent households have frequent contact with a partner. Thirdly, the category of single parenthood is of diverse composition and changing proportions including a declining proportion of widowed and increasing proportions of divorced and never married single parents. Situations may also vary significantly in terms of support and financial security available, but generally the never married are more likely to struggle on low income.

The figures for those living alone show a significant increase in recent decades. For example, in 1998, 12% of people lived in single person households compared to 3.9% in 1961. These comprised 12% of households in 1961 and 28% of households in 1998, since by definition these are the smallest household units. However, pausing here for a moment may alert us to some of the complexities behind these apparently straightforward figures. The routes to living alone are diverse and it may be that many who live alone do not do so through a positive decision of their own. This can certainly be the case for elderly people through the death of a partner. The figures for those under retirement age may therefore be more indicative of positive choice. These comprised 4% of all households in 1961 and 12% in 1996-1997. But how exactly are single person households defined? Take the example of a house divided into three separate flats, each let out to a student. Each flat may count as a single person household, but is this quite the same as people living alone in separate dwellings? What if each student in each flat shared common kitchen facilities and a television room? Do they still live alone or constitute single person households? Whether for definitional purposes they do or do not, presumably, qualitatively, their domestic lives would be quite different from those living in isolated and self-contained flats or separate dwellings. Furthermore, statistics only take a snapshot view of the domestic situation. Presumably, some of these students would return to families during vacation times. Longer-term profiles would therefore more realistically show the varying domestic situations experienced than any snapshot measurement could.

Although people can now be more open about gay and lesbian relationships, it is difficult to obtain any accurate measure of the changing extent of these relationships in society due to powerful past taboos. As part of the moral uniformity of the post war decades, people with homosexual inclinations had to either repress these tendencies or face the risk of criminalisation or 'corrective therapy'.

One feature of gay and lesbian relationships is that they are free from the imposition of conventional male and female gender stereotypes. Hence, there is more scope for negotiation of roles which tend to be more egalitarian than in heterosexual relationships. This was indeed found to be the case in Gillian Dunne's (1999) study of lesbian households.

In a growing number of countries, people in same sex relationships have been able to acquire legal recognition. In most of these countries, a distinction is made between same sex partnerships and heterosexual marriage, with the former referred to as 'civil partnerships'. This is essentially a distinction of legal terminology and status based on religious sensitivities, although the exact legal differences vary somewhat from society to society. Same sex civil partnerships were pioneered in Denmark in 1989, to be followed by Norway and Sweden in 1993 and 1994 respectively, France in 2000, Germany in 2001, and Britain from 21 December 2005. Other countries and some states or localities in countries with federal political systems such as Argentina and Australia have followed since.

In Britain, the established position of the Church of England is that the purpose of marriage is to fulfil god's purpose by promoting a committed and faithful relationship between a man and woman for the procreation of children. The term 'marriage' holds a degree of religious connotation and the state has recognised this by limiting single sex partnerships to civil status, officiated by a registrar at approved premises. However, the status of civil partnership does confer on partners legal equalities to that of married couples, for example in terms of taxes and benefits, protection against domestic violence and rules regarding migration and nationality.

At the time of the introduction of civil partnerships, it was estimated that in Britain approximately 4,500 would be granted in the first year. This figure was actually exceeded by over 10,000. As not legally defined as marriage, breakdowns of these relationships are not referred to as divorce, but as 'dissolution'. However, the procedure follows a similar one to that of divorce whereby the partnership must have endured for at least a year and face irretrievable breakdown.

On the one hand, such reforms can be seen as the government's response to demands for gay rights and an advance in social tolerance. However, it has also been suggested by Jennie Bristow that following decades of decline in the number of marriages and substantial increases in numbers of cohabiting couples set to continue, this is more of a 'top down' initiative by a government which is worried when people live their lives 'beneath the radar of the state'.

Holland (April 2001) was the first country to completely eliminate the distinction between same sex and heterosexual marriage, followed by Belgium in 2002. In Holland, 2,400 same sex marriages were officiated in the nine months of 2001, whilst for the twelve months of 2003 the number had fallen to 1,500.

The Papacy, as the custodian of Catholic traditionalism, strongly opposes same sex partnerships, and the Pope has recently referred to homosexuality as an "intrinsic moral evil". More surprisingly, therefore, the third country to pass legislation enabling same sex marriage was Spain in 2005 where a substantial majority of the population still see themselves as Catholic. The Roman Catholic Church and many conservatives bitterly opposed the reforms of a socialist government, which also passed legislation to speed up the process of divorce.

Both Canada and South Africa have since passed legislation allowing same sex marriage. However, the situation in the United States is complicated as laws apply on a state-by-state basis. Whilst California has recognised same sex civil partnerships and Massachusetts marriage, a broader debate has emerged in which attempts are being made to pass a constitutional amendment prohibiting legal recognition of such partnerships.

In late 2006, opposition between religious traditionalism and state reform on issues of sexuality and discrimination surfaced in Britain regarding adoption. It became possible for same sex couples to adopt in 2005. The Catholic Church, which runs a small number of adoption agencies in England and Wales, opposed the placement of children for adoption through its own agencies with single sex couples in civil partnerships which, based on religious scriptures, it did not recognise as marriages which had to be a union of man and woman. The timing of this statement of opposition related to the 2007 Equalities Act which makes it illegal to discriminate against anybody on the grounds of sexuality, including cases of adoption by same sex couples. In its response, the Catholic Church threatened to close its adoption agencies if it were forced to comply.

Responses to changes in family life

There have been a variety of responses to changes in family life in both society and in sociology. For example, one position adopted is that despite evidence of lifestyle diversity, the nuclear family still remains the standard family form in contemporary British society. An alternative view sees the diversity of modern family life and evidence of high divorce rates as alarming indicators of the breakdown of the family and a sign of a broader social malaise. For yet others, evidence of growing diversity of lifestyle should be viewed positively as indicative of the emergence of a more pluralistic and tolerant society. These positions can be briefly elaborated as follows.

Representative of the first position is Robert Chester. Much of his argument is based on the way that statistics on family life are viewed. Increased cohabitation and declining marriage rates amongst the young during the 1980s were interpreted by Chester as a period of adjustment as the young were delaying the age at which they married. Whilst in 1981, households with married parents and their children comprised only 32% of all households, being on average larger units, they comprised 49% of people. Additionally, since these figures were only a snapshot of family life, they did not show the fact that a majority of people lived in a nuclear family at some time in their life. For Chester, the nuclear family was thus still a majority institution. However, since his writings, the above figures have shown a significant decline and the argument now appears to look rather dated.

The political ideology and social policy of new right Conservatism leads quite directly to the second position. The new right, whilst liberals in economics, felt that moral values were becoming too liberal in terms of tolerance of alternatives to the nuclear family. Singled out for particular concern was the increase during the 1980s in the number of never married single parents. It vexed the new right that what was viewed as irresponsible behaviour often required state support and therefore the placing of additional tax burden on others, including those who already supported conventional families.

New right social policy, which intended to encourage traditional family roles and responsibilities, included new child support arrangements and care in the community. Set up in 1993 to pursue absent parents, the Child Support Agency operated to assert traditional family responsibilities of male provider for female child carer by imposing financial contributions on absent parents. In so doing, it aimed to combine the purpose of enforcing moral responsibility with saving treasury expenditure.

De-institutionalisation and the promotion of care in the community had the effect of placing an enhanced burden of care, especially for the aged, on the shoulders of female relatives. For example, research by Nissel and Bonnerjea into care for the handicapped elderly found that, on important care activities, for each one minute contributed by husbands, nineteen minutes was provided by wives.

Rhona Rapoport is representative of the third position identified above. This stance commends the diversity of family and lifestyle types which have come to characterise contemporary life in democratic societies. For Rapoport, tolerance of such diversity is seen as enhancing people's human rights to choose to live as they wish.

The leadership of the British Conservative Party under David Cameron is attempting to reposition the party a little more toward the latter position by retreating from past new right ideological hostility against single parents and supporting legislation introduced by New Labour for single sex civil ceremonies. Despite such reforms, the New Labour government continue to emphasise the importance of stable traditional heterosexual family life and are looking at ways to encourage single parents to return to work when their youngest child is twelve years old rather than sixteen. Indeed, in a 2008 welfare green paper, it has been proposed that this age be reduced further to seven. There appears to be a degree of convergence between the main political parties in the acceptance of family diversity without either fully embracing it.

Pause and reflection

As suggested earlier in this chapter, both Marxist and functionalist perspectives tend to be locked into a rather dated analysis of society and the family in which the traditional form of the latter fits into the broader structure of the former. For example, the emphasis placed by functionalism on the nuclear family tended to claim superiority of and universalise from a model of family life that was dominant at a time when the perspective was at the height of its influence in the 1950s. This indicates an inherent conservative weakness in the functionalist perspective – it takes what is, argues that it therefore serves social needs, and makes supporting justifications. Although the perspective should be able to anticipate and explain changes in the family as part of the mutual adjustment of institutions as society changes, functionalism has tended to remain synonymous with the 1950s model of the family. Furthermore, it is questionable whether it is possible to go far enough within this framework to explain changes in the family and relationships in the contemporary context of globalisation.

Symbolic interactionism was argued to be a more flexible perspective through which to understand the diversity of contemporary family life. However, as a micro perspective, it has far less to say about the broad social and historical changes which have brought about this diversity. Some contemporary approaches have attempted to explain diversity within this broader perspective.

Contemporary sociological perspectives on the family

A number of theorists are in broad agreement that society has in recent decades been changing fundamentally and that modernist explanations and concepts are no longer adequate for explaining contemporary society. These theorists can be divided into the two main camps of postmodernists and high modernists.

Postmodernism – almost anything goes

For postmodernists, there is a clear distinction between modern and postmodern society. The hallmark of modern societies, and derived from the Enlightenment of the seventeenth to eighteenth century, was the idea of progress through rational analysis as this enabled informed intervention and planned social improvement. Absolute truth could be based on scientific certainty to guide human intervention to improve the world. Classical sociological theory itself developed scientific credentials and the prospect of applying social engineering to improve the condition of society.

The idea of a single rational based truth coincided with pressures toward appropriate ways of life. Thus a consensus of values, such as those regarding the superiority of nuclear family life in the 1950s, would tend to provide a single and constraining moral certainty.

However, postmodernists argue that what is know and taken as true or normal is based on cultural setting and is relative to time and place. There have been fundamental changes in contemporary societies which affect people's choices, identities and understanding of the social world. It is argued that a postmodern era has emerged in which there has been a breakdown of faith in the scientific certainties and uniform moral standards that were more typical of modern societies.

Social change has taken the form of a growing diversity of lifestyles and the recognition that different types of knowledge and ways of life are relative and open to choice. This process has been enhanced by the impact of globalisation. Society has fractured into a diversity of cultures, types of knowledge and judgements about how to live. In this context, no one way of living can be judged as superior and imposed by others. In postmodern society, there is no single overriding moral consensus. Lifestyle can be increasingly based on individual choice, so long as it does not transgress the like rights of others.

For writers such as Baudrillard, postmodern society is a world of fast communication and media images in which people are free to choose from an array of lifestyles and identities as they search for successful formulas for their lives in an ever changing social world.

Judith Stacey emphasises that high technology and globalisation have brought about rapid change and the need for flexibility in people's work lives which brings forth the need for adaptive changes in their personal and family lives. Within this context, Stacey conducted small scale research in the United States which suggested that in the post industrial region of Silicon Valley, people engage in innovative adaptations in their lives to the extent that there no longer remains a single family life norm. This advanced region was selected because it was argued that it provides an image of postmodern conditions which will increasingly emerge across society.

For postmodernists, bewildering choice and relativism in terms of truth and lifestyle are here to stay. There is no likelihood of the emergence of a new single family form generally agreed to be the model to conform to and no detectable direction of change other than that of growing diversity.

High modernism – relationships at the end of nature

Ulrich Beck distinguishes between first modernity (capitalist industrial society up to the 1960s) and contemporary second modernity, the latter being referred to as 'risk society'. Adopting a similar position to that of, Giddens, Beck relates a decline in traditional social constraints to the process of individualisation, which accompanied first modernity and has reached a new level in second modernity. By progressive individualisation, Beck means that the scope of choices facing people in their daily lives has massively increased, as, for example, the constraints of family life, social class and gender stratification decrease. Acquiring freedom from constraints, people have to take on the burden of navigating their own way in life. Their intimate relationships therefore become more important in an insecure world. However, the guidelines for these relationships must now also be fashioned more by the partners themselves. This openness means that trying to make a relationship work can increasingly become be a source of conflict based on different expectations.

Anthony Giddens conceptualises contemporary society as at a high modernist stage of development. This stage is characterised by a change in the nature of people's commitment to intimate relationships which reflects a breakdown of social structures and personal commitments and ties more typical of modern society and the emergence of a more fluid social condition.

In 'The Transformation of Intimacy', and 'Runaway World' Giddens put forward a broad ranging model to explain changes in the nature of intimate relationships. According to this model, in pre-modern societies, families were built around the economic imperative. For most, the severe conditions of life were not conducive to the development of romantic intimacy as the basis for attachment. High infant mortality rates meant that the social tradition of marriage for procreation was embedded in and worked in harmony with the needs of nature.

A key feature of the modern era was the application of reason to the aim of improvement, which promoted social change. Thus, the hallmark of the modern period was growing 'reflexivity' – the need to weigh up and monitor situations. This period saw the emergence of romantic love as the basis for attraction and the binding of individuals in marriage. Acceptance of the rituals of marriage and family bonds formed the basis of tradition in the modern era.

In contemporary or high modern societies, improved health and declining infant mortality rates have meant that populations have become self-sustaining at low reproduction rates. Consequently, such societies contrast to those of the past in that sex becomes freed from the need for and emphasis on procreation and advances in contraception enable people to acquire more choice on whether or not to have children. In this sense, intimate relationships exist at the end of nature. The separation of sex from reproduction enables key modernist and traditional assumptions on family life undergo fundamental change.

Firstly, Giddens argues that relationships tend to become contingent. Rather than being constrained by the finality of having chosen the right person and pressures to remain together come what may, partners strive to achieve purer relationships in which the continuance of each is contingent of emotional rewards and satisfactions derived. This means that reflexivity reaches new levels as partners continually reflect on the purity of the relationship and whether or not to continue within it.

Secondly, a diversity of relationship types can emerge. This diversity allows individuals greater choice in the construction of their self-identity and the opportunity to experiment and shape their own lives. As part of this diversity, the greater tolerance of same sex relationships is not just associated with more liberal attitudes and a decline in traditional family values but is a further logical consequence of the separation of sexuality from reproduction.

Thirdly, sociologically, it is now more appropriate to refer to 'coupling' and 'uncoupling' than to marriage and divorce. There are now higher levels of cohabitation and although the institution of marriage retains some popularity, it is a 'shell institution' whose contents have changed since decisions on whether to remain together are now more based on individual choice in seeking a pure relationship. Marriage remains a possible ritual commitment and tradition which can help to stabilise a relationship, but this is now more a matter of free choice for couples. Although often still a traumatic experience, divorce or uncoupling now holds little stigma and it is recognised as a relatively high possibility for those who enter into relationships. Marriage or coupling now introduces new risks into people's lives at a very personal level as many of these relationships will break up.

Fourthly, Giddens optimistically suggests the advance of tolerance, freedom and equality in sexual relationships mirrors political advances that are taking place in society and globally. There is a parallel between the advance of democratic freedoms and personal relationships based on equality and mutual respect. The ways of democracy undermine the confines of tradition and embrace global cosmopolitanism – the contact of a diversity of cultural traditions in a climate of tolerance. There has been an increase in the number of cosmopolitan families as globalisation brings together people from different social and ethnic backgrounds. By contrast, fundamentalism is an attempt to re-impose traditional inequalities and constraints. For Giddens, issues of gay rights, marriage and gender equality are at the centre of the battle between the forces of cosmopolitan tolerance and often religious based fundamentalism.

4: Sociology of Education

Abstract

This chapter begins by alerting the reader to the fact that a sociological approach to education cannot be based on generalising from personal educational experiences. In place of the personal view, various theoretical perspectives are utilised – functionalism, Marxism, interactionism, postmodernism and high modernism – to offer a range of explanations of the relationship between education and broader society.

At a more empirical (evidential or factual) level, social, historical and political factors are reviewed to help provide an understanding of the influences behind educational developments.

Issues of genetic inheritance versus social environment regarding intelligence and educational achievement are raised. These are related especially to social class and also to gender, to which a variety of sociological arguments and research findings point to the importance of environmental factors.

As an exercise in applying the sociological imagination, the concept of meritocracy in society and education is explained. The reader is guided through some of the issues involved to help arrive at assessments of the degree to which the British education system is meritocratic.

Statistics on educational achievement and the associated issues of educational standards and the worth of qualifications are presented and discussed.

The question of the complexity of our educational system and the issue of diversity and choice are related to political thinking. They are also shown to be relevant to the question of meritocracy and central to theories of postmodernity and high modernity.

The sociological challenge

The English educational 'system' is complex and diverse with different regional and local patterns of provision. This issue of complexity and choice will be reviewed later. The challenge that first needs to be addressed is to recognise that our attitudes toward education generally, and different types of school and the process of selection more specifically, are likely to reflect our own educational experiences. These experiences and attitudes may run deep. Do we have a general loathing for grammar schools? Do we sympathise with the aims of comprehensive education? Do we admire the excellence of independent education? Whatever they are, our personal judgements and their implications in terms of our broader view of the educational system are likely to be based on our personal experience. This may make it difficult to engage in impartial analysis of the educational system. Yet, as sociologists, we must be vigilant against the bias of our personal experiences. How can we attempt to achieve this?

We need to raise our awareness of potential bias by stepping back and examining our own experiences and attitudes. By so doing, we can become prepared to study and evaluate sociological theories and explanations of education in a more open minded way. These theories offer frameworks to make sense of education systems within social and even global contexts. We can apply sociological concepts systematically and analyse to what conclusions they take us. We can also review research findings. As a result, our own views on education may be refined or even fundamentally changed. We should not fear this possibility, but recognise it as the reward of engaging in sociological thinking.

Definition of main concepts

One way to look at education sociologically is to identify a number of **functions** that it performs. 'Functions' of education refers to ways in which education operates to the benefit of society. For functionalists, these functions tend to be viewed as universal requirements – in one form or another they are necessary to all social systems.

Through the **economic function**, education imparts appropriate skills, knowledge, behaviour and values which enable individuals to perform effectively in work situations and support themselves and their families. Economic productivity and the prosperity of businesses and society itself are dependent on the effective operation of this function.

The processes through which people are selected for different types and levels of education are referred to as the **selective function**. This function is closely connected to the economic function since selection in education feeds through to positions in the occupational and social structure. If pupils are selected through competition to achieve and progress academically entirely in terms of their own abilities and effort, sociologists refer to the existence of opportunities for **contest mobility**. In a society of educational opportunity, education would service an open occupational and social structure in which allocation of position is based on individual merit. Such a society is referred to as a **meritocracy**.

Education is also an important vehicle for the **transmission of culture**. Culture used in this sense refers to society's traditions, values and identity which are communicated through language and symbols. Functionalists emphasise that education helps society to achieve both continuity and cohesion through conveying a shared cultural identity from one generation to the next.

Social order is promoted through the **social control function**. Through following rules and regulations and showing respect for authority within educational institutions, education lays the groundwork for a society of law-abiding citizens. For functionalists, this is vitally important because however effectively the other functions are preformed, society is likely to be damaged by high levels of disorder if there is no agency to adequately socialise the young into accepting a certain level of compliance.

The officially stated content of subjects is referred to as the **formal curriculum**. Teaching, learning and assessment are guided and constrained by course curriculum. However, **hidden curriculum** processes and influences may also operate alongside the formal curriculum. As an example of the impact of the hidden curriculum, an issue highlighted by feminists has been the effect of gender stereotyping. This can work in a variety of ways. School timetabling of subjects based on gender stereotyping can make it difficult for males or females to take certain subjects. Teachers may think in terms of gender stereotypes when advising students on choice of courses and careers. The content of academic materials can also affect pupils' choice of subjects and how they relate to them by conveying positive or negative gender messages. These processes can affect pupil's experiences, opportunities, self-perception and levels of achievement and have been the focus of much educational reform.

Returning briefly to an overview of the functions of education, it should be emphasised that the above distinctions that have been made are somewhat artificial and divided up to assist analysis. In the real world, these functions intermingle. For example, the impact of them all can be identified in the economic sphere. The economic function, viewed in a restricted sense, provides the economy with variously educated and skilled workers. But also the way that the selective function operates has an important bearing on the matching of abilities and skills to occupational roles. The key question here is the extent to which selection takes place more through privilege or merit. Again, the cultural values transmitted may be more or less favourable to enterprise culture. And social control, in requiring certain levels of obedience to authority and the structuring of the school day according to timetables, can be viewed as preparation for acceptance of authority and structured routines by the individual in work institutions. Clearly, viewing the combined effect of functions in this way helps to identify the importance of the hidden curriculum in educational processes.

How can viewing the education system through the concept of functions assist in developing understanding? It enables the analyst to take a macro view and think through the types of policy changes that may improve the functional effectiveness of education to benefit society. But this is a top down approach. Subordinating all to the functional needs of society tends to lose sight of the needs of individuals. It is therefore also important to think through what this type of society would amount to in terms of individual autonomy and self-fulfilment.

Founding sociological perspectives on education

Functionalism and Marxism are major founding perspectives on education. They are both macro theories – they locate an understanding of educational process within their own analyses of the broader social system. However, these perspectives differ fundamentally in their view of the nature of that broader system and therefore the role of education in society. For functionalists, education, like the family, is a vital element of the social bedrock. It should contribute toward the maintenance of an efficient and stable society. To do so effectively, the way that it operates must synchronise with the needs and key characteristics of the broader social structure. Therefore, as society changes, so must the education system. Locating an understanding of education within this holistic approach of functionalism alerts us to the priority of firstly gaining an overview of the key features of society and how it changes. Only then can sense be made of the changing nature of educational provision.

Functionalism – education services a meritocratic society

When adopting a broad historical vantage point, functionalists point to the relatively closed structure of social hierarchies in pre-industrial or traditional societies (at their height under feudalism in the Middle Ages). This means that there were few opportunities for people to rise above their place of origin in the social order. The sons of the wealthy were the main beneficiaries of formal education through having virtually exclusive access to private tutors and elite higher educational institutions. Their formal studies included traditional subjects – for example theology, philosophy, law, and Latin – which, if they did not live off the inheritance of an estate, prepared them for entry into elite professions such as the church, the law or government office. Through their privileged assess to education, they would also develop the etiquette, manners and leadership qualities appropriate to their social rank.

The commercial ranks may have been able to purchase a form of education for their sons. The type of education would very likely have been relevant to commerce and placed an emphasis on such practical areas of study as trade, commercial law, arithmetic and accountancy.

For the vast majority of peasants and labourers, there was little or no provision of formal education. Instead, children assisted parents in their work from an early age. Whilst occasionally a wealthy benefactor may assist in enabling a child of lowly social background receive an education, such assistance was in the gift of the patron. It was a personal favour and certainly not an established right. This type of personal relationship is referred to by Parsons as 'particularistic' – it was particular to personal inclinations.

To sum up, in traditional society, the selective function of education synchronised with and helped to perpetuate a relatively closed social hierarchy. The position of parents within the social structure largely determined access to and type of education received by their sons and largely denied to their daughters. Education, or lack of it, itself served to perpetuate privilege or disadvantage from generation to generation and access to education bore little relationship to individual talent.

Functionalists argue that, by contrast, modern industrial societies develop highly open social hierarchies and require a well educated and highly trained workforce. New technology requires that people are prepared for higher levels of work skills. The development of new and more specialised occupations leads to highly differentiated occupational structures. To prosper in a dynamic and more integrated world of industrial competition, modern industrial societies need to utilise their human resources far more effectively than did traditional societies. Consequently, the allocation of people to occupations must take place according to their assessed ability rather than by birthright. Educational provision has to adapt to these broader social changes. The development of educational institutions requiring universal access and offering opportunities for achievement and success based on individual merit, liberate successive generations from educational provision once tied to family background and offer opportunities for occupational and social mobility. In modern industrial societies, the selective function in education adapts to synchronise with the needs of a more meritocratic society. Parsons refers to education provided as a matter of right and selection by impersonal and impartial standards as 'universalistic' – rules are applied impartially and formally to all.

Emile Durkhiem, writing around the turn of the twentieth century, was acutely aware that modern society has to balance the maintenance of order and stability with that of merit and individual achievement. Compared to pre-industrial societies, a more competitive and meritocratic system could increase social disharmony if an excessive focus on individual achievement promoted a preoccupation with the self and raised individual expectations. To counteract the socially damaging effects of excessive individualism, Durkheim emphasised that society needed also to impose realistic constraints on individual ambition and remind individuals that they also have obligations to society.

To this effect, the school effectively works like society in miniature, moulding and preparing future citizens. For the benefit of society, as well as encouraging individual competition in pupils, education must impose order and a sense obligation by the individual to the collectivity. Schooling should therefore nurture in the individual a sense of pride in and identification with the collectivity and the institution. It must expect obedience to rules and regulations and the acceptance of the school hierarchy. The school promotes social cohesion amongst its pupils through developing its own collective rituals (school assemblies and award ceremonies) and sense of respect for its symbols (the school badge and mottos). These rituals and symbols tying the individual to the collectivity find their equivalent in society in the form of nationalistic sentiments and reverence for such powerful symbols as the national flag and anthem. As well as their formal curriculum content and the promotion of academic learning, the study of such subjects as history, literature and social studies would perform the important (hidden curriculum) function of developing a sense of shared national identity.

Talcott Parsons agreed with Durkheim regarding the importance of education in the promotion of shared values and a sense of national identity. However, in adapting functionalism to an American context, Parsons placed greater emphasis on education as promoting competition in a social system with an occupational hierarchy which is highly differentiated in levels of monetary reward. It was important that members of society shared meritocratic values and that society was seen to be meritcratic. Although emphasising the individual, the shared values of enterprise and fair individual competition would then be the bond which held society together as people accepted their position within the social order as the rightful outcome of this fair competition.

The link between economic incentives in the occupational structure and academic competition was drawn by Davis and Moore in 1945. They argued that society's occupational hierarchy represented an income differentiated ladder of opportunity, with educational achievement based on merit providing an important key to occupational success.

Marxism – education perpetuates the appearance of a meritocratic society

Whilst functionalists emphasise the importance of education to a harmonious, integrated, efficient and meritocratic modern industrial society from which all to some extent ultimately benefit, Marxists point to the negative aspects of the capitalist nature of modern societies. They view capitalist society as divided by economic and social class inequalities which tend to be perpetuated from one generation to the next. In that sense, Marxists maintain that, despite appearances to the contrary, capitalist societies are not as different from the closed social structures of the past as functionalist accounts propose. Marxists challenge the view that education under capitalism can ever select impartially to educate according to assessed ability and then match individuals to appropriate occupations and rewards.

Various insights have been developed from this perspective. One is that education assists social control in the workplace through promoting the acceptance of authority within an institutional context and oversupplying the labour market in terms of the skills required. It has been argued from this perspective (for example, Braverman, 1974) that capitalism has, in fact, brought about deskilling in the workplace as advances in the division of labour narrow down more jobs to highly repetitive processes, make labour more easily controlled, and reduce it to the experience of a meaningless activity. From a Marxist perspective, the real economic function of education is to ensure that workers can operate efficiently in the workplace whilst accepting authority and boredom and acquire sufficient skills to enhance their own efficient exploitation.

The appearance of meritocracy is conveyed by reference to a small number of high profile cases of rapid social ascent. The importance of this appearance is that it encourages people to believe that the system is fairly based on individual competition. This both encourages personal application and, for those who fail, the tendency to view their failure in terms of personal blame. However, for Marxists, the overwhelming reality of the selective function under capitalism is that it reproduces from one generation to the next social class related differences in opportunity.

From a classical Marxist position, class is determined by the means of production. Viewed this way, education primarily assists those who own the means of production and benefit from the labour of others. However, Marxists also look at class in terms of occupational level. Applying this approach to class, Bowles and Gintis (1976) conducted research on senior students in a New York high school. They found that those of average I.Q. showed great variation in their achievement of qualifications and levels of occupational success. Additionally, level of qualifications obtained did not correlate closely with occupational levels achieved. Those of high I.Q. did tend to achieve higher qualifications than others, but the researchers argue that the development of I.Q. was related to length of stay in education and that this related more to opportunities deriving from privileged social background. Overall, Bowles and Gintis argued that differences in social class background had a substantial effect on time spent in education, measured I.Q., qualifications gained and occupational success. Social class background therefore showed a higher correlation with educational and occupational achievement than did individual ability. They conclude that rather than education performing a meritocratic selective process for the allocation of future occupational roles, social stratification, in terms of the impact of student's family background, imposes a non-meritocratic, class based selective process on educational performance and occupational outcome. Education only appears to select according to individual ability, but for capitalism it is crucially important that this appearance is maintained. In reality, the key function of education in capitalist society is to help perpetuate the false consciousness of meritocracy within education and society to justify massive economic inequality, whilst in reality social class privilege and disadvantage tend to be passed down the generations.

Pierre Bourdieu has offered a more cultural explanation from a Marxist perspective. He argued that dominant social classes were able to impose their culture into the education system as the legitimate medium for success. The culture of the higher social classes tended to be more highbrow, whereas that of the working class more allied to pop culture. For Bourdieu, there is nothing academically superior in the former, but it reflects the yardstick for assessment which derives from class power.

The power to impose one's own culture as the medium for success is referred to by Bourdieu through the term 'cultural capital'. Since much of a person's culture is acquired during early socialisation within the family, children enter school with different class cultural advantages or disadvantages in an educational system where the culture of the dominant social classes is imposed as the worthy measure of success. This culture is not just about academic criteria but also relates to behaviour, manners and taste. The function of this monopolisation of educational culture is to minimise working class pupil's educational success and access to the higher occupations. This is achieved through their withdrawal from an environment in which the odds are stacked against them and by relative examination failure. The purpose of exams from this perspective is to offer the appearance of fairness and merit, since all students who sit them know that they take the same exams at the same time and under the same examination conditions. However, given the effect of different class cultures on exam performance, certification formally legitimises upper and middle class success and working class failure.

From this viewpoint, the transmission of culture in education does not, as functionalists maintain, take the form of a neutral national cultural consensus for the objective and meritocratic assessment of performance. It is class based, and its real function resides in maintaining social class privilege for some and disadvantage for others.

Symbolic Interactionism – self agency versus labelling

Interactionism opposes both Marxist and functionalist accounts of educational systems as being too deterministic. By this it is meant that these macro theories emphasise the determining effect of broader social structures on educational outcomes and pay little attention to the micro level of classroom situations as environments that are more autonomous from these broader processes. By contrast, symbolic interactionists explain pupil behaviour and performance by focussing on processes that take place within classrooms. They look at how pupil's self concepts emerge in these situations and affect their performance.

As explained in Chapter 2, from this perspective Mead claimed that self-identity is a product of both the passive 'me' and the more assertive 'I'. Whilst the 'me' tends to internalise externally imposed identities, the 'I' attempts to impose its own sense of self into social situations. There is therefore also the potential from this perspective for explaining educational processes in a more individualised way. To what extent has this potential been utilised in sociological research?

Interactonist research has often focussed on the impact of labelling on student self concept and performance. It has shown that labels applied by teachers to pupil's behaviour, sometimes associated with the streaming process, can have a powerful impact on student self-concept, behaviour and academic performance. In this sense, interactionism has sometimes not been able to avoid falling into its own determinism – individual behaviour still tends to be viewed as socially determined, but by social forces operating at a micro (classroom) level. This perspective has also sometimes related labelling in the classroom to the broader social structure (for example social class), as will be shown in the later section on sociological research.

However, research conducted by Margaret Fuller (1984) strongly cautions against assuming that labelling necessarily leads to predictable and pre-determined outcomes. Her study of black girls in a London comprehensive school found that they strongly resisted negative stereotyping which they were determined to prove wrong by their application to their studies. This enhanced their educational success.

Educational change in social and historical context

In pre-industrial England, sons of the wealthy landed classes had access to an elitist and traditional style of education whilst those of the commercial classes were equipped with a more commercial, practical, and scientific based education. The education of children of manual workers and agricultural labourers would largely comprise the direct acquisition of work based skills and worldly wisdom through assisting their parents in their occupations. Most females were denied access to education, save the possibility of involvement in religious orders.

A complex mixture of fortuitous factors lay behind the Industrial Revolution which was apace in England by the late eighteenth century. The development of practical and scientific educational in dissenting academies in the eighteenth century, to which we will shortly return, was part of the complex picture. However, throughout much of the nineteenth century, as industrialisation developed, educational provision showed only limited advance and on an ad hoc basis with minimal state involvement. Some continental countries that had industrialised later than England were introducing state organised educational systems before England. For example, by the mid nineteenth century, Germany and Holland were developing systems of elementary education. Given the apparent connection between industrial modernisation and the need for a more highly skilled workforce and the emergence of a more merotocratic society, why was state education in England relatively slow to develop?

To begin to answer this question requires going beyond education systems and looking at cultural values, religion and social class dynamics. A strong culture of laissez faire (self support through individual enterprise and hard work) prevailed in England through the middle decades of the nineteenth century. This was a value system which particularly appealed to the successful industrial middle classes. England was the first country to industrialise and the process had therefore not been state planned. The benefits of non-intervention had apparently proved themselves. The rising entrepreneurial (risk taking owners of private enterprise) classes thus associated freedom and prosperity with the values of individualism and private enterprise. Individual success and freedom was associated with freedom from the state.

This view was also linked to the preservation of religious freedoms. The industrial middle classes had a long tradition of religious beliefs which dissented from the Church of England. Consequently, they sometimes sent their sons to dissenting academies of their own religious persuasion (for example Quaker) where they would gain a more scientific and practical education. Since they paid for their own children's education, many felt entitled to resist also paying for state education of working class children through higher taxation. Furthermore, many feared that state sponsored education would interfere with their freedom of religious persuasion through the imposition of the religion of the established church. It was also feared by some employers that a more educated working class may push up their labour costs and further that, in their defence of a highly ordered society, these people may forget their social station.

There were therefore powerful forces of cultural, religious and social class self-interest which help to explain why the introduction of state education was delayed in this country. How, then, can the advance of state education later in the nineteenth century be explained? A number of factors coincide quite closely with the timing of the introduction and extension of universal elementary education dating from Forster's Education Act of 1870.

1) To explain the first factor, a distinction needs to be made between social class and social status. Social class is to do with social levels or strata identified in terms of occupational bands, whereas status refers to social groupings who share a common culture in terms of taste, manners and lifestyle from which they derive a certain level of social prestige. The latter decades of the nineteenth century witnessed a decline in the values of laissez faire enterprise culture. The reasons for this are complicated, but one thesis (J.W. Wiener 1981) argues that an important contribution to this decline was the greater use of public schools by the entrepreneurial classes. Viewed culturally as Philistines by more elite status groups, they sought gentlemanly status for their sons. This could be achieved by utilising their economic resources to send their sons to public schools. However, it was in this environment that they became ingratiated into a culture of disdain for industry.

2) England's waning economic performance, partly explained by the above, meant that other countries were closing the lead in economic modernisation that England had once established. These later developers appeared to have benefited from the provision of universal elementary education. The economic function of universal education in the context of international competition was therefore apparent to governments.

3) There also existed a fear that, by being left to their own devices and setting up discussion and reading groups, the working classes were beginning to educate themselves and in so doing often spreading politically subversive ideas. This situation could get out of control. To counteract it, the state could promote the social control function by imposing a form of education which provided the indoctrinating experience of rote learning and 'safe' god fearing religious messages.

Despite legislation in 1876 and 1880 to require compulsory full-time school attendance for children up to the age of 10, elementary education and a rote style of learning was all that was available to most pupils without parental means, whatever their abilities. And despite educational reforms early in the twentieth century which offered more grammar school places to able children of working class background, access to secondary education at the age of 11 remained largely fee based up to the end of the Second World War. This meant that even as the minimum school leaving age was gradually raised to 14, most pupils without parents of means had to remain in elementary school.

Educational reforms followed both the First and Second World Wars. Each time, the low level of education of war recruits had been identified. Additionally, wartime promises of reform in a range of policy areas including education were made to either circumvent the risk of political radicalism (First World War) or to raise wartime morale (Second World War). The reforms introduced after the Second World War can be seen as based on a collectivist consensus which emerged during the war and remained relatively intact for at least two decades afterwards. Generally, this consensus between the main political parties and across much of society favoured state intervention to protect the vulnerable whilst enhancing opportunities for the able irrespective of their social background.

Against the backdrop of this consensus, educational reforms contained in the Butler Act were implemented by the post war Labour government in 1946. They included both the extension of the minimum school leaving age to 15 and the transition from primary to some form of secondary schooling at the age of 11 for all children within the state system, along with the abolition of fees for access to state secondary education. With the barrier of parental inability to pay fees removed, it was expected that standardised intelligence testing through the introduction of the 11+ exam would perform a selective function to channel pupils with different levels of ability into different types of state secondary school. The reforms were therefore expected to enhance pupil's equality of opportunity to demonstrate their inequality of ability irrespective of social background, and then to educate them accordingly. These were therefore meriocratic principles which when applied in the selective process of the 11+ test for entry into the new largely tripartite system of secondary moderns, technical schools and grammar schools, were expected to show significantly improved access for able working class children to the academically challenging grammar schools.

However, research from the 1950s indicated that there was, in fact, little change in the access of children from working class backgrounds to grammar schools, proportionate to those from middle class backgrounds. During the 1960s, political party divergence opened up with the Labour Party supporting comprehensivisation and the Conservatives more intent on retaining the tripartite selective system. For Labour, comprehensive schools, which would take in pupils across the entire ability range within their catchment area, linked in with the idea of the promotion of a modern classless society. Yet even with the growth of comprehensive education, social class differences in achievement levels remained.

Traditional sociological research:

1 Social class - the seemingly impenetrable barrier to equal opportunity in educational achievement

Much post war educational research focussed on the issue of working class access to grammar school and levels of academic achievement. Given the meritocratic reasoning behind the post-war reforms, research tended to focus on establishing whether pupils of working class background were the main beneficiaries as may have been anticipated. In fact, much evidence showed that class related differences in terms of access and achievement remained relatively unchanged. For example, research conducted by J.W.B. Douglas (The Home and the School, 1964) compared the GCE O level performance of students of similar high measured ability but different social class backgrounds and found that performance levels declined in correlation with descending social class background. A far greater proportion of able lower working class students were also leaving school at the minimum leaving age.

Later research carried out by Halsey, Heath and Ridge (1980) found that, in terms of school leaving age, qualifications obtained, and entrance to university, the performance of youngsters from all social class backgrounds improved when pre-war and post-war cohorts were compared. However, in terms of their relative underperformance, the position of children of working class background remained largely unchanged. Their chances of entering grammar school were three times less than that of children from professional and managerial backgrounds – a proportion little different from pre-war figures.

What are the main approaches to explaining these persisting social class related differences in levels of educational success? At a general level, a distinction can be made between explanations that emphasise differences in natural or innate abilities and others which refer to the predominant influence of environmental factors. The first approach tends to be more prevalent within psychology. For those adopting this position, such as Hernstein and Murray in the United States, the relationship between social class background and level of educational achievement is seen as largely the result of social class differences in inherited intelligence levels. As far as this genetic inheritance argument goes, the data may appear to fit the interpretation. It would also enable evidence of limited levels of social mobility to square with the view that society is nevertheless meritocratic, in that there exists equality of opportunity but working class children inherit lower levels of innate ability which tend to keep them in their class of origin.

There are a number of major problems with this interpretation. Firstly, it may be questioned whether it is possible to measure innate intelligence levels that have not been influenced by environmental factors. Secondly, even if working class parents are less intelligent than middle class parents whose occupations may demand higher intellectual qualities, there is no evidence from laws of heredity that from this starting point these same intelligence levels will be directly inherited by the next generation. Laws of heredity suggest that differences in innate intelligence are more likely to be randomly distributed throughout the class structure. Thirdly, the inheritance argument tends to be further undermined by a large body of evidence showing different levels of educational performance related to social class background when comparing children of similar measured ability. Fourthly, it is highly questionable whether testing only measures intelligence levels. For example, practice can often improve test performance but access to the opportunities for practice is likely to be a socially constructed inequality.

Whilst not denying the existence of innate differences in intellectual ability (nature), sociological explanations attribute far more importance to environmental factors (nurture) in influencing educational achievement. One broad category of explanations emphasises the impact of differences in social class cultural environments. Culture, in the sociological sense, refers to shared usage of language, values and understandings. An early explanation of the persistence of social class differences in levels of educational achievement which comes under this category of explanation was developed by Basil Bernstein (from 1961). He identified the importance of different class related linguistic codes. Bernstein argued that speech codes developed in working class families tended to be restricted. By this, he meant that communication takes place in the form of descriptive vocabulary. Grammatical form is often incomplete because it assumes that others have a shared knowledge of the particular circumstances to which it relates. In correcting children, parents are more likely to issue imperatives along the lines of 'don't do that or else...' By contrast, middle class families tend to use relatively elaborated speech codes. This form of communication is more grammatically rounded, it tends to use abstract concepts, and provides more detailed explanations. In correcting children, parents are more likely to explain 'you should not do that because...'

Before even attending school, children are socialised into the linguistic code of their social class as a way of communicating. As the mode of communication used by teachers within schools tends to conform to the elaborated speech code, working class children are at a social class disadvantage in getting onto the frequency of communication and expressing themselves in a way deemed to be appropriate in that context. It could also be added that intelligence testing tends to rely on pupils showing that they can deal with abstract concepts, that more working class pupils tended to fail their 11+, and that secondary modern schools were designed as appropriate for children who thought in more concrete terms, thus being heavily populated by children of working class parents.

Another approach which emphasised a cultural dimension to educational achievement was adopted by Herbert Hyman (1967). In a study of a range of research findings in the United States, Hyman explained educational achievement differences mainly in terms of different class values. He argued that the cultural values of the poor place less emphasis on personal achievement than those of the middle class. They also place less value on upward occupational mobility and educational striving. Children from poor backgrounds become socialised into these more fatalistic cultural values which do not prepare them well for success in education. Although Hyman acknowledged that these values are in part a realistic reflection of the lesser opportunity that society offers the working class, the greater emphasis in his analysis is that it is the negative value system of the poor which is the barrier to their success within a society of opportunity. The key to combating the problem is therefore instilling, through education, values of individual competitiveness into pupils from more deprived backgrounds at the youngest age possible to help them to reach their potential.

As identified in a previous section, Pierre Bourdieu offered a cultural explanation of working class relative educational failure. In this Marxist interpretation, the power of the dominant social classes to impose their culture as the means of assessment disadvantages the working class. From this position, it is unlikely that such educational disadvantage can be overcome, even with the best of intentions, whilst society remains divided into economically dominant and subordinate classes.

Barry Sugarman's cultural explanation (1970) related educational achievement to time horizons associated with parental occupations. Working class and middle class occupations tended to promote different time perspectives. The career structure of middle class occupations meant that planning for the future and making sacrifices now – referred to as 'deferred gratification' – would be recognised to pay off in the long run. As working class occupations did not tend to have a long-term career structure, but instead a wage structure that peaked quite early in life, they tended to encourage more of a present time orientation or 'live for today' approach to life. These different outlooks could influence children's orientation to education, which for success required individual application and deferred gratification.

Other explanations of differential achievement place less emphasis on class cultural values. One such is Douglas' (1964) research, which has already been referred to. Douglas identified parental attention to children in the pre-school home environment and interest in their children's education as particularly important to children's educational achievement. It was claimed, through measuring parent's school visits, that the middle classes expressed a greater interest in their children's educational progress. However, Douglas also related educational success to other class connected phenomena such as the child's health, the size of the family, study and living conditions, and the quality of the school. There were therefore a mixture of cultural and material social class factors affecting pupil's achievement.

For Raymond Boudon (1974), position in the class structure is more important than aspects of class culture in explaining class differences in educational attainment. Given different class background starting points, Boudon argued that it would be misleading to suggest that working class youngsters with horizons for working class occupations hold more fatalistic values than middle class youngsters aiming for middle class occupations. He emphasised that educational systems offer various potential educational pathways and exit points, and argued that pupils engage in a rational process of costs and benefits analysis, which are partly but not exclusively economic, in making their educational decisions. The different class backdrops to these decisions means that pupils of different social class backgrounds may well come to different but equally rational decisions regarding their educational options. For example, the transition from school or college to higher education is a potential exit point where decisions have to be made. The prospect for a pupil of working class background of embarking on a higher education course which could lead to a profession may entail a distancing, both geographically and socially, from family and friends and the need to adjust to new social circles. Since such a decision may not carry much support from family and friends who may not share these horizons, potential costs may appear to outweigh benefits. By contrast, in considering pursuing the same pathway, the pupil from a middle class background may assess that the benefits outweigh the costs as their family expects and supports further study and friends make similar decisions. For Boudon, both decisions may be equally rational and made by individuals but they take place against the backdrop of the class structure which they then feed back into.

Nell Keddie (1973) applied an interactionist approach to the study of streaming in a comprehensive school. Although the research was focussed at a micro level, it raised broader questions regarding stereotyping and the relationship between streaming and social class. Keddie found that, in a school that adopted streaming but also ran a course that was not meant to be taught in a differentiated way, teachers gave pupils from different streams differential access to course knowledge. 'A' stream pupils were viewed as academically able and easy to work with and so were given access to abstract curriculum knowledge. 'C' stream pupils were regarded as less able and seen as more difficult to work with because they tended to think in a concrete way. They were likely to speak up if their concrete experiences contradicted the teacher's subject knowledge. When this happened, their contributions tended to be dismissed. Keddie thus found that schooling tended to reward the ability of the predominantly middle class 'A' stream students to conform to the requirements of the curriculum and penalise the more critical contributions of the predominantly working class 'C' stream students.

Research by Paul Willis (1977) is unusual in that it was conducted at a micro level within a broader Marxist framework of analysis. In so doing, he came to some rather different conclusions than to where most mainstream Marxist approaches lead. In his small scale study of 12 'lads' of working class background, he found that their response to the school environment, which they experienced as alienating, was to develop a counter culture in which they avoided school work, played up, and ridiculed others whom they viewed as conformist swats. Whilst the 'lads' valued the superiority of street wisdom and quick wit, they also knew how far to bend the rules. According to Willis, they realistically anticipated their working class occupational destinations and so did not value academic conformity and achievement. By so doing, they became confirmed in their expected occupations. Willis also studied the 'lads' when they entered the workplace. He found that their school counter culture had prepared them with a type of pre-vocational experience in preparation for a workplace in which the quick wit and manipulation the rules were part of the shop floor culture in coping with tedium. They did not feel that they were either just down beaten failures at school or suppressed in the workplace.

The above explanations comprise just a limited selection from a body of well established sociological research and explanations of social class differences in educational achievement. Given the variety of influences identified, it is hardly surprising that substantial class related achievement differences have remained so persistent despite reforms of the education system which would seem to be designed to enhance equality of opportunity to succeed. At first glance, explanations in terms of the inheritance of social class differences in intelligence could appear to fit the facts of class related differences in educational achievement levels. However, sociologists focus more on the impact of the social distribution of influences and opportunities for personal development and achievement to explain the same facts. The above explanations suggest, from a sociological viewpoint, that it is more the impact of different class based life chances on educational performance that is inherited than genetic differences in levels of intelligence.

2 Gender – changing social and educational horizons

Sex differences between males and females are biological differences imposed by nature. The term gender refers to socially constructed differences in identity related to sex differences rather than the view that such identity differences are biologically predetermined. As in the study of social class, sociology adopts a mainly environmental or nurture emphasis in explaining differential educational achievement in gender terms.

Research has long established that girls have tended to perform better than boys up to about the middle stage of secondary school. They then used to fall behind the performance of boys and were less likely to stay on at school. Such a turn around could be explained in terms of a combination of different socially constructed gender expectations and discriminatory practices.

During the post war decades, the expectations for many girls were that a future housewife role required little consideration of occupational striving and the necessary educational qualifications. These social expectations were often reproduced across a range of educational and general reading materials, appearing most prescriptively in Housekeeping Monthly in 1955 which explained how a woman should run the home, serve her husband and know her place. Even in the early 1970s, Sue Sharpe found that the girls in her London based research saw their futures mainly in terms of marriage and gave aiming for a career little consideration (however, as many of the girls were of working class background, the possible combined effect of class and gender on their outlook cannot be discounted).

Discriminatory practices up to this time included gender quotas operated by some local authorities. Given the superior performance of girls at the 11+ stage, a number of authorities would raise the pass mark for girls compared to that for boys so as to level out the proportions of males and females entering grammar schools.

Females had also experienced widespread prejudice and discrimination in the workplace. Women who took on 'men's jobs' often faced extreme hostility. More generally, they were often denied promotion, offered lower rates of pay to men, and in some occupations were even expected to give up their work if they married.

Early feminist writers such as Betty Friedan (1965) were challenging the restriction on their self-fulfilment that the traditional housewife role was argued to impose on so many women. By 1970, the emergence of feminist consciousness in a number of western societies focussed on challenging female disadvantage in a broad range of social contexts. Studies within education were beginning to reflect this change by paying more critical attention to gender issues. One area of attention was that of traditional sexual stereotyping, which related to presumed fixed and innate differences in abilities and predispositions and cast females as natural carers and males as their providers. From at least one strand of feminist thinking (radical feminism), views which emphasised these immutable differences were in fact male ideology – the ideas supported social arrangements through which males exercised power over females.

Studies focussing on the impact of socialisation in forming gender identity held liberating potential, since, if the effect was shown to be substantial, reform to the social environment could bring about reformed gender identity. Research conducted during the 1970s and 1980s paid greater attention to the impact of early gender socialisation within the family and playgroups through the different treatment of boys and girls and different toys they were given to play with. School reading and teaching materials also came under greater scrutiny. For example, content analysis of stories in school books by researchers such as Glenys Lobban (1974) often revealed gender stereotypes of male adventurousness and female domesticity.

A further issue was that subjects themselves were often gender stereotyped along the lines of maths and sciences being natural male subjects, whilst humanities and domestic science were natural female subjects. Traditional gender related subject choices were then sometimes reinforced by assumptions built into school timetabling and often supported by teacher guidance. Researchers were also studying ways in which some subject texts were written which assumed one gender or the other to be the natural audience. And observational studies found widespread evidence of male dominance in classroom participation.

Reflecting the climate of growing awareness and criticism of gender inequality, the Sex Discrimination Act was passed in 1975. One consequence of this legislation was that the practice of operating different 11+ pass levels for boys and girls became illegal. Other social changes would encourage significant improvements in the educational performance of females. One was the perception of enhanced employment opportunities for women. This was associated with the expansion of service sector employment and examples set by some highly successful female role models in business and politics. An enhanced social and political climate of enterprise culture values during the 1980s emphasised the individual striving of career women as opposed to the earlier more collectivist feminist protests. At the same time, rapidly rising divorce rates arguably placed greater importance on females to recognise the need to be able to achieve financial independence. These changes may be seen as the backdrop of both enhanced opportunities and motivations for the dramatic progress in female educational performance which will be outlined later. This remarkable improvement provides a powerful argument against those who argue that substantially different intellectual capacities are built into the nature of males and females.

Education – contemporary developments

1 The promotion of diversity and choice

In the context of Britain's waning economic performance, debate from the mid 70s was increasingly focussing on the appropriateness of educational provision to cater for the needs of the economy. In sociological terms, concern across the political spectrum was emerging about the effectiveness of the education system in performing its economic function.

When the Conservative government came to power in 1979, they were intent on reforming education and improving economic efficiency and competitiveness. As well as placing greater emphasis on vocational education, the issue of enhancing equality of educational opportunity with reference to social class background tended to be downgraded, with greater concern being placed on raising overall standards. From a new right perspective, it was argued that this could best be achieved by marketising the education system - introducing reforms into the public sector to create a competitive environment similar to that of the private sector.

A policy promoting greater diversity of schools was aimed at enhancing (parental) choice. As things stood, selective education was allowed to continue in those areas that had retained grammar schools. Many local authorities were converting to comprehensive provision, whereas in some localities grammar schools coexisted alongside 'comprehensives' which were therefore strictly speaking not comprehensives at all. Most schools were coeducational, but some had single sex intake. Faith schools, partly funded by churches, offered further options in many local authorities.

New right reforms extended this diversity. City technology colleges, funded by both central government and business and specialising in science, technology and business subjects, were established in a small number of urban localities. Schools could elect to become 'grant maintained'. These schools 'opted out' of local authority finance and control, were funded directly from the government, and were run autonomously by boards of school governors. Some introduced highly selective intake procedures, whilst others did not. The government also introduced the Assisted Places Scheme. This provided means tested support for able children of poorer families to enter independent schools.

Alongside this growing diversity of provision, uniformity within the state sector was enhanced through the introduction of the national curriculum and periodic standardised testing. This uniformity formed the basis of publicly accessible information on academic achievement. On the basis of standardised information compiled in the form of published league tables, it was intended that schools would have to become more publicly accountable for their performance and that parents would be able to make enlightened decisions on the best schools for their children to attend. Schools needed to be more competitive as intake quotas were no longer guaranteed and funding followed their ability to attract pupils. All this meant that schools had to become better at marketing themselves.

Another element of educational diversity remains the independent school sector. Independent schools, as privately run charitable organisations, rely heavily on parental payment of fees for their children to attend. Within this sector, the more exclusive and prestigious schools are referred to as public schools. At secondary level, public schools usually have an entry age of 13, which coincides with completing private preparatory school, and pupils are required to have passed the common entrance exam. Many public schools offer boarding facilities and a number have retained single sex intake.

New Labour were as determined as the Conservatives to promote diversity and competition within education and to impose a demanding inspection regime, all to promote high educational standards. In fact, their reforms have sometimes relied on Conservative support in Parliament. Although entrance within the state secondary system now operates largely on a non-selective basis, the government has not actively promoted the abolition of the remaining grammar schools. Whilst grant maintained schools have reverted back to local authority funding, with most becoming foundation schools, their governing boards have retained a high level of decision making autonomy. City technology colleges have largely joined the ranks of city academies, set up to improve educational performance in deprived and underachieving inner city areas. City academies are run as self-governing trusts, which are partly supported by private funding and expertise. Specialist schools, allowed to select up to 10% of their pupils in terms of their specialist ability, have been established in sports, modern languages, technology and the arts. Comprehensives are being encouraged to become specialist schools and the establishment of new faith schools has government support.

The Labour government is requiring all new schools to operate as self-governing trusts, organisations partly supported by charitable foundation partners and run by their own boards of governors. In the long run, all state secondary schools are expected to become either specialist or academy trusts. Overall, local diversity and autonomy, market competition, parental choice, and the driving up of standards, measured by examination performance, have remained central features of government policy on education.

2 An emphasis on examination performance – onwards and upwards?

Educational achievement is conventionally viewed as synonymous with exam grade performance. This allows ease of statistical measurement of performance across the student population to establish trends of change. In a more personal way, examination performance is annually symbolised in the media by students receiving their (usually high grade!) results. What do the statistics show? One of the most remarkable trends is the opening up of a gender gap in GCSE and A level as the performance of girls has improved more rapidly than that of boys. Since the introduction of the GCSE exam in 1988, the performance of girls has moved ahead of boys in each year up to 2002 with the exception of 2001. As a result, the GCSE figures for August 2002 showed that 62.4% of girls' entries achieved a grade C or above compared to 53.4% for boys. 5.9% of girls' entries achieved an A* grade compared to 4.1% for boys. Likewise, at A level, girls have been consistently outperforming boys in pass rates. What has changed is in the achievement of A grade passes. During the early 1990s, boys slightly outperformed girls in the achievement of top grades. A reason for this given at the time was that girls tended to play it safe compared to boys who were more likely to have the confidence to go for broke. However, recent figures show that girls are now outperforming boys in terms of A grade performance, and increasingly so. In August 2002, 21.9% of girls' entries achieved an A grade pass compared to 19.3% of boys'. This represents a threefold increase in their lead compared with 2001 figures.

On a subject basis, girls have extended their lead in performance in those areas where they have more traditionally outperformed boys (the arts and humanities) and are increasing their participation and moving ahead of boys in most of the traditional male subject areas (in science subjects). The latter advance has been assisted by the impact of the national curriculum, which requires all students to study sciences, and the use of less gender biased texts.

In the light of the above figures, attention has focussed on the problem of relative male underachievement which is usually explained in terms of laddish culture and behaviour, especially amongst those from poorer backgrounds. On the other hand, it has been suggested that a greater proportion of coursework assessment has favoured females who tend to be more methodical in their application to their studies.

The overall performance figures for 2002 indicated an improvement on those of the previous year. At GCSE level, A-C passes increased from 57.1% to 59.9% and A-G level grades reached 97.1%. Additionally, the number of students fast tracking to take GCSE exams at the age of 15 or under was more than double that of the previous year. A level passes (grades A-E) showed the largest annual increase, climbing from 89.8% to 94.3%.

The general trend in examination performance has remained an upward one. By 2006, A-C grade passes at GCSE reached 62.4% and the number of A* and A grades increased by 0.7% on the previous year's figure to 19.1%. The figures for 2007 had further improved to 63.3% and 19.5% respectively, whilst the proportion of fast tracked students (fifteen year olds or under) had reached 14% of all entries. The 2006 A level figures for A-E grade passes reached 96.6%, and A grades achieved improved by 1.3% on the figure for the previous year to reach 24.1%. By 2007, A-E passes improved further to 96.9% and the proportion of A grades awarded increased by a further 1.2% to reach 25.3%. By comparison, the A grade figure for independent schools rose from 41.3% of entries in 2002 to 47.9% in 2006 and remained almost unchanged at 47.8% in 2007.

In comparing the academic performance of girls and boys, the figures for 2006 and 2007 offered the first indication that the gap opened up by girls over boys may be starting to close. In GCSEs for 2006, the achievement gap in A* and A grades narrowed compared to 2005 by 0.5%, but still remained at 7.7%. This gap narrowed by a further 0.2% by 2007 and the A* to C grade performance gap narrowed by 0.6% between 2006 and 2007. At A level, between 2005 and 2007, boys closed the gap on girls slightly in the achievement of A-E passes, but between 2005 and 2006, girls had increased their lead over boys in achieving A grade passes.

One explanation for this modest reversal is that a number of schools have selected more adventure and action based texts for study which boys tend to find more appealing – an interesting reversal of past feminist crusades to make texts more female friendly at a time when boys were out performing girls.

The performance of ethnic minority pupils has generally improved more rapidly than that of white students in recent years. This has sometimes been from a relatively low base of achievement. For example, in GCSE grades A*-C, the performance of black Caribbean students has improved by approximately 6% over the two years leading up to 2006 to reach 41.7% and black Africans by 5% to 48.3%. At the higher end, the figure for Chinese students improved in the year up to 2006 by 6.8% to reach 74.2%.

When figures are broken down in terms of ethnicity, gender, and living in poverty, the poorest performers appear to be white boys from poor backgrounds. Research conducted by Cassen and Kingdom (2007) for the Joseph Rowntree Foundation found that 62% of white boys who take free school meals appear in the bottom 10% of performers in education, a figure far higher than for equally poor Afro-Carribeans. The research identified an anti-education culture amongst classmates and at home a poor learning environment and limited language communication as part of the problem.

Overall, regular annual improvements in performance statistics have raised much debate over the question of standards. What light can sociology shed on this matter? The problem is that approaching this issue is difficult to reduce to a purely technical matter. Opposing positions adopted tend to develop around an emphasis on innate ability versus environmental influences and issues of broader political ideology. The argument that the improving statistics show an erosion of standards tends to be based on the view that innate ability follows a standard distribution curve for the population as a whole and does not significantly advance over time. This position often lies behind the criticisms of those who identify with the political right. It is argued that annual improvements in success bear little relationship to real improvements in performance or overall levels of intelligence and can only be achieved through the erosion of standards. Ruth Lea, of the Institute of Directors, has used the term 'grade inflation' – the watering down of performance required to achieve grades and give a statistically misleading suggestion of improvement - to express this position.

However, an alternative interpretation is that standards have been maintained and that the statistics indicate real improvement in performance. How is this possible? In the case of A levels, environmental changes, such as more effective filtering processes, are having an influence. Because schools are concerned about the publication of their performance in league tables, there are pressures to discourage the entry of students who are regarded as risky prospects for exam success. Additionally, the introduction of AS levels has enhanced the process of filtering through self-selection. By taking AS levels after one year, students are able to make decisions on which subjects they will drop and which they will continue to study through to A level. The fact that the largest annual increase in A level performance has coincided with a 6% drop in entrants following the introduction of AS levels appears to offer confirmation of these effects of self-selection.

During and since the summer of 2003, a number of universities have been expressing concern regarding problems of differentiation. As more students were passing A levels with top grades, concern was raised over the growing difficulty of using these grades to separate out the most able students. Students themselves were increasingly finding that top grades were no guarantee of gaining access to popular and competitive courses and the most prestigious universities. As a consequence, more universities have been setting their own entrance exams and looking to alternatives to A levels which will better differentiate levels of student ability and performance.

In schools, one response has been an increasing uptake of the more demanding Advanced Extension Award which replaced special level papers from 2002. This exam, aimed at the top 10% of A level students, requires the demonstration of a deeper level of subject understanding. Universities occasionally make the Advanced Extension Award part of an offer. The government has also become involved in piloting a toughening of A level questions with the aim of introducing more challenging A levels from September 2008. The changes to be introduced will include a movement away from structured exam questions and the requirement of more extended answers, as well as an A* grade for those who achieve 90% or above in their final exams.

A further development has been an increasing take up in schools of the International Baccalaureate Diploma which combines core and optional elements into a broad education. This offers highly differentiated outcomes ranging from certificates in individual subjects for those who do not pass the diploma overall to a top end of achievement equivalent in UCAS points to that of six grade A A levels. A leading examining board is also piloting a baccalaureate type qualification which adds to three A levels a paper in general studies, critical thinking or citizenship and a piece of extended essay or project work.

3 The expansion of higher education

Higher education has witnessed massive expansion in terms of student numbers since the early 1960s. For example, during 1962-3, approximately 216,000 students were in full-time higher education. By 1997-8, the figure had risen to approximately 1,200,000, with 34% of all 18 to 19 year olds entering higher education. The percentage has continued to rise slightly since, with 36% of 18 year olds going on to full-time higher education in 2000. However, different rates of access for those of different social class background have remained remarkably entrenched. In 1991-1992, when 23% of 18 to 19 year olds were entering full-time higher education, 55% from professional background gained access whilst from unskilled manual background only 6% went on to higher education. By 1997-1998, these figures had risen to 80% and 14% respectively. Yet when one looks at entry in terms of gender, there has been a massive increase in female participation to the point where females are now entering higher education in significantly higher numbers than males.

Student finance has changed to accommodate increased participation. Up to the mid 1990s, undergraduate students in higher education were supported by local authority grants. These grants were means tested in that parental income was taken into account. Students whose parents were on modest incomes would receive the full grant, whereas those whose parents earned higher salaries would have their grants reduced by an assessed amount of parental contribution. Higher education fees were also paid by local authorities. By the late 1990s, grants had been phased out and replaced by low interest loans and charges for fees were introduced. The latter initially were paid up front, but repayment has since been deferred until a certain level of income is obtained through employment.

From the start of the 2006 academic year, top up fees were introduced. This allowed universities to increase fees from the old flat rate of £1,100 per year up to £3,000 per year. Most universities imposed the full increase. At the time it looked as if the cost may have had a detrimental effect since the number of students enrolled fell by 3.6% compared to 2005. However, closer scrutiny suggests that the decreased numbers for 2006 followed a surge in entry in 2005 as many students who would have otherwise taken a gap year went straight to university to avoid paying the higher fees which a delay would incur. This interpretation is born out by the 6.4% increase in applicants to British universities for 2007. Of these applicants, 221,523 were female and 173,784 were male. Unsurprisingly, subjects which attracted the greatest increase in applicants have been vocational subjects such as business and administration (a 25% increase) which offer the prospects of a quicker clearing of student debt. Such economic pressures have therefore encouraged students to choose courses most obviously linked to the economic function of education.

As more qualifications are being achieved at all levels of the education system, their value in the labour market has tended to decline and more or higher level qualifications are required for particular jobs. This phenomena is referred to by the term 'credential inflation' and means that individuals are under pressure to obtain more qualifications to just stand still in the labour market. At the same time, to pay for this expansion in provision, a higher level of burden is passed from governments, keen to limit public expenditure, down to individuals and families.

4 Meritocracy – advance or retreat?

The concept 'meritocracy' has been previously introduced and refers to a society in which achievement is based on individual effort and ability alone. As well as being central to the debate between major theoretical perspectives, this is a term which has been applied positively by politicians to our educational system. As an exercise in sociological thinking, we should now be able to apply this concept systematically to scrutinise educational opportunity. The following points would appear to be salient:

1   In terms of educational achievement at GCSE and A level, entry to higher education and success in higher grade degree passes, it would appear that there have been significant advances toward a more meritocratic educational system for females. However, there is more doubt, as we shall see in another chapter, about whether this translates sufficiently into equal opportunity with males for occupational success.

2   Regarding the enhancement of market forces in the school system, a key issue is that of social class differences in utilising the system. In an increasingly diverse system, there is strong evidence suggesting that middle class parents understand it better, know how to get the best from it, and are better able to prepare their children for success, for example through paying for private tutors. Working class parents are more likely to accept sending their children to a local school which may include poor performing schools in run down areas. Therefore, if parents are given greater choice in the schools attended by their children, this would appear to enhance class related differences in children's educational opportunity and suggest a retreat from meritocracy as family based life chances play a greater role in educational access again. Phillip Brown uses the term 'parentocracy' to express this changing emphasis.

3   The massive expansion of higher education may at first glance appear to further meritocracy within education as more people are offered the opportunity to pursue their studies. However, increasing access may not advance meritocracy when to do so a new funding system has had to be introduced in the form of the replacement of student grants with loans. The loan system introduces financial hardships and pressures which are unlikely to be experienced uniformly across the social classes.

Those of working class background who are considering entering higher education may be faced with a painful costs / benefits analysis in which the calculation of future debt can be of overriding importance and off-putting. Of those who enter higher education, the greater financial pressure that some students are likely to be under and the consequent temptation to combine paid work with study is likely to undermine a more level playing field of academic achievement.

Research conducted in 2005 by the Higher Education Funding Council for England appears to bear out these concerns. It was found that students from poor and ethnic minority backgrounds were under greater pressure to work during term time. Figures showed that about 30% of these students worked for twenty hours a week or more. Many felt under pressure to skip lectures and give in poor work. Evidence indicated that students who devoted fifteen hours a week or more to work had only a 62% chance of achieving a first class or upper second class honours degree compared to those who were able to devote their time fully to their studies. Furthermore, there was evidence that students of working class background who completed their studies were likely to end up with bigger debts. It could therefore be argued that although the grant based system could only support a smaller HE intake, and in that sense was more elitist, it operated more meritocratically.

4   Part of educational diversity has been the retention of the independent sector. At the pinnacle of this sector reside the prestigious public schools, entry to which is essentially based on social connections and parental ability to pay high fees. These schools offer enhanced access to elite universities and the exclusive higher echelons of the top professions. Whilst politicians of the major political parties have been keen to refer positively to meritocracy, they usually prefer to remain silent on this vestige of privilege which flies in the face of meritocracy. It may be suspected that this omission is an attempt to discourage the layman from engaging in joined up thinking in this area. By contrast, sociology encourages us to think systematically and follow where logic leads us when applying such concepts to our educational system. In so doing, assertions by politicians about meritocracy in education may turn out to look superficial and unconvincing.

Contemporary sociological perspectives on education:

Postmodernism – the liberating potential of education

According to postmodernists such as Lyotard, contemporary societies are entering a stage which is very different from past traditional and modern societies. A hallmark of traditional or pre-modern society was the predominance of religious dogma and superstition. Religion provided an all embracing metanarrative (system of thinking) which claimed to provide a single truth and education reflected this. However, during the eighteenth century, Enlightenment thinking, in the form of scientific and rational criticism, undermined religious dogma and promised the realisation of intellectual liberty and human progress. The development of modern education was the product of this Enlightenment optimism of the modern period. However, postmodernists argue that this promise has disappointed as modern society substituted one claim to a single truth, the metanarrative of religion, by another, the metanarrative of rational analysis and the methods of science. Postmodernists claim that rational and scientific thinking itself became repressive by imposing its logic and methods on society and education as the only criteria of truth. They argue that with the emergence of contemporary postmodern conditions of social and cultural diversity, faith in a single and indispensable foundation for certain knowledge collapses and along with it the modernist metanarrative.

For postmodernists, contemporary societies entering the postmodern era become increasingly pluralistic and comprise diverse cultural and consumer interests. Education must reflect this by moving away from belief in the absolute truth of science and rational thinking and the imposition of a standardised system. Education under postmodern conditions needs to become diverse in provision and relativistic, questioning the ascendancy of any single type of education and the idea of a single absolute truth. Rather than moulding, controlling and restricting individuals, education should be a diverse resource that can be utilised by people to cater for their diverse and changing needs. Whether pursued for purposes of lifestyle image, general interest, personal fulfilment or the acquisition of work skills, there should be no single standard against which any of these purposes can be deemed universally superior.

For proponents Usher and Edwards, postmodernism challenges the favoured status to work related skills and the emphasis placed by governments that education should be organised primarily along such lines. Contemporary educational provision needs to be part of a society of growing diversity of choice and lifestyle as it becomes increasingly utilised by individuals who - as in the case of other products they consume – may use it to seek status and convey an image. Furthermore, there is nothing intrinsically superior in formal classroom teaching and learning, but assisted by advanced technology, a diversity of approaches and settings are becoming available. For postmodernists, only by such varied and flexible provision and a relativistic view of knowledge itself can education become truly liberating.

High modernism – education for adaptation

One of the leading high modernist theorists is Anthony Giddens. For Giddens, rational thinking associated with the Enlightenment is viewed in a more positive way than by postmodernists. The high modernist view is that in contemporary society science and rational thinking can still demonstrate superiority over other forms of knowledge. It is still the basis for understanding society and guiding progress, albeit under more challenging conditions of social complexity, globalisation and rapid technological change.

High modernists view education in the context of rapidly changing high tech knowledge economies. In this context, constant updating of work skills is a vital element of education as societies compete to attract inward investment in a global competitive market. Governments need to play an active role in encouraging individuals to update their work related skills. Individuals cannot expect to complete their education at a fixed point in life but must be prepared to engage in lifelong learning.

Britain's New Labour government have tended to follow this line in promoting a more flexible culture of education in the globally competitive conditions of. People have been encouraged to embrace advances in technology and constantly acquire new skills, benefiting both themselves and the economy. New computer technology has both required the mastery of new skills and enabled learning to occur in a diversity of settings, including people's own homes through an expansion of distance learning made possible by the internet, and the development of outreach centres.

These challenges both offer opportunities and introduce strains and burdens into people's lives as they struggle to respond to a rapidly changing world and risk getting left behind.

5: Social Stratification

Abstract

Developing personal awareness of one's position in a social hierarchy and a range of associated experiences and opportunities may be a starting point for understanding social stratification. However, the reader is alerted to the fact that this would not be an appropriate point from which to make generalisations about the nature of stratification in society. This chapter will show that approaching the area sociologically requires a more detached and systematic approach.

It is important to gain a broad social and historical perspective on stratification in contemporary western societies or Britain more specifically as part of a considered assessment of the degree of openness of the social structure. For this purpose, an understanding of the basic features of more closed stratification systems is introduced.

Social class is a well established feature of stratification and the question of why and issues of how sociologists measure it and some of the problems that this entails are raised. However, there are other dimensions to stratification in contemporary society than social class. In this chapter, gender, ethnicity and status will also be considered, indicating the complex nature of social stratification.

In approaching this subject, the reader is encouraged to recognise connections across different topic areas since the social world does not exist in sealed compartments. Links are made from themes raised in this chapter to those in previous chapters. For example, understanding gender stratification can be related to the impact on the family of industrialisation and more recently the expansion of the service sector. Evaluating the extent to which contemporary British society is meritocratic requires an understanding of issues of meritocracy in education.

Established theoretical approaches of functionalism, Marxism and Weber are introduced to help the reader develop an understanding of some of the founding concepts used and explanations of stratification dynamics. However, some important concerns are also raised and a consideration of contemporary theories is intended to assist the reader in gauging the continuing viability or otherwise of these founding approaches.

The sociological challenge

In a general sense, social stratification refers to social hierarchy which is divided into layers comprising different levels. These layers or strata (stratum in the singular) are structured in terms of inequality in the social distribution of resources deemed within a society to be important. Such resources typically include wealth, income, knowledge and lifestyle. Access to these resources will be socially structured, for example by legal title of property ownership, rules of inheritance, and strategies that some people adopt to exclude access to resources by others.

If social stratification simply referred to social layering in terms of the unequal distribution of resources, the problem for the sociologist would remain that of identifying the key points at which the boundaries between layers takes place. This is a very complex matter as stratification includes various dimensions such as social class, social status, gender and ethnicity. These dimensions interact with each other and impose their own distinctive layering on society. At present, it should be added that the existence of a degree of shared values and common outlook amongst people which distinguish them from others can be a good guide to stratification levels.

The study of social stratification poses a number of problems. One may be the tendency to deride other societies and cultures from the viewpoint of the society to which we are accustomed. As analysts, it is important to guard against the block that ethnocentricity puts on understanding and be prepared to ask, for example, how position in society tends to be justified to women in Islamic culture.

Furthermore, we may take for granted a certain view of stratification within our own society. As sociologists, we need to be prepared to give careful consideration to evidence which challenges these taken for granted assumptions. It may be a sobering thought to appreciate that in the future, others may look back with incredulity at what we take for granted regarding social stratification in a similar way to the way we view stratification in past societies.

In Britain, sociologists have traditionally viewed social class as the major dimension of stratification. However, they are now grappling with understanding the changing and complex impact of the interaction between class and other dimensions of stratification such as status, gender and ethnicity. As well as being confronted with this complexity, as sociologists we must remain vigilant that our personal experiences may bias us to overemphasise or underemphasise the importance of any of these categories.

Definition of main concepts

The term **social class** refers to a social category based on economic factors. This may include levels of wealth but the established emphasis in sociology is to measure social class in terms of occupational levels and categories. **Social mobility** refers to the extent of upward and downward movement experienced by individuals throughout an occupational hierarchy. It is usually measured in **intergenerational** terms, comparing the occupational level achieved by members of one generation with that of their parents. By definition, when position is **ascribed**, social mobility will be extremely low (in theory non-existent), and when it is open to **achievement** we expect to find relatively high levels of social mobility. However, even within quite open social structures, some groups may attempt to enhance **social closure.** This refers to strategies adopted to preserve exclusive access to valued resources by denying access to others. Examples of social closure are most apparent amongst the establishment who tend to utilise top public schools to enhance entry to elite professions.

In sociology, **social status** refers to the judgements made within a society regarding the prestige of a social group and its members. Although status is culturally defined by social values given to different ways of life, knowledge and possessions, it is not always easy to separate it out from social class. As in the case of social class, if status is ascribed, the social structure fixes people into the stratum of their birth for life. Such a stratification system is referred to as **closed**. Examples of relatively closed societies include slavery, feudalism, caste society and apartheid, all of which will be reviewed later in this chapter. By contrast, **achieved class** or **status** is associated with an **open stratification** system which enables individuals to occupy positions in the social structure derived from personal characteristics, primarily effort and ability, whatever the status or class of their family background. Most modern industrial societies are recognised as relatively open stratification systems, although sociologists disagree over the exact extent to which they are so and the varied importance of social class, social status and other features of stratification.

These other dimensions of stratification include those of gender and ethnicity. **Patriarchy** is a term used to emphasise gender based stratification in which men have power over women. This may exhibit itself in terms of gender related concentrations of people in different occupational spheres and levels, inheritance practices and domestic responsibilities. Values supporting such gender related inequalities, usually with reference to different presumed male and female qualities and capacities, are referred to as **sexist**, and to the extent to which they are viewed as distorting reality would be referred to as **sexist ideology**.

Discriminatory practices against ethnic minorities form the basis of ethnic stratification. Such discrimination may concentrate ethnic groups in certain occupational spheres and levels as well as residential areas. Attitudes which justify discrimination in terms of racially based notions of superiority and inferiority are referred to as **racist**, and, in a similar way to sexist views can take the form of **racist ideology**.

The concept **life chances** refers to the quality of life and standard of living associated with a position in the social structure. Life chances can include access to and in turn derive from levels of education and healthcare. There is a close correlation between life chances and the distribution of wealth and income in society. However, inequalities in life chances may be more of less determined by family background in more or less closed stratification systems respectively. Thus, in comparing different societies or societies at different times in history a key question to ask is, to what extent are people constrained by inherited life chances or to what degree can they rise above them and create their own life chances? Ultimately, life chances can be measured by such indices as socially patterned differences in life expectancy and infant mortality rates.

The concept of a **meritocracy** has been already introduced in the context of education. It is a term that has often been applied to modern industrial societies which are viewed as open stratification systems, enabling social mobility to be based on individual merit. It is therefore a useful concept against which to measure such stratification systems.

A glimpse at closed stratification systems

History offers many examples of relatively closed systems of stratification in which life for the majority was often brutal and oppressive. However, even in the most oppressive societies, social hierarchies were supported by justifying ideas and values as well as by coercion. Viewed at a social and historical distance and with the knowledge that we now have, the ideological nature of these values may often now seem clear.

Slavery is a system of stratification most commonly associated with the early civilisations of the Greeks, Egyptians and Romans. Although in detail slavery exhibited different features between these societies, a characteristic common to all of them was that there existed legally recognised and enforced social inequality through which slaves were owned by others. Often taken through conquests, slaves would be put to a variety of tasks from heavy labour in mines or the building of monuments to teaching or even running estates. The main curb on the treatment of slaves by their owners was their continuing use as productive labour. Control could include coercion in the form of the threat of physical punishment or inducement of fear of offending the gods. There were usually hierarchical grades within the slave stratum and in some cases control may take the form of inducement through the possibility of slaves working to obtain freedom from slave status.

A more recent example of slavery was found in American history. During the slave trade, Africans were transported to the southern states and put to work on plantations. Their lives were highly regulated by their white masters. Slave status was reinforced by beliefs in black racial inferiority and the encouragement of the slave population to adopt Christian values of the virtue of humility. The institution of slavery was only formally abolished in 1865 following the defeat of the south in the American Civil War. However, it took a further century and the emergence of the Civil Rights Movement by the early 1960s for a fundamental challenge to remaining racial segregation and disadvantage to become effective.

Caste stratification was peculiar to traditional Indian society. In this form of social hierarchy, a rigid form of stratification was sanctioned by the religious beliefs of Hinduism. The strata (varna) of this society were closed by rules limiting association and prescribing appropriate behaviour. Brahmin priests, as men of learning – and often also significant owners of land - formed the upper varna. Central to the Hindu teachings which they conveyed were the ideas of reincarnation and the relative purity of the different varna. The priestly caste lived the purest life, conducted religious ceremonies and administered the law. In descending order of purity followed the warrior, trader and labouring strata. Below them were placed the outcastes who engaged in the most degrading occupations. Acceptance of this closed hierarchy was perpetuated by the belief in reincarnation – a concept referring to a continuing cycle of rebirth after the death of the physical body. Prospects for future life were tied to conformity in the present life. To defy the codes of one's caste would lead to rebirth into a lower caste, whilst conformity could lead to rebirth into a higher caste. Fatalism in the here and now, conformity, and merit were therefore intertwined and a closed stratification system was supported by the appeal of social mobility through reincarnation. Likewise, one's current position could be justified by one's supposed behaviour in a previous life.

In **feudal** societies, life was essentially agrarian and lived out in local communities. Feudal life was typified by European societies during the Middle Ages. The key to power was land ownership, and this was concentrated in the hands of the two upper strata (estates), the nobility and the church. The third estate, or commoners, comprised mainly small landowning peasants and landless serfs. The latter worked the land of the nobility and the church. They were required to give both produce and labour to their landowners and lived under inferior legal rights. Opportunities for social mobility were very limited as this section of the population were kept in perpetual servitude.

In this social system, deference was expected by the upper orders from those of the lower estates. By tracing their noble lineage back through many generations, the landed orders were able to claim the inheritance of leadership qualities through appeal to the notion of superior social breeding – a concept which harmonised well with the practice of animal breeding in an agrarian society. The social forces which would disturb this balance in the rural hierarchy would later emanate from a section of the population who resided more on the margins of this defining relationship – the more urban based traders, merchants and industrialists.

Apartheid refers to a system instituted in South Africa shortly after the Second World War and which lasted until 1992. Under this system, a white minority dominated non-white groups defined, in descending order, as mixed race or coloured, Asian, and black. Under this system, racial segregation was enforced in public places and black South Africans forced to live in separate shantytown homelands. Given these segregated regions, members of a racial group would take care to avoid straying into a territory closed to them. Blacks who worked as domestics for whites would have to show an ID pass and often work at night. Even when working in the same occupations as white workers, the wages and conditions of employment of black workers were inferior. Infant mortality was far higher within the black than the white population. Political gatherings were banned and discontent ruthlessly put down by police or military force.

This system which kept blacks down was justified by reference to theories of racial types which had grown to prominence during the period of colonial expansion of the nineteenth century. Such theories maintained that different races contained different genetically inbuilt characteristics and that the white race had demonstrated its superiority of intelligence and determination over the blacks. In the hands of an apartheid regime, this reasoning could be used to justify the need for maintaining racial purity and making taboo racial intermarriage. The life chances of blacks could be kept vastly inferior to that of whites and this in turn could provide 'evidence' of black inferiority.

Although racial stratification was the defining feature of apartheid, other elements of stratification were discernable. For example, the white stratum mainly comprised groups of British, German and Dutch extraction, with the former at the top of society tending to control the economy, and the other groups often owning land. Whilst Indians and Asians were often less poverty stricken than blacks, race would remain a barrier to social mobility which application and the acquisition of money could not overcome. Within the black stratum, social divisions would take the form of tribal groupings, with Zulus tending to comprise the dominant group. Throughout all strata, patriarchal relationships tended to prevail with girls brought up to be good wives and domestic servants.

Founding sociological perspectives on social stratification

There are three major founding perspectives on stratification – functionalist, Marxist, and Weberian. Each are macro perspectives, ie. they adopt a broad view of social structures. As traditional perspectives, they all analyse stratification in terms of social class, although not all do so exclusively.

Functionalism – the realisation of an open social structure

It is often useful to consider the social and historical context in which social theory emerges to more fully appreciate its leaning. Functionalism is traceable back to the French social philosopher Auguste Comte who was writing in a period of French history following the Revolution of 1789. Comte regarded European societies at the height of feudalism, around the twelfth century, as stable and well established social hierarchies supported by shared dogma in the religion of Catholicism. Following a long period of decline, the Revolution finally swept away feudal society in France. The problem diagnosed by Comte in the post Revolution period was that of protracted social instability. The old social order had been overthrown but a new and stable order had not yet emerged. The social ill of instability needed to be remedied.

Through Comte, functionalism emerged as a reaction to the socially destabilising effects of the French Revolution and the desire to re-establish social order and stability. As such, the perspective emphasises the normality of stable social hierarchy. To underpin social stability, modern societies, just as much as traditional societies, need their own supporting value systems which members of society share and adhere to. Functionalism, as it has developed since the works of Comte, has remained true to this heritage.

Comte's ideas were built on by Emile Durkheim. For Durkheim, modern industrial societies are like organisms which grow in size and complexity. Technological advances extend the division of labour and promote an increasingly complex occupational structure. State education plays key functions in maintaining the social structure. It promotes the shared values necessary to build social consensus as well as the need for obedience to authority and conformity to rules. Education also helps to select and train people for appropriate occupational roles and positions in the social hierarchy. People's acceptance of their position in this hierarchy has to be justified according to shared values appropriate to modern industrial society. This society requires the efficient utilisation of human talent. The process of educational and occupational selection and the prevailing social values are therefore those of a meritocracy – social position is achieved according to effort and ability.

The distinction between the feudal social order and that natural to modern industrial societies is clearly established in the writings of the American functionalist Talcott Parsons. For Parsons, social hierarchies are a prerequisite of stable societies. Value systems must reflect the nature of the society - they must synchronise with the needs of society if stability is to be maintained. So what were the main features of feudal society? Life was local centred, agrarian and based on tradition. Religious thinking prevailed. The social hierarchy was relatively closed. People married within their own stratum and the chance of movement out of the stratum of birth was for most highly unlikely. In this type of society, social superiors expected shows of deference from those of lower social rank. The minimal social mobility that existed was likely to derive from sponsorship by a known patron. Parsons refers to this type of relationship as particularistic – opportunities were dependent on particular personal relationships.

By contrast, modern capitalist societies are large, impersonal, complex, integrated and interdependent social structures with a high division of labour. They are noted for their dynamism and efficiency in the quest for profit. However, conflict in one area of society can cause widespread disruption. It is therefore important that as well as striving for individual success, people accept their position within the stratification system as justly arrived at. For Parsons, American capitalism best typifies appropriate values around which social consensus can be based in modern societies. These values include enterprise, competition, individual achievement and self-support.

The occupational hierarchy will need to be a highly differentiated hierarchy of income. This is because in modern complex societies the highest occupations place great demands on their occupants who must have acquired sophisticated planning, managerial and organisational skills. Social efficiency requires that, at this and other levels of the occupational hierarchy, there is a close match between the ability of those who occupy roles and the demands of the occupational role. Consequently, there is maximum utilisation of human resources and the resultant productivity levels enable materialistic values and goals to be realised.

To effectively utilise the pool of talent in society, the social structure of modern industrial societies must be a relatively open one. High levels of upward and downward social mobility will be likely as members of society are sifted for appropriate occupational roles based on their individual ability and effort. Compared to traditional societies, position must be acquired through individual competition according to impersonal and universally applicable performance criteria. Parsons refers to such relationships as universalistic. The shared values which correspond to this type of society are those of a meritocracy – a hierarchy of social inequalities which is justified by the widespread belief that whatever position an individual attains closely reflects their abilities and efforts.

In the post war years, Davis and Moore focussed on the nature of this occupational structure by referring to it as a 'ladder of opportunity'. They argued that stratification is a feature of all societies as it is a 'functional prerequisite' of societies to place people in different roles. The form that this process of allocation takes in modern industrial society is that in an open and competitive social structure, society benefits from talented people moving up into demanding occupations. High income differentials are justified as the motivating factor which enhances competition. They offer due return to talents in scarce supply in society and compensatory reward for the sacrifices made by individuals in extending their education and training.

At this point, it may be beneficial to raise a number of questions that are critical of the functionalist perspective. The reader is recommended to pause and think through these questions with reference to evidence where possible. Firstly, does not the emphasis on consensus, order and hierarchy tend to underplay the existence of conflict between social strata? Secondly, to what extent is belief in meritocracy shared throughout society or the wishful thinking or self-congratulation of a minority who may or may not owe their success entirely to individual merit? Thirdly, what degree of income differential is necessary between upper and lower level occupational levels in a meritocracy to motivate individual competition? Fourthly, to what extent does the free market in labour or strategies of professional self-interest determine these income differences? Fifthly, how can the relative functional importance to society of different occupations be assessed? Sixthly, to what extent do the workings of the free market coincide with the functional importance of an occupation? Seventhly, how can the very stratification system that is meant to separate out talent and motivate individuals and create a level playing field of competition work when inequalities produced in one generation become unequal life chances which impact on the opportunities of next generation? The reader may be able to add further questions to this list to reflect on.

Marxism – capitalism remains a class stratified social structure

Marxist theorists strongly dispute the meritocratic nature of modern capitalist societies. For Marxists, capitalist societies are highly stratified in terms of class division. Furthermore, this division contains inbuilt class opposition, which Marx believed would eventually become open conflict and destroy capitalism.

Marx used the term class more broadly than most sociologists. He maintained that class stratification, based on economic factors, has existed throughout much of human history. Once early societies had settled and developed rudimentary means of production, they were able to produce more wealth than was necessary for the basic subsistence of the community. The surplus above subsistence enabled inequalities of wealth to emerge. These inequalities became institutionalised and transmitted down the generations through the recognition of private property, laws of inheritance and private ownership of the means of production. Through their consolidation of wealth, those who owned the means of production acquired the power of a ruling class and were able to exploit the labour of others who were kept in a state of subsistence. However, throughout history, the means of production have developed, accompanied by the emergence of new classes who own them. Conflicts in which aspiring ruling classes owning modernised means of production challenge established ruling classes are the motive force of social change as societies move by revolution through a series of different social and stratification types.

Marx, then, developed a theory which attempted to explain the existence of economic based social stratification throughout history. It placed ownership of the means of production at the centre of an analysis of class conflict and social change. The key social relationship in stratified societies is between those who own the means of production and those who own only their labour power. Just to subsist, the latter are compelled to supply their labour to the service of the former. As political power, broadly defined as the ability of some to impose their will over others, derives from economic power, the owners of the means of production constitute the ruling class and those whose labour they utilise the subject class. The power of the ruling class enables them to engage in an unequal exchange relationship with the subject class in which the latter do not receive full remuneration for the labour that they contribute to the productive process. Marx refers to this shortfall as class exploitation. This is the means by which resources become further accumulated in the hands of a minority and the means of production consolidated. It is also the basis of class conflict between the ruling and subject class.

How can this broad sweeping theory be applied to the stratification of modern capitalist societies and how did the latter emerge? Marxism offers an explanation of how capitalist societies grew out of feudal societies. In feudal societies, the main means of production were land, animals, agricultural buildings, machinery powered by natural forces and hand implements. The owners of these means of production were the major landowners who used the labour power of serfs to work the land. Serfs were agricultural workers who toiled the land but did not own it. They lived in a state of perpetual subsistence, bonded to landowners who extracted economic surpluses from their labour.

Although landowner and serf was the defining class relationship of feudalism, other gradations and occupations existed. Some peasants were small landholders who worked their own land. Craft workers made goods for the market. Others were occupied in trade, commerce and industry. It was amongst these latter groups, involved in forms of enterprise and risk taking, that moneyed wealth was gradually accumulating.

This increasing wealth accumulated by the owners of early industrial means of production was assisted by the competitive drive to apply advances in science and technology to make the productive process more efficient. The development of powered machinery and factory production drew increasing numbers of workers from rural and agricultural pursuits to industrial employment in expanding towns. The consequent expansion of industrial wealth by employers gave them the political power to challenge the social ascendancy of the old landed elite, enabled the transfer of class power to a new entrepreneurial elite, and marked the transition from feudalism to capitalism. These new relations of production were contractual relations between employer owners of the means of production and waged employee. They were also new divisions of conflicting class interest.

For Marx, although all class societies by definition contain opposing class interests, open class conflict is often averted. To understand how this is possible, the superstructure and infrastructure need to be defined and their relationship explained.

Institutions and ideas are referred to as the superstructure whilst the economy and the class divisions and stresses that it generates are referred to as the infrastructure. The function of the superstructure is to contain and dissipate class conflict generated by exploitation in the infrastructure. For example, the police and the courts can often control outward signs of social discontent. However, that discontent can often itself be averted through control of the consciousness of the subject class. This is achieved through the process of ideological distortion of reality. Ideology refers to a plausible but systematically distorted image of society. The ruling class are in a position to project this image - under capitalism justifying social arrangements in terms of freedom of contract and justice - onto the subject class. The purpose of these ideas is to encourage acceptance, conformity, and application and hide the reality of exploitation. Internalisation of an ideologically distorted view of society leads to false consciousness in the subject class. For example, the institution of private property is upheld by dominant social values and enforced by the law of the land protecting rightful owners of property from theft. There is widespread public awareness that such behaviour is criminal and detailed statistics available on such crimes. However, from a Marxist perspective there is one form of crime which is continuous but hidden – class based theft in the form of exploitation. Ideological distortion hides this reality through the concept of rightful profit.

Marxists agree with the functionalist analysis that social systems tend to generate ideas that promote consensus. However, Marx maintained that the beneficiaries of that consensus are not society as a whole, but primarily an exploiting class. There are tendencies within capitalism, though, toward the opening up of class conflict. Marx argued that factory conditions depress the level of work skills and concentrate increasing numbers of workers together. Although workers under capitalism are better off than serfs under feudalism, they are being exploited by a class whose wealth has increased even more through combining their labour with highly efficient means of production. Through this tendency for wealth to polarise, the rift between the classes will become more evident, especially during those periods when the economy malfunctions, producing mass unemployment and pushing wages down. It is at such times that ruling class ideology is likely to be seen through and a common class consciousness emerge between workers. Exploitation becomes recognised. The solution of class revolution becomes evident. The majority class then rise up against the minority class and take the means of production into common ownership. By such means, according to Marx, a communist society would replace capitalism. Since the means of production become commonly owned, this society would by definition be a classless society.

Marx's theory of classes and capitalism was based on his condemnation of a free enterprise system which emerged in mid-nineteenth century England. This raises certain questions regarding the contemporary relevance of Marxist theory in relation to which the reader is recommended to pause and reflect upon. For example, under entrepreneurial capitalism, private enterprises were often owned and run by individuals or families who made the key decisions and took the profits or faced the losses. There was a clearly defined capitalist class. But is this now the main form that capitalism takes? The expansion of large corporate enterprises in the twentieth century has arguably put trained managerial employees and professionals who are not driven solely by profit maximisation as the basis of personal wealth in charge of the decision making process. Furthermore, who now owns private enterprise? The development of joint stock companies has enabled millions of people to become shareholders. As such, whilst most of these people need to work for a living, they are also, according to the Marxist model, part owners of the means of production, and therefore have a foot in each of the classes as defined by Marx. Is it not the case that these changes, combined with improved standards of living, would suggest, contrary to Marx's predictions of radicalised workers and class revolution, the emergence of a new form of capitalism; one with which a large middling stratum of de-radicalised workers will tend to identify? What other weaknesses in the Marxist stratification model can the reader identify and analyse?

Weber – the importance of social status

Like Marx, Weber provided a conflict theory of stratification. He agreed with Marx that social class derives from economic factors. However, by contrast, Weber maintained that stratification is not exclusively reducible to social class, but includes status and party dimensions. Furthermore, class formation does not take place exclusively around the means of production. For Weber, occupations in the competitive labour market require different skills and qualities from workers. In return, they offer different levels of remuneration, security and perks. Social classes are formed and can be analysed through the clustering of occupations that are alike in these rewards and distinguishable from other occupational groups.

Social groups do not necessarily relate to a competitive labour market passively but struggle to maximise their returns. They may adopt strategies and use power in an attempt to control the labour market. Sometimes, the threat or use of collective action may be the strategy applied in the attempt to maximise rewards or improve terms and conditions of employment. In some occupations, strategies of restricting entry compared to demand for services are used to bolster rewards. Workers are therefore not necessarily as powerless under capitalism as the Marxist model suggests. For Weber, life chances and opportunities are less determined by inheritance and more created by purposeful action.

Weber identified the growth of large bureaucratic organisations as a key feature of modernisation. This process gives rise to an expansion of white collar occupations and classes around the middle of the stratification system. He disputed the Marxist analysis of tendencies toward social polarisation into two opposing social classes, the necessary emergence of a mass working class consciousness, and the inevitability of revolution.

Weber defined social status in terms of prestige judgements. A person's occupation (social class) and income level may affect their social status, but essentially status is to do with lifestyle. A status group therefore share a similar type of lifestyle. Although range of likely lifestyles will be linked to occupation and income, a person's position in social status terms may have some autonomy from their social class position. For example, status can be derived from living in a particular residential area. Although a residential area may tend to attract residents from similar occupational groups and levels of income – ie classes in Weber's terms – there is unlikely to be a hard and fast correlation. A status group include people from different social classes, and a social class can cut across status groups.

Culture, in the form of taste and manners, can be a more important dimension of status judgements than economics. People who are well off financially may be judged as brash by others who are less well off. Thus, during the nineteenth century, some who claimed high status by virtue of established wealth and cultured upbringing looked down on those who had achieved new wealth through business enterprise as

'Philistines' in terms of their perceived lack of culture. The response of the latter was sometimes to use their new made wealth to enhance the status of their children by sending them to public school.

Party was a further dimension of stratification for Weber. It brings together people with shared interests and aims and can therefore include identification with mass political parties and pressure groups. Common party identification may or may not correlate closely with peoples' social class or status. For example, in the case of a trade union which is fighting for the interests of a particular section of workers, party identification and class stratification are likely to be closely associated. However, party can bring together people from different class and status groups to pursue shared aims, even if the aims are pursued for different reasons. Opposition groups to new road building schemes can illustrate this point. Such groups have been known to bring together major local landowners and other local residents, concerned primarily with issues of quality of life and property prices, and geographically mobile members of new environmental pressure groups that advocate direct action. These people are likely to be highly distinguishable in terms of class and status differences. They may often have little time for each other. Yet, under such circumstances, there have been examples of local residents providing meals and washing facilities for direct action environmental protesters.

To sum up, Weber's model suggests weaknesses in both functionalist and Marxist stratification models. For example, the remuneration of groups within the occupational structure may not simply reflect the functional importance of an occupation or the workings of the free market as the functionalists maintain. Instead, in the struggle for resources, it may derive from strategies pursued by occupational groups, such as limitation of entry, to enhance the market position of their members.

Furthermore, stratification is a highly complex and multidimensional phenomena. There are many possible combinations of position in class, status and party that people occupy as well as forming shifting alliances with others as they engage in the pursuit of their interests. For Weber, attempts by Marxists to reduce an analysis of stratification to that of class related to the means of production alone will lack subtlety and distort reality.

Social stratification – traditional sociological issues and research:

1 How to measure occupational class

A major interest in studies of stratification in modern industrial societies has been the measurement of social mobility – the amount and extent of movement of people up and down the social hierarchy. If the extent of social mobility could be quantified, evidence would be provided of the degree of openness of modern social structures as potential meritocracies. But how can social mobility be reliably measured? The conventional means has been for sociologists or government officials to construct occupational scales which bracket occupations into a hierarchy of categories usually referred to as social classes. Such scales can be used in research as standard measuring devices to quantify the frequency and range of movement up and down the social structure, usually by comparing occupational levels between the generations. Traditionally, only the occupations of males figured in the measurement and if females were included in social mobility research their occupational level was deemed to derive from that of their husband's occupation.

Constructing occupational scales poses certain problems. For example, what criteria should be used for grouping occupations into categories and deciding on the number and positioning of class divisions? Should the criteria be based primarily on level of income, skill, social prestige, power in the workplace, etc. associated with an occupation or a combination of these? If the latter, what is an appropriate formula for that combination? These matters remain open to dispute. And whichever emphasis if given, there remains the problem of placing all occupations in a society into their appropriate groupings. It is not surprising, then, that a number of different occupational scales have been devised.

The Registrar General's scale, constructed by the government's statistical department and used from 1921, was the first occupational scale to be applied in Britain. It originally comprised five occupational categories – two of which were predominantly white collar and three predominantly blue collar. To remain relevant to subsequent changes in the occupational structure, the scale was reconstructed in 1971 as a six class scale by the addition of a further white collar category. The positioning of occupations on the scale was intended to reflect public perception of the relative advantage of different occupations but has been criticised by sociologists for its lack of theoretical underpinning.

Other occupational scales have been constructed with guidance from sociological theory. The major perspectives utilised have been Weberian and Marxist. Scales which take their lead from Weber tend to base occupational classification on a combination of occupational position in the competitive labour market and extent of authority in the workplace. By the first of these criteria, occupations would be classified in terms of levels of pay and other material rewards, job security and career prospects, and associated life chances. On the second criteria, major factors would be degree of power, control and autonomy that the job gives the worker in the workplace. These combined criteria would be applied to guide decisions in the construction of the scale with regard to the positioning and number of class categories in society.

In 1972, John Goldthorpe constructed a scale based on Weberian theory and has applied it in the Oxford Mobility Studies. This scale initially (it has since been revised) comprised seven occupational categories which were bracketed into three main social classes. The term 'service class' was used to apply to the two occupational categories of higher and lower professions. Higher professional occupations included managers in large companies and amongst lower professionals were high grade technicians. An 'intermediate class' comprised the three occupational categories: routine clerical work, small business proprietors and self-employed, and lower grade technicians and supervisors. Finally, a 'working class' consisted of two occupational categories – skilled manual work, and semi and unskilled manual work.

Marxists dispute the theoretical basis upon which such scales are constructed. They emphasise that, despite the various subdivisions of occupational categories that could be devised, there still remains a majority working class, defined by the necessity to sell its labour, and a capitalist employing class. Marxists such as Braverman have acknowledged that there has emerged some degree of gradation between these two main strata. For example, upper managerial employment could be part of an intermediate and marginal class who, despite their reliance on a salary, are well paid to do the bidding of their employers with whom they largely see eye to eye. However, Marxists maintain that conventional scales misleadingly construct separate class categories within a working class and are largely unable to pay recognition to the existence of a capitalist class.

Erik Olin Wright's development of a more elaborate scale of twelve finely graded occupational categories raises the dilemma faced by Marxists of constructing scales to measure class in contemporary capitalism. On the one hand, a scale that remained based on the simple division between owners and non-owners of the means of production is likely to appear over simplistic and outmoded. On the other hand, in their complexity, scales such as Wright's have been criticised for their departure from the classic Marxist model and have further proved difficult to operationalise (apply in research).

2 Measuring social mobility

Before reviewing and evaluating some findings on social mobility, the reader may find it beneficial to consider the meaning of social mobility at an individual level. The question to ask regarding 'intergenerational' mobility is how does an individual's occupational level compare to that of their parent's (traditionally father!)? Has there been upward or downward mobility and to what extent, or has the position remained about the same? This must, of course, only be a starting point to help grasp the meaning of intergenerational social mobility. Individual perceptions of the openness or closed nature of the social structure may reflect people's immediate experiences, but these are unlikely to be representative of broader social patterns. Sociologists attempt to measure the patterns of social mobility across society. This is achieved through the statistical analysis of measurements taken from a sample of the population. The measuring devices used are occupational scales.

Since the Second World War, a number of social mobility studies have been conducted in Britain and abroad. Some studies have made comparisons of mobility rates between societies. Comparisons can also be made over time to measure whether levels and patterns of social mobility are changing. By taking representative samples from a population, mobility studies are able to make generalisations of their findings to the broader population from which the sample has been drawn. Traditionally, studies were based on the assumption that family units were headed by a male breadwinner. Consequently, the occupational category of the dependent family would derive from the location on the scale of the male breadwinner's occupation. These studies essentially focussed on measuring the social mobility of males by comparing occupational levels of sons with that of fathers.

The findings of social mobility studies offer a statistical basis against which can be assessed the degree of openness of the social structure (traditionally, for males!). Information can be conveniently summarised in table form. Tables, as illustrated overleaf, comprise a grid of data on which a statistical comparison of father's and son's (the horizontal and vertical dimensions respectively) occupational level for society is summarised.

The following table (overleaf) summarises the findings of the Goldthorpe research into occupational mobility in England and Wales in 1972. Occupational mobility has been traditionally taken as a measure of social mobility. The information is here compiled in the form of an 'outflow' table. This means that the table takes as its base or starting point the father's occupational level and from this measures the percentage of sons from each of the father's occupational backgrounds who end up in each occupational category themselves.

David Goldthorpe, Oxford Mobility Study, England and Wales
Outflow Table

		Son's Occupational Category, 1972								
		1	2	3	4	5	6	7	Fathers in sample	
						No.	%			
Father's	1	**45.2**	18.9	11.5	7.7	4.8	5.4	6.5	688	7.3
	2	29.1	**23.1**	11.9	7.0	9.6	10.6	8.7	554	5.9
Occupational	3	18.4	15.7	**12.8**	7.8	12.8	15.6	16.9	694	7.3
	4	12.6	11.4	8.0	**24.8**	8.7	14.4	20.5	1329	14.1
Category	5	14.2	13.6	10.1	7.7	**15.7**	21.2	17.6	1082	11.5
	6	7.8	8.8	8.3	6.6	12.3	**30.4**	25.9	2594	27.5
	7	6.5	7.8	8.2	6.6	12.5	23.5	**34.9**	2493	24.6

In Goldthorpe's research, a scale using seven occupational categories, as referred to in the previous section, has been used. In the table, the 1-7 category column on the left refers to the father's occupational background. The figures in each box running across each row indicate the percentages of their sons who were in each of the seven column headed occupational categories. At the end of each row are given the total number of fathers in the sample in each occupational category and these figures converted into percentages to indicate the relative size of each category in the father's generation.

How to read the table can be illustrated in the following way. The 11.5% figure in column three of the top row means that 11.5% of sons from occupational category one background (father's occupation) were working in group three occupations and the 6.5% figure at the bottom of the first column shows that 6.5% of sons from occupational background seven were in the occupational group one category. The same approach can be applied to any figure on the table and it is worth pausing to work through with a number of the figures .

To interpret the table requires a broader view and an element of judgement. One approach would be to assess how far the pattern of evidence suggested that society was removed from a completely closed stratification system. If the stratification system were completely closed, the bold figures in the diagonals would all read 100% and all other cells would contain 0%, showing that all sons worked at the same occupational level as fathers. This is clearly not the case – some intergenerational social mobility is clearly evident. However, the highest figures do fall on or near to the diagonal. These figures further indicate that the highest levels of self recruitment come from category one and category seven occupational backgrounds and that those from group three backgrounds are the most occupationally mobile.

Another approach would be to compare the research evidence with the expected distribution of figures within a completely open social structure. In such an open structure, the figures would be more evenly spread across the rows and certainly much higher toward the corners opposite the diagonal, indicating high levels of long range social mobility. Impediments to this openness can be judged from the research figures which show that whilst 45.2% of males from category one backgrounds are found in category one occupations, only 6.5% appear in category seven employment and 34.9% from level seven backgrounds are in level seven occupations whilst only 6.5% achieve level one occupations.

On the other hand, compared to the findings of a study previously conducted by Glass *et al* in 1949, there is evidence of higher levels of long range social mobility. Although the findings are not strictly comparable as different occupational scales were used, the earlier research showed that only 1.5% of males from category one backgrounds were found in category seven occupations and 0% from category seven backgrounds achieved level one occupational status.

3 Analysing society in terms of meritocracy

There is a close link between an open social structure and a meritocracy, but the two are not exactly the same thing. Since a meritocracy is a society that enables individuals to reach occupational positions entirely in terms of their own efforts and abilities, its existence presupposes an open social structure. Research statistics on social mobility in the occupational structure offer a good measure of the openness of the social structure. However, there are complications to consider. It can be argued that a society that appears to exhibit a degree of social closure may still be highly meritocratic. How can this apparent contradiction be reconciled? It has been suggested that social mobility levels that on the surface fall short of the expectations of a meritocracy may be the consequence of social class related differences in levels of intelligence and (or) effort. If this is the case, it could be claimed that society offers equal opportunities to all, but that social mobility levels short of those expected in a meritocracy can be explained in terms of these differences in levels of ability and effort related to class background.

A strong advocate of this explanation is Peter Saunders. His arguments derive from a Conservative new right perspective. This position offers a strong defence of the liberal democratic institutions and individual freedoms of capitalist societies. It is emphasised that the dynamism of such societies is enhanced by substantial inequalities of occupational income, which promotes individual competition. A highly differentiated occupational reward structure is therefore the motivator for individual success. As the main criteria for success are effort and ability, success does not just benefit individuals exhibiting these qualities, but by appropriately placing people in suitable occupations it enhances living standards for all through the efficient utilisation of human resources. A highly differentiated income structure can thus be legitimised, as can the accumulation of private wealth based on achievement.

Saunders argues that class linked differences in individual ability and effort go a long way toward explaining the differences in occupational outcome of people from different social class backgrounds. And whilst he acknowledges that modern Britain is not perfectly meritocratic, his research also indicates that ability is closely associated with occupational destination and that where differences in ability alone cannot sufficiently explain variations in level of occupational achievement, then differences in individual motivation, related so social background, also have an important impact.

In considering these arguments, there are reasons to be cautions or critical of Saunders' position. Firstly, the proposition that there are ability differences based on social class background requires examination. The importance of educational opportunity and achievement to meritocracy has already been established in the previous chapter. Here, it was argued that evidence of class related differences in inherited ability are not compelling. These ability differences will therefore have very limited effect on explaining levels of closure in social stratification from one generation to the next. Instead, it has been argued that class related differences are built into the assessment of intelligence and educational performance. The educational system is therefore bent toward the middle classes and through the extra help often available their children can be supported toward success in the education system. Such a class based distortion built into education will have consequences for both educational and occupational achievement to the extent that occupation is based on educational achievement.

Furthermore, if levels of motivation and individual effort are related to social class, the argument can be taken in different directions. If those of manual working class background tend to be more fatalistic in terms of their occupational destination, then it can be argued, as did Hyman, that it is these negative values which act as self imposed barriers to success within a basically meritocratic society. Alternatively, from his research of a group of working class lads, Willis suggested the explanation that in their lesser effort to succeed at school and aspire to higher level occupations than their fathers, they make a realistic assessment of the limited opportunities available to them within a society which was far less meritocratic.

A number of other reasons to be cautious in claiming British society to be highly meritocratic can be made. One of these is to do with changes that take place within the occupational structure. The size and makeup of occupational classes changes over time. For example, during the post war decades, there was a period of rapid expansion in professional occupations. However, the fertility rate of the middle class was lower than that of the working class. During this period, it was difficult for expanding professional occupations to sufficiently recruit from the young of the middle classes alone to fill all posts. Under these conditions, Goldthorpe's research indicated greater levels of upward than downward mobility. This particular pattern of social mobility enabled more people of manual working class background to gain access to middle class occupations without threatening to displace many from middle class backgrounds. It is therefore doubtful whether such opportunities for upward mobility should be equated with meritocracy and they are likely to be highly contingent on the conditions identified.

A further problem for the meritocracy thesis is that whilst a totally open social structure is a prerequisite for a meritocracy, a high level of social mobility is not in itself sufficient proof of mobility through meritocratic means – that of fair and legitimate competition based on individual effort and ability. Levels of social mobility derived from marriage or through criminal activity would hardly equate with the normally accepted means of meritocratic success.

A weakness of general occupational scales is that they lack the precision to measure social mobility levels at the very pinnacle of society. For example, on the Goldthorpe scale, the top occupational category comprised 7.3% of the sample of fathers and by implication the size of that category in the population. This class had grown to 13.6% of the son's generation. However, a researcher's focus of interest may be in measuring social mobility into the 'elite'. In occupational terms, this category will include such professions as ambassadors, senior judges, high ranking officers in the armed forces, members of parliament, high ranking civil servants, and directors of major industrial, banking and insurance companies. This group borders onto a propertied upper class and in total comprises only about 0.1 – 0.2% of the adult population. Occupational scales which do not have a separate social stratum to reflect this will not be subtle enough to measure mobility across this point. Furthermore, in general social mobility studies, only about 1 or 2 participants from this category per 1,000 in a representative sample of the population are likely to be included. There will therefore also be insufficient participants for statistical purposes to measure levels of social mobility into elite occupations.

An alternative approach could be to select a sample of people comprising entirely those in elite occupations. Such groups, however, tend to be closed to the enquiries of prying sociologists. The study of this stratum needs to be approached from another angle. One way of going about this is to obtain a measure of the percentages of people in elite professions who have attended the most exclusive public schools and compare these figures with those of other occupations or for the rest of the population.

A massive disparity in favour of the elite occupations does in fact exist which offers strong evidence of non-meritocratic elite self-recruitment.

According to Peter Saunders, 'a meritocracy is like a race where everybody lines up together at the start'. Assuming that this is a close account of the basis of opportunity in society appears to be a remarkably superficial view. Even if competition for occupation and income level is largely based on ability and effort, this does not explain how the resulting accumulation of wealth and its inheritance squares with a meritocratic society. The distribution of wealth is even more unequal than that of income. Saunders defends the legitimacy to pass on legally acquired wealth to others. However, the problem here is that even if wealth in one generation is entirely achieved by merit, through right of disposal to descendants it would then not remain acquired by meritocratic means to that and to subsequent generations.

Another way of approaching these issues is to imagine the creation of a meritocracy from a social blank slate. For the first generation, all would start, as Saunders suggests, on an equal footing to compete for occupations in terms of ability and effort. Assuming the motivation for competition to be substantial inequality of income associated with different occupations and assuming a system of private property and inheritance, it is quite obvious that the meritocracy would be undermined in the following generation through the inheritance of different life chance starting points based purely on luck, offering some the advantages deriving from their parent's achievements and others the disadvantages of their parent's lack of achievement. These advantages and disadvantages can include different study conditions and educational privileges, and differences in nutrition, health and access to levels of healthcare. Such factors are often interrelated. It is well documented that the physical and health condition of those of manual working class background are generally inferior to those of middle class background. Individual competition for academic achievement and occupational status will not be taking place on a level playing field.

The above qualifications have related primarily to social class. In terms of class stratification, although modern Britain (and like western democracies) is a relatively meritocratic society by general historical comparisons, evidence and arguments show it to be substantially short of being a pure meritocracy. However, there is also an ideological dimension which may colour assessment of this area. Functionalists and supporters of the new right find meritocracy to be compatible with capitalism. In fact, they tend to utilise the concept of meritocracy to justify massive inequality of income as a motivator for competition and the achievement of social mobility. Critics from the left tend to question the need for vast income differentials and are likely to be more cautious of the extent to which modern capitalist societies are meritocratic. Indeed, as suggested earlier, it could be argued that there is a logical contradiction between capitalism and meritocracy.

Meritocracy can only be more comprehensively evaluated when other dimensions of stratification such as gender and ethnicity are also considered and questions raised regarding the continuing existence of institutions of privilege and status deriving from birthright. Our political leaders are often keen to appeal to the concept of Britain as a meritocratic society but less keen on engaging in or encouraging joined up thinking in this area. Pursuing this logical analysis too far may raise awkward questions which point to the incompatibility of some of our social institutions, from which many of them and their children have been beneficiaries, with the realisation of a meritocracy. Indeed, following such an analysis, the reader, at a personal level, may have come to feel more or less comfortable with the idea of meritocracy in principle or practice. However, as a sociologist, the aim should be to enlighten, not obscure. An attempt must be made to step outside of society and assess it in terms of a comparison with the logical outcome of the application of such concepts as meritocracy.

Class stratification – changing but how?

Linked to the areas of dispute between the founding theoretical perspectives on stratification (functionalist, Marxist and Weberian) are a number of interpretations of changes in the class structure. One such interpretation was the embourgeoisement thesis. This thesis was rooted in the experience of growing affluence of the late 1950s and early 1960s and was associated with such writers as Jessie Bernard. It was essentially argued that the traditional working class was declining in size and the middle class expanding. More specifically, as a feature of economic modernisation, traditional working class occupations, such as dock work, mining and agricultural work, were undergoing long-term decline. Blue-collar employment on modern production lines was expanding and enabling workers to earn incomes comparable to the middle classes. In the resultant mass consumer society, affluent blue collar workers were apparently adopting the lifestyle and status and even political views associated with those in middle class occupations

There are clear theoretical implications of this interpretation. One is that Marx's analysis of the essence of class conflict to capitalism and predictions of class polarisation were mistaken. Marxist analysis could be seen as increasingly dated and redundant as capitalism became able to transcend class conflict and evolve toward a single middle class society. This emphasis on 'middleclassness' as a basis for shared values and social integration would certainly align embourgeoisement with the theoretical position of functionalism.

It is now well established that the embourgeoisement interpretation was undermined by research conducted by Goldthorpe and Lockwood in the early 1960s. By focussing on a sample of affluent blue-collar workers in the Luton area, this research found that in terms of their relationship to work, their lifestyle and their political attitudes, these workers were neither traditional working class nor middle class. Such findings point to a more differentiated stratification system implied in Weber's perspective.

A rival interpretation of changes in the class structure from a Marxist perspective pointed to the process of proletarianisation. Supporters of this position, such as Harry Braverman, maintained in the early 1970s that despite absolute improvements in standard of living and the expansion of white-collar occupations, a mass working class still existed. It was argued that through modernisation, many blue-collar occupations had undergone a process of 'deskilling'. From the early decades of the twentieth century, craft skills were being replaced by low skilled and narrowly designed repetitive production line work. Workers on production lines experienced a loss of autonomy and heightened alienation in the workplace. Furthermore, by the 1970s, the expansion of white-collar employment was increasingly in the form of low skilled work with little autonomy and responsibility and few promotion prospects. Deskilling was therefore also a feature of a growing section of white-collar work. The proletarianisation thesis maintained that modern capitalism contains a mass working class which is identified by a common experience in the workplace. That experience is one of declining skill levels, autonomy and responsibility; processes common to an increasing number of both blue-collar and white-collar workers. Consequently, from a Marxist perspective, it is false consciousness for deskilled white-collar workers to distinguish themselves as middle class and separate from working class blue-collar workers. Occupational scales which make this distinction are themselves faulty measuring devices.

Of the various criticisms of Marxist interpretations of the class structure, one of the most challenging has been the decomposition thesis which was associated with Ralf Dahrendorf. Dahrendorf argued that rather than the class structure of modern capitalist societies crystallising into clearly opposed camps as Marx predicted, it was in fact breaking down. In a complex occupational structure, the blue-collar 'working class' was fragmenting into a number of occupational stratum comprising growing proportions of skilled and declining proportions of unskilled workers. More blue-collar workers were becoming owner-occupiers of their homes and achieving comparative prosperity. The 'working class' were therefore breaking down as a discrete stratum and experiencing a decline in common class consciousness.

Additionally, the class of entrepreneurial owners of the means of production associated with an earlier phase of capitalism that was so criticised by Marx, had been eclipsed in modern capitalism by the emergence of larger joint stock companies which relied for their finance on a mass of investors. Through the spread of shareholding, a significant proportion of the public, as investors in private enterprise, were becoming part owners of the means of production. The ambiguity posed for classical Marxist class analysis is clear, since most of these investors would also be in employment and therefore, according to this perspective, also often proletarian.

Dahrendorf's model suggests a more open and meritocratic social structure in which class conflict gives way to individual competition and a wider variety of people feel that they have a stake in the system. Contemporary capitalism had percolated power down to shareholders and thus become democratised. Such features of late twentieth century capitalism identified by Dahrendorf as challenging the contemporary relevance of the Marxist model were actively promoted by new right policies through which privatisation spread shareholding and home ownership in Britain to more people than ever before during the 1980s and early 90s.

Gender stratification – liberation and inequality

The term gender refers to socially constructed identity associated with biologically determined sex differences. Gender identity and gender roles change as society and its institutions and values change. Socialisation of gender identity is not necessarily a uniform process across society and identity varies between societies. Furthermore, males and females do not comprise undifferentiated stratification groups. Gender stratification is cross cut by other forms of stratification such as class, status, ethnicity and age as gender stratification itself cuts across these. The reality and analysis of gender identity and stratification is therefore highly complex, and although the two are linked, this section of the chapter will focus on the latter.

Educational opportunity, work and family relationships are key dimensions of gender stratification. How these have changed can be viewed in historical terms and the following comments related back to previous chapters on the family and education.

In pre-industrial Britain, quite a high proportion of economic production took place in domestic settings, combining work and family relationships. Although productive domestic based work was often divided along gender lines, later notions of male (working) breadwinner and female (non-working) housewife were little recognised. Housework was likely to have been allocated to children.

Gender role segregation took on a new and pronounced form following the Industrial Revolution. As the productive process moved outside of the home, work was becoming defined in terms of this external setting in which workers were employed in large numbers in the pay of an employer. The introduction of the Factory Acts offered some degree of protection in the workplace for women and children, making them less attractive labour. By the second half of the nineteenth century, women were becoming increasingly excluded from factory work and consigned to the home. Within the home, they engaged in domestic activities which were no longer regarded as work. This gender based reconfiguration and the redefinition of work is sometimes referred to as the rise of private or domestic patriarchy, supported by the ideology of domesticity in which the 'natural' caring and serving qualities of females suited them to domesticity and dependence on the male wage earner, the latter often exhibiting opposition to the employment of women as a threat to their employment security.

Throughout the nineteenth century, entry to many professions was closed to middle class women and the main employment available for working class women was that which reflected their perceived natural role: domestic service.

During the first half of the twentieth century, patterns of employment for women fluctuated greatly. Two world wars required the mass mobilisation of women into the workforce, often engaging in heavy-duty work to support the war effort. However, at the end of each conflict it was expected that they would return to their domestic duties so that men, if they returned, could rightfully reclaim the jobs that they had temporarily vacated.

After the Second World War, more women resisted pressures to vacate their jobs, but were often faced with male hostility and powerful government propaganda to resume their portrayed primary domestic role. However, from the 1960s economic change and feminist challenges to traditional gender roles were bringing about a feminisation of the workforce. From about this time, with the growth of service sector employment, more women were entering the workforce. By the 1970s and 1980s, further changes in the form of de-industrialisation and arguably also deskilling opened up lower grade clerical opportunities that were mainly taken up by women.

At the most general level, at the turn of the twenty first century, the workforce in Britain (and other western societies) includes an almost equal proportion of women and men. However, when scrutinised more closely, there is evidence of continuing gender inequality in terms of patterns of concentration, segregation and stratification.

Firstly, in Britain women are far more likely to be concentrated in routine clerical level occupations than men. As a result, they tend to experience a different pattern of social mobility to that of men. Marshall *et al* indicated in the 1988 Essex Mobility Study that women are both more upwardly and downwardly mobile from a variety of occupational backgrounds as they tended to converge in the routine clerical occupational stratum.

Secondly, more women than men work part-time or under flexible work conditions. This may be of advantage of both employers and to women with domestic commitments, but such employment is usually in the 'secondary' sector of the labour market which is marked by low wages, poor employment prospects and employee insecurity.

Thirdly, there remains a degree of gender related horizontal segregation in employment. Horizontal segregation refers to separation into different occupational spheres. There remain marked concentrations of women working in catering, cleaning, selling, education, welfare and health, and men in construction, extractive industries, the armed forces, police and security services, and science and technology.

Fourthly, evidence remains of significant gender differences in occupational level achieved. Gender is therefore an element of vertical segregation in the stratification hierarchy. As a general rule, there is a correlation between the higher levels of pay and status in an occupation and a declining proportion of women employed at these levels. Key occupations in which women have not progressed far, despite evidence of occasional successes, include the legal profession and the police. Even in those occupations where women are more concentrated, such as in teaching and social work, they predominate in the lower levels and participate in declining proportions at the higher managerial and professional levels. In occupations in which males are concentrated, women are usually quite a rarity in the upper echelons.

Although gaining access to employment in virtually equal proportions to males, it can be argued that through a combination of horizontal segregation and vertical stratification, women's opportunities remain more limited, suggesting that patriarchal power also remains well established outside of the family.

Despite legislative advances against discrimination and for equal pay during the first half of the 1970s, and the impact of more recent EU legislation, women are still paid lower hourly rates to men, work shorter hours, are more likely to be in part-time employment, obtain lower pay for equivalent qualifications, and are more likely to be employed in the insecure secondary labour market. Even when comparing the hourly rates of males and females working full time, females still only earn about 80% of male rates of pay.

There is also evidence that growing economic and social polarisation during the 1980s and 1990s had a greater impact on females than males. Whilst, particularly from the 1980s, the number of single, usually female, parents living in poverty has been increasing, a growing number of women, although remaining minorities, have entered professional and managerial positions. This latter improvement may be set to continue as more females are entering higher education than males.

Of particular concern to feminists has been the implications of care in the community policy which was promoted in Britain from the early 1990s. Research has shown that much of the caring takes place within the family and that the burden falls excessively on females. The costs involved in taking on this burden can be substantial. For example, as well as loss of earnings, carers lose out on making extra pension contributions. They are also likely to have missed out on retraining and promotion prospects and may find it difficult to return to work. On top of these career and economic penalties, carers risk suffering anxiety and isolation which can affect their health and well being.

Measuring gender stratification – a case for individual assignment?

Traditionally, sociologists such as Goldthorpe have measured the stratification position of the family unit in terms of the occupational position of the male head of the household. Powerful social expectations supporting the housewife role meant that if women did work, opportunities were restricted, employment was often recognised as temporary and their earnings were seen more as a supplement to the family income. As the husband's commitment to employment was usually the greater, it could be argued that his employment position in the occupational structure should be taken as the benchmark for the social class of the family unit. At a time when gender stratification was marked but largely accepted, this dimension of stratification tended to be overlooked by sociologists focussing primarily on class stratification based on male occupation.

Women have since entered the labour force in far greater numbers. More females are now self-supporting and independent through employment, make significant or major contributions to a family income, or are the sole supporters of a family. It is therefore often felt to be unrealistic to measure the position of women in the stratification system in terms of the occupation of males assumed to be heads of households. The picture is a mixed one. Despite evidence of a clear break from past expectations limiting females to a largely domestic role, there is still evidence of substantial vertical and horizontal segregation in male and female employment, working to the detriment of the females. Consequently, measuring the social class position of females in terms of the occupation, where it is possible, of a male partner, would hide these differences and the degree of gender based occupational stratification that still exists.

Alternative approaches to the measurement of class position of females have been developed which either allocate position on an individual basis (for example Michelle Stanworth and Arber *et al*) or, if the family remains the unit of classification, take female employment into account (for example Heath and Britten). However, various complications and difficulties arise. In the case of families or partnerships, if both partners work, they may hold similar level occupations. In such cases, there would appear to be little problem or difference in measuring social class whether assessed individually or jointly. But would it be realistic to accord the same stratification position, individually or jointly, to a partnership where only one partner works at the same occupational level as another with both working? Furthermore, if within a partnership both partners work but at different occupational levels, is it appropriate to allocate each to a different social class or more realistic to refer to the unit as a cross-class unit? Alternatively, is it viable to just take the highest occupational position in a partnership, whether that of the male or the female, and read the social class of the partnership from that designation? Answers to such questions also have implications for the measurement of intergenerational social mobility, the findings of which will be influenced by the base point used for comparison between the generations.

Because of the close relationship between occupation and social class, radical feminists are likely to maintain that measuring stratification by occupation, however approached, may indicate little more than a gendered dimension of social class stratification. This does not bring out other aspects which, they argue, make gender stratification primary to and more fundamental than class, in particular the oppression of females by males in a broad range of social relationships and the existence of sexist attitudes, etcetera.

Furthermore, the nature and extent of gender stratification varies significantly between different ethnic groups.

Differentiating race and ethnicity

The view that the human race can be divided into racially distinct categories based on skin colour, each with different biologically inbuilt characteristics and capacities, developed in European thinking as white Europeans colonised different parts of the world. During the nineteenth century, this view of racial types was commonly linked to evolutionary theory, which viewed the white race as the most advanced. It gained further prominence and the kudos of science in the early twentieth century with the emergence of the eugenics movement. However, the scientific basis behind the view of innate and fixed racially distinctive characteristics has to a large extent been subsequently discredited.

Sociologists usually prefer to use the term 'ethnicity' to that of race to identify different groups. Ethnic characteristics are based on environmental as opposed to biological factors. Distinctive ethnic identities are formed by the process of socialisation into distinctive cultural traditions, languages, and perceptions of ancestry. Viewing people in terms of ethnicity avoids attributing fixed and inbuilt racial traits and although ethnic groups may fall along racial lines, ethnicity also emphasises distinctions within general racial groups such as white Irish or Italians. However, the sociological problem does not finish there. A key sociological question is why, despite the discrediting of the assumptions behind racial types, racism and ethnic intolerance still exists within society? Some answers are indicated in the following section.

Post war immigration and models of stratification

Although there have been various population movements into Britain throughout history, it was only after the Second World War that black ethnic minorities were entering the country in substantial numbers. Post war reconstruction created a situation of low unemployment. As some of the white population were experiencing upward mobility, labour shortages existed in areas of unskilled manual employment. Against this backdrop, the British Nationality Act of 1948 offered relatively open access and rights of permanent settlement for citizens of Commonwealth countries and recruitment drives were launched abroad.

During the 1950s and 1960s, the main flow of immigration was from the Caribbean. Employment of this ethnic group was particularly focussed in relatively poorly paid and unskilled work in public transport and also in the National Health Service.

By the 1970s, immigrants into the country were now coming more from India, Pakistan and Bangladesh. Again, employment was mainly taken up at unskilled level but these ethnic groups were concentrated more in the areas of textile work and engineering. Very few ethnic minority workers during these decades acquired employment in managerial positions.

To sum up, immigrants settling during this phase, mainly from Commonwealth countries, experienced both substantial horizontal (occupational) concentration and vertical stratification into lower level occupations.

Tensions often arose between host and immigrant populations. The basis of this was both cultural and economic. As clearly identifiable groups, immigrant workers brought with them what were perceived by sections of the indigenous population as alien beliefs and ways of living. They were also often perceived as competing for and taking jobs from the white population. The response of the host population was therefore often unwelcoming and resentment could surface in the form of racism and hostility. Such hostility surfaced in the first race riots in Notting Hill in 1958.

How could the stratification position of recently arrived immigrants be understood sociologically and what would the future hold? Different stratification models, especially with reference to black immigrants, were developed to attempt to explain the dynamics of this situation, two of which have been frequently cited: the immigrant – host model and the white racism model.

The immigrant – host (or assimilation) model, initially based on research conducted by Sheila Patterson, holds many of the characteristics of functionalist theory and is a position which tends to find favour with the political right. It starts from the position that before the arrival of immigrants, the host society shares a common national identity and consensus of values and that there exists a stable class hierarchy. New immigrants are initially concentrated in occupations toward the bottom of the occupational structure. Although they share class disadvantage with some of the white population, they also experience cultural separation. When the host population experiences an influx of people unfamiliar in their appearance and ways, the response is often one of ignorance, suspicion and hostility which can take the form of racism. These animosities have a destabilising effect on society. However, in time, ethnic minorities become assimilated into the culture of the host society. Consequently, hostility, racism and discrimination decline, minorities become integrated across the class structure and can take up their position more on merit. A new social stability is established, and the overriding form of stratification and disadvantage for all alike is social class. Only resistance to assimilation on the part of ethnic minorities through the retention of their cultural traditions and separateness will continue them subject to racial stratification and for this the problem is seen to be of their own making.

An alternative interpretation of the dynamics involved is that it is the persistence of racism (values) and racial discrimination (action) from the white population which keeps ethnic minorities separate from white society in a largely disadvantaged position at the foot of society. This analysis is sometimes taken in the direction of Marxist criticism. According to this position, the persistence of racism under capitalism can be expected. Like sexism, it operates as a false consciousness, dividing and weakening a common class. Ethnic minorities often provide (as do women) a reserve army of cheap labour. Sections of the white working class are therefore vulnerable to media generated hostility toward immigrants who are scapegoated as the cause of their insecurity. The policies of far right political parties can hold some appeal within these sections of the population. From a Marxist position, although in theory many ethnic minority people are part of a broad working class, it is the false consciousness of white racism which excludes them from the white working class at the base of society. Because racism and racial discrimination are viewed as a consequence of the class structure under capitalism, there is little room for optimism in effective assimilation.

Ethnicity and occupational profile – diversity remains

From the early 1960s, and particularly with economic slowdown during the 1970s and the recession of the early 1980s, legislation was passed which effectively placed increasing restriction on non-white immigration. These restrictions were followed by a tightening of asylum regulation as more people wanting to enter the country were pursuing this alternative channel. With a stemming of immigration, most of the black ethnic minority groups now comprise majorities of second or even third generation British citizens.

Compared to their predecessors, what is the contemporary pattern of ethnic minority participation in the occupational structure? Valuable information for the period 1998-2000 has been provided by the Labour Force Survey. It shows that when ethnic minorities are taken together, differences in the occupational profile compared to that of white British are very small. The same applies when the figures are further broken down by gender. However, when the information for individual ethnic groups is studied, the picture is a very complex one of distinctive profiles.

For males, evidence of occupational concentration indicates some continuity with past patterns of employment. Pakistanis remain highly represented in manufacturing, Bangladeshis and Chinese in hotel and catering, Afro Caribbeans in transport and communications and Indians in transport and communications and manufacturing.

In terms of occupational level, Chinese and Indians figured in larger proportions than whites in professional, managerial and technical occupational categories, but the proportion of Bangladeshis in these occupations was substantially lower than that of whites. In the largely manual partly skilled and unskilled occupations, Indians figured in about the same proportion as whites but the percentages for Bangladeshis and black Caribbean groups were substantially higher.

For females, the figures showed that significantly larger proportions of Chinese were employed in professional, managerial and technical occupations than whites, but that smaller proportions of Pakistanis and Bangladeshis were employed in these groups than whites. A smaller proportion of Chinese than white women worked in the partly skilled and unskilled occupations, whereas a substantially higher proportion of black African women were employed at this level. The latter's participation rates were also high. Relatively high proportions of Pakistani and Bangladeshi women were also employed in this category, but Bangladeshi women have the lowest rate of participation in employment outside the family. This reflects traditional family life and the values of Islamic culture and is a reminder that the study of stratification should also look at different patterns of family life and the distribution of power and resources within families.

A fairly consistent pattern emerges across the range of ethnic groups in which women tend to have lower occupational positions than men. The biggest gender difference in professional, managerial and technical occupations is amongst Indians where 47% of males are employed and only 33% of females. However, some groups provide exceptions. For example, there are higher proportions of women than men from black Caribbean, other black and black mixed groups in these occupational categories.

In partly skilled and unskilled occupations, figures for female participation are consistently higher than for males with the exception of black Caribbean workers where 27% of employed males and 24% of females work. Clearly, a fuller understanding of these figures would necessitate more detail on actual occupations worked in.

Gender stratification appears to be a fairly enduring pattern across white and a range of ethnic groups. Furthermore, evidence suggests that ethnic minority females generally are less differentiated in terms of income and occupational level from white females than is the case in comparing ethnic minority and white males. For some feminists, despite variations between the ethnic groups, this is taken as evidence of the overriding significance of gender stratification. As women are generally concentrated toward the lower end of the occupational structure, there is less room for differentiation.

In terms of equality of achievement, the evidence at a general level is positive but in detail remains mixed. The occupational restructuring accompanying economic modernisation from the 1980s has drawn in ethnic minorities so as to narrow the occupational profile differences between themselves and white British workers. Overall, their vertical positioning is converging with white workers. However, there remain greater differences between specific ethnic minority groups than between ethnic minorities as a whole and the white population in terms of both vertical stratification and horizontal differentiation.

Figures of occupational distribution within general categories only reveal part of the picture. For example, evidence of more ethnic minority men now employed in the professional, managerial and technical category tends to hide the fact that relatively high proportions work in more precarious positions of self-employment.

Furthermore, information on general categories of employment does not reveal the disparity of earnings and expenditure that still exist between the different ethnic groups and the white population. For example, evidence provided in Social Trends (2002) shows that the average income of Bangladeshi men is approximately only half that of whites and that average household expenditure for Bangladeshis is less than half that of whites.

Account should also be taken of hours worked, conditions of employment and treatment in the workplace, job insecurity and risk of unemployment, on all of which there is some evidence of ethnic disadvantage. Ethnic minorities have traditionally been concentrated in less secure employment. Thus, during the recession of the 1980s which hit manufacturing very hard, Pakistanis, Bangladeshis and Afro Caribbeans became unemployed at about twice the rate of whites. However, when employment picked up, that was also quicker for these groups than for white workers. This pattern of effect on ethnic minorities has been referred to as 'hyper-cyclical'.

Racial discrimination – grounds for optimism?

What evidence is available on racial discrimination practiced by employers and to what extent is the situation changing? To measure behaviour in such an emotive and sensitive area, the use of covert (concealed) methods may be necessary. Such an approach was adopted in research conducted by D.J. Smith and published in 1977. In this research, applications were submitted from applicants of white and ethnic minority background with matched work histories and qualifications for a range of blue collar and white collar jobs. Employers' response to blue collar applicants indicated a tenfold preference of whites to blacks, and in the case of white collar applicants, those with names indicating Asian or West Indian background were 30% less likely to be even offered an interview than white applicants.

To what extent are ethnic minorities still disadvantaged by racial discrimination? In small scale covert research employing hidden recording devices, journalists in a BBC documentary (Black and White) visited the Bristol area in an attempt to measure racial discrimination by employers and landlords. Taped and filmed evidence of racial discrimination was evident in this area. When the journalists followed up advertisements for jobs and accommodation, that which was unavailable when the black applicant turned up sometimes became available when the white applicant appeared later.

Another approach to the question of racial discrimination has been to conduct self-report surveys. National surveys conducted by the Policy Studies Institute have asked ethnic minorities about their experiences of racial discrimination. There was evidence here of differentiation between ethnic groups in their perception of being victims of racial discrimination. Measurements taken in the 1980s and 1990s reveal a consistent pattern that about 25% of West Indians perceived that racial discrimination had led to them being refused a job. The figures for Asians were substantially lower. Of course, the problem with such research is that the findings are based on subjective judgements and can be difficult to interpret. Whilst complacency should be avoided, it is at least an ironic possibility that the high figures of discrimination experienced are partly the product of more enlightened times and a greater sensitivity to being the victims of discrimination.

New anxieties

More recently, the issues of ethnicity have again returned to the theme of immigration. New concerns and hostilities have been raised in the media regarding suspected bogus asylum seekers who are in fact economic migrants, and levels of illegal immigration. Furthermore, as the European Union has expanded eastwards to include countries such as Poland, a shortage of skills in the building and construction trade in particular, but also the attraction of vacancies for unskilled labour in areas such as agriculture, has attracted workers from such countries to Britain. As documented in the 2008 BBC 2 series 'White Season', the concentration of these workers in such towns as Peterborough has often been accompanied by hostility from locals.

Contemporary sociological thinking on social stratification:

1 The decline of social class?

Social class has previously been defined as primarily based on economic differences. Class stratification therefore reflects the distribution of wealth and income in society. In a class stratified society, stratification primarily takes the form of different occupationally grouped strata within which people experience similar levels of income, as well as life chances and experiences and a degree of consciousness of their distinctiveness from people in other social classes.

Social stratification by economic class was a well established feature of modern societies and a predominant theme in the sociological tradition. Class societies, offering prospects of social mobility but also imposing barriers to it, represent a position in stratification terms somewhere in between the extremes of closed and open social hierarchies. However, much sociological debate has emerged over the continuing prevalence of social class in the way that contemporary societies are stratified. Doubts over the salience of class stratification have taken various forms. From the late 1960s, both gender and ethnic stratification have gained greater attention and sociologists have come to realise the complex and sometimes unpredictable ways in which class, gender and ethnicity interact.

Furthermore, a pattern of evidence suggesting the declining significance of social class has been emerging. For example, Dahrendorf argued that social classes were decomposing or breaking up and Crewe has indicated the declining importance of social class as an influence on voting behaviour.

2 The growing importance of social status?

Social status has previously been defined in terms of values and ways of life that people aspire to and the acquisition of objects, all of which accord individuals and groups levels of social prestige. The link between status and economics tends to relate more to what people do with their money than how they have earned it. How people attribute symbols of status to the objects of possession and how owners derive status from these objects can be illustrated by the experience of changes in treatment on the road that a person may experience with a change in the type of car driven!

Some sociologists, particularly amongst postmodernists and high modernists, argue that, in affluent consumer societies, social status is replacing social class as the predominant form of social stratification. From a broad historical perspective, the social structures of contemporary societies are relatively open. In a more open society, people are likely to feel free to aspire to symbols of success rather than being resigned to accepting their inherited position in the stratification system. Consequently, the importance of status awareness in a more open social structure may be eclipsing that of class consciousness in a class stratified society. In relatively open status societies, people tend to compare themselves with others and base their sense of self worth on the signs of status achievement that they can project. This heightened awareness and comparison with others can lead to new psychological anxieties associated with what Alain de Botton refers to as 'status anxiety'.

Postmodernism – the demise of social class

Postmodernist writers tend to adopt the farthest position in claiming demise of social class. Their broad view of history distinguishes three phases: traditional, modern and postmodern. In traditional society, both possessions and behaviour were largely prescribed by one's position in the stratification system. The meaning of objects was therefore bound up with and reinforced precisely demarcated social relations (taking on the ways of those higher in the social structure risked the charge of impersonation – the non-legitimate copying of social 'betters'). As the old structure broke down and modern industrial societies emerged, enhanced social mobility opportunities led to competition for objects as confirmation of (new) status.

Now, in postmodern society, it is not the social relations which determine the meaning of objects, but the acquisition of possessions as status symbols which determine social relations. Objects become less desired in terms of their subsistence need or purely functional use and more in terms of the status they convey. It is the symbols that are desired by consumers and changing fashions fuel insatiable desire. It is now the goods and their associated symbolic status which form social differences rather than the reverse of the past. In this sense, 'authentic' social boundaries have collapsed, only to be replaced by those based on a superficial and ephemeral world of fashions in relation to which individuals have a high degree of freedom available for 'self-assembly'.

Postmodernists tend to emphasise the positive aspect of these changes. Such a position is adopted by Pakulski and Waters who argue that in postmodern society concern with social class has much diminished. This is because the productive capacity of contemporary society has made the old social class battles based on economic necessity redundant. The achievement of economic security has led to a society preoccupied with the acquisition of products and the leading of lifestyles more for the images that they convey.

It is argued that economic security thus enables people to choose products and lifestyles more freely. As a result, social status becomes increasingly decoupled from social class, and even for people at similar income levels, status based on lifestyle choice – cultural differences – comes to distinguish groups. It is increasingly possible for those living on more modest incomes to aspire to higher status than others better off by adopting prestigious lifestyle choices.

The values, lifestyles and fashions associated with social status are ever changing. Furthermore, individuals are relatively free to change their personal lifestyle choices. Social stratification therefore enters a new level of fluidity.

High modernism / late modernism – the individualisation of risk

Not all sociologists who believe that contemporary society has entered a new phase are quite so convinced of the complete demise of social class or so positive regarding the process of individualisation as postmodernists tend to be. In the works of writers such as Anthony Giddens and Ulrich Beck, the hallmark of high modern or late modern societies respectively is the emergence of new types and levels of risk.

In modern society, the need to create wealth and conquer poverty were the key aims of science and technology. For Beck, in this context the unequal distribution of limited resources and risks in life prioritised social class in peoples' experience. By contrast, late modern society is characterised by the fact that material need has been largely met. Despite the fact that inequalities of class societies remain, new risks, which are the consequences of development, have emerged. These risks include nuclear hazards, environmental damage and possible global economic meltdown. The geographically widespread nature of such risks means that people right across societies are vulnerable to their effects, against which wealth can only offer limited protection. Exposure to risk therefore becomes more equalised. As they operate across and tend to dissolve both class and national boundaries, the way that they are experienced becomes more individualised. For example, in the face of rapid technological change, people need to prepare for frequent retraining and career change. Innovation and the risk of unemployment no longer hit manual workers hardest but tend to spread their impact more equally across the lives of workers. In such a risk society, individuals are left equally free of career structures and class constraints to navigate their own way reflexively (always having to weigh up options and adapt) through life.

Globalisation and liquid modernity – the polarisation of mobility, the domination of capital and the detachment of the individual

Theorists disagree on the impact of globalisation on social stratification. The most optimistic position is adopted in the neo-liberal approach of Ohmae who sees in globalisation evidence of movement toward a 'borderless economy'. For Ohmae, this is a world of mobile capital and free enterprise capitalism. Governments most go with the grain of change and work to promote such open global economies by which in the long run all will benefit.

Not all writers on globalisation are so likely to downplay the importance of social divisions. For Zygmunt Bauman, globalisation, accentuates differences in mobility chances which fall along class lines. This has led to increased social polarisation which works to the detriment of workers.

In modern societies (as explained in Marxist theory), in social and work hierarchies, employers and workers had relatively fixed positions and relationships. Social class and industrial relations included direct conflict and settlement with both sides locked into mutual dependence. The potential for disruption by organised workers introduced the threat of uncertainty for business managers and owners.

Bauman argues that in contemporary conditions of global capitalism, wealth has polarised and has been accompanied by a polarisation of mobility chances. Given the greatly enhanced mobility of capital and information made possible through the cyberspace of contemporary global technology, the enhanced threat of disengagement of capital has become an uncertainty to workers who remain more geographically rooted. For Bauman, mobility, wealth and power polarisation now fundamentally disadvantages workers and frees them from the possibility of effective collective response.

Bauman uses the term 'liquid modernity' to refer to the fluidity of advanced societies. In such societies, individuals become detached from collective action and forced into a freedom of taking responsibility for their self-determination in situations of transience and uncertainty. This environment leads to increasing social polarisation as geographically mobile global elites become disengaged from the masses who, through the provision of labour, are relatively tied to their localities and left to struggle with this new 'freedom'.

Postmodernism celebrated the emergence of positive individual freedom to choose identity and transcend class ties. For Bauman, only elites really have this privilege. The freedom that workers now find themselves placed in is not the positive freedom of the old entrepreneurial middle class. For many, the experience is primarily of the negative aspect of freedom – the freedom of being cut adrift, like it or not, from the confines of a secure class structure. Individualisation in the contemporary context means de-identification and the perpetual burden of uncertainty and striving for identity (for many of the poor throughout the world, not even this negative freedom is available). This leads to new conflicts in the form of 'recognition wars' in which people attempt to impose both their own identity and force identities onto others. A key resource here is use of PRs, spin doctors and access to the mass media. Furthermore, growing insecurity can lead people to the search for culprits and popular government responses in the form of toughness on crime and immigration.

6: Research Methods

Abstract

This chapter begins by alerting the reader to the problem of the intrusion of personal bias into everyday knowledge about society and emphasises that sociology requires a methodical approach and a sound evidential base for the study of society. A limited number of key terms and concepts central to research methods are then introduced and clarified.

A simple framework is adopted to cover a range of research methods. These methods are organised in terms of whether information is gained primarily through asking questions, through observation, or through utilising documents. However, it is also shown that, by their nature or through their varied applications, methods may be located in other than just their primary category. The methods are explained in terms of how they are used and strengths and weaknesses are considered. Reference is also made to the positivist and interpretive dimensions in the methods outlined.

It is explained how founding perspectives argue different positions on how best to understand society and what the aims of sociology should be. Distinctions are made between positivist, social action, symbolic interactionist and ethnomethodological perspectives. It is shown how these perspectives hold different implications for how to approach research and the types of methods preferred.

Some contemporary approaches to sociological research are introduced which raise a number of fundamental questions regarding established canons of sociological research: these approaches question the certainty of knowledge, the nature of researcher / subject relationships, the possibility of value neutrality and the very status of sociology. The more extreme position of some postmodernists even dismisses the possibility of establishing the truth and dismisses the traditional assertion that sociological knowledge is superior to any other knowledge about society.

The sociological challenge

In our daily situations, we all hold a stock of knowledge about the social world. This knowledge may seem to be self evidently correct and adequate for our everyday purposes. It may be only when events take place which challenge this knowledge that we are likely to engage in more thoughtful scrutiny of what we have previously taken for granted. In sum, in our everyday lives we are likely to hold a pragmatic view of society – what we take as true or adequate remains relatively unchallenged all the time that it gets us by.

From where do we acquire our everyday knowledge about society? Its main sources will include our immediate experiences, hearsay information from others, and information from the mass media; sources which vary in their impact, overlap, and complement or contradict each other. By such means, our attitudes and opinions are formed and influenced. We may be vulnerable to misrepresentation and manipulation but we are also likely to be conspirators in the process as we select information and interpret the world to confirm our beliefs through our choice of friends and associates, newspapers, television programmes and internet information.

Further consideration of the influences contributing to our everyday knowledge reveals how unreliable this may be as a basis for understanding society. For example, experiences vary from individual to individual and the world of our immediate social experiences is very small. How far, therefore, is it valid to generalise our knowledge of society from these limited experiences? They may be quite unlike the experiences of people of different gender, social class, ethnicity, age, and with different life chances, etcetera. Our immediate experiences help to form our attitudes and opinions. These we may share with those whom we choose to be our friends and acquaintances. The potential for reinforcement of our attitudes and opinions can therefore be great, but these are the means through which we filter our understanding of broader society.

We also need to rely on the mass media for helping us frame the bigger picture – for example on global events. Even if we are cautious, suspecting that information is being distorted or that we are being manipulated, the key question is how can we check the truthfulness of what we are being told? Is it enough to review alternative sources of media information when we cannot check hardly any of this information by direct experience? Furthermore, if the media is an important vehicle of agenda setting in the public domain, what can we know about issues or events that tend to remain off the agenda altogether?

Most sociologists would agree that as an academic subject, sociology can not be just an assemblage, even a well organised one, of the stock of everyday knowledge that exists about society. To be so would often be to reproduce everyday bias, subjectivity and selectiveness and it would not be possible to assess the superiority of one person's viewpoint on society to that of another. Most sociologists adopt the position that sociology must generate its own superior findings through procedures which stand up to rigorous scrutiny even though these findings are never foolproof or undisputed or final truths. These findings may be of varying levels of interest for people in their everyday lives or even fly in the face of common sense knowledge or assumptions. However, it is the educative role of sociology to feed back its findings not just to its own academic community but to members of society and to encourage people to examine their taken for granted assumptions.

So just where do we place sociology in providing a sound understanding of society? Having emphasised its superiority to common sense knowledge, some cautionary points need to be raised:

1 There is much debate within sociology over the nature of rigour and the uses and virtues of different methods of obtaining information.

2 There is rarely any single method by which a particular area can be uniquely and conclusively researched.

3 In the study of any single topic area, different methods can provide different types of data and lead to different or contradictory findings.

4 However well established and conclusive the findings of a piece of research may be at a particular point in time, the fact that society is constantly changing necessitates ever new research and explanations.

5 A particular difficulty for sociology is that sociologists, as people, are deeply implicated in the subject of their studies. They are also lay members of society who hold their own values, attitudes and prejudices about society. These are likely to intrude into the research process, thus questioning the claim to superior academic credentials.

The purpose of this chapter is to examine the approaches and methods that sociologists use to obtain information about and develop an understanding of society. This examination will indicate some of the strengths that sociological research offers in obtaining reliable and valid information compared to that of everyday knowledge. It will also go further and encourage a critical assessment of the methods used by sociologists. Finally, consideration will be given of new approaches which question the traditional methodological assumptions that sociological research must aim for value neutrality and non-directiveness and which even attack the possibility of sociologists achieving superior knowledge of society to that of the layperson.

Definition of main concepts

A basic distinction in research methods can be made between whether the sources of information used are of a primary or secondary nature. **Primary** information is that which has been compiled by the researcher in the form required for the research. This is likely to include information obtained through social surveys or participant observation. **Secondary** sources of information are those which were originally compiled by others for non-sociological purposes. Official statistics and personal documents are likely to fall into this category.

The social survey is a commonly used method in sociology. In social survey research, the terms interviewer, interviewee and respondent are used. An **interviewer** is the person eliciting personal verbal feedback from another or others – the **interviewee(s)** – in a social situation which is organised for the purpose of focussing responses to questions deemed to be relevant to the research. This definition implies quite a formal social encounter, offering the interviewee little scope in influencing its direction. However, some styles of interviewing are less formal and allow the interviewee more control as to their input or even the course of the interview itself. Like an interviewee, a **respondent** is the subject of research, but this term is reserved for those supplying information in survey research which does not involve a personal verbal interview – for example, those who take away a questionnaire to fill in themselves or those who partake in mail or internet surveys.

The technical terms population and sample are closely connected. In sociological research, the term **population** refers to a clearly defined category of people to which the research applies. Research into voting behaviour may take the 'British electorate' as the relevant population, or a study of the causes of homelessness may define its population as 'those living without access to accommodation in Nottingham'. A **sample** is a small selection from a population for purposes of inclusion in the research. The aim of taking a sample is to make the research process efficient, or in many cases even possible at all, usually by obtaining a precise micro replication of the features of the population for analysis. Two key points emerge from this: 1) the sample must be selected so that it is as representative as possible of the profile of the population from which it is drawn, and 2) the findings of the research based on the sample can then be generalised back to the population from which the sample was taken, but not beyond.

In Chapter 2, a distinction was made between **positivist** and **interpretive** perspectives. A sociologist's orientation toward one of these perspectives may influence their research strategy and choice of methods used. A connection between these different perspectives and the types of methods preferred will be briefly indicated. However, it should be appreciated that sociologists often do not adopt a hard line approach of exclusively positivist or interpretive orientated methods and research strategies.

Positivism emphasises that society is little different from the natural world and can thus be analysed in hard scientific terms. Sociologists who incline toward positivism will be looking to demonstrate that natural scientific method and precision has been undertaken in their research. Consequently, they will tend to devise precisely pre-planned and tightly controlled research strategies to obtain the type of information that they know they want. To assist in precision of measurement, they will prefer to use methods which can supply **quantitative** information – that which is viewed as hard data and can be expressed in numerical form. Methods which can be used in this way and supply this type of information include the social survey, the experimental laboratory method and the analysis of official statistics.

When research procedures have been precisely specified and controlled, their use can be carefully replicated by others in further research. It is frequently suggested that this means that a researcher should be able to repeat the same controls and procedures on a similar sample of people and obtain the same results. This is an over simplistic and incorrect assertion. It would be more accurate and precise to say that positivist type methods such as the social survey or laboratory experiments should provide the same findings when repeated if another researcher had used the identical method on the same participants at the same time. Consequently, confidence in the comparability of findings between different research projects can be high. If researchers apply the same methods and procedures at different times or places and obtain different results, it is likely that the difference is substantial and not due to the vagaries of the method or the way in which it has been used.

Research which emphasises natural scientific procedures and the possibility of precise replication is considered to be high in **reliability**. This criterion of rigour is of primary importance and viewed as a strength in positivist and quantitative research.

By contrast, **interpretive** sociology emphasises that understanding society can only be possible through a more subjective approach. Theorists who tend to identify with an interpretive stance will emphasise the importance of gaining insight into the meanings behind peoples' actions. Research will more likely be viewed as a continuous learning process. The methods and strategy used must therefore allow researchers to constantly review procedures and evidence and enable refinement of insight to take place. The preferred methods will tend to be those which generate **qualitative** information – that which is aimed at promoting quality of insight into the worlds of others and which may lend itself more to narrative than to quantitative expression. Methods particularly suitable for interpretive type research include participant observation, in-depth interviewing and the study of personal documents.

Interpretive sociologists emphasise that priority should be placed on establishing certainty that the researcher is measuring what they claim to be measuring. Research procedures must therefore allow the researcher greater flexibility to engage in a learning process whereby closeness to the outlook of social actors can be established. If this is achieved, then rigour takes the form of establishing a high level of **validity** in the findings, which provides a key strength in interpretive and qualitative research.

Positivist approaches tend to be weaker in establishing the validity of their findings. This is because they usually pre-structure research around researcher's meanings and adopt a greater clinical distance from the subjects of the research. Interpretive approaches are criticised for lacking sufficient reliability as each piece of research relies heavily on the subjective judgements and interpretations of the researcher and cannot be precisely replicated by others.

The range of research methods

The methods of research used by sociologists are many and varied. It is rarely the case that any area of study can only be approached by using a single method which is deemed to be exclusively suitable. Various factors can influence the methods(s) used and the way that they are used. These factors can include the amount of time available, the level of funding and manpower constraints and the ethical judgements of researchers. Another important area of influence relates to the researcher's theoretical leanings since certain methods can be seen to have affinities with particular theoretical approaches adopted. Furthermore, as all methods have their strengths and weaknesses, it is quite common for sociologists to utilise more than one method in a research project to maximise overall rigor. This approach has been variously referred to as methodological pluralism or triangulation.

The benefits of triangulation can be argued in different ways. On the one hand, it can be emphasised that using a variety of methods enables the research to establish a closer approximation to the truth than when using just one. On the other hand, society may be viewed as a multi-layered and sometimes contradictory reality, the complexities of which are often only apprehended through the use of a rich variety of research methods.

Research methods can be classified in various ways. One common approach has been to place them on a positivist – interpretivist scale. Although this dimension can rarely be completely ignored, other approaches have been adopted. For example,

McNeill and Chapman (2005) comprehensively organise methods into the following chapters: social surveys, experiments and comparative method, ethnography, and secondary data.

The author of this text will apply two levels of organisation to a range of research methods. The first level will refer directly to the methods themselves and the categories employed will be derived from answering the simple question 'how do sociologists obtain information?' The resulting categories used will be: through asking questions, through observing behaviour, and through utilising documents. Methods will be classified in terms of their primary categories but as they can be applied in a variety of ways some will also require mention in other categories. Furthermore, methods may overlap or one method can encapsulate others.

The second level of classification will relate methods to a range of theoretical perspectives: positivism, social action theory, symbolic interactionism, phenomenology and ethnomethodology, critical theory, feminism and postmodernism.

How do sociologists obtain information?

1 Primarily through asking questions

Most people have had experience of being interviewed, for example through participation in market research. Such an encounter is usually within the scope of a **social survey**. The social survey is a highly pre-structured research method. By this is meant that the type of information, wording of questions and size and nature of the sample are precisely defined at the start. In a social survey, where interviewing is used, this usually follows a highly structured and standardised procedure in which questions are read by the interviewer from a research tool, the questionnaire. The location of survey interview situations may vary with the nature of the research and could take place, for example, in the street, the interviewee's home, the workplace or an office of the interviewer. In the context of survey research, the interviewee is simply restricted to answering the pre-set questions and the encounter is quite brief and formal. This enables a large number of people to be interviewed and the aim is to generate a mass of information in the form of data which can be statistically analysed.

Survey questions are not only delivered in the form of face-to-face interviews. Other approaches include allowing respondents to fill in the questionnaire themselves, telephone interviewing, mail questionnaires, newspaper and magazine questionnaires, and e mail surveys. Linked to the formality of this method and the quest for quantifiable data is the style of questioning. In many surveys, a large proportion of the questions are closed ended – they only offer the respondent choice from pre-determined categories in selecting their answer(s). The purpose of such questions is to readily provide data for statistical analysis. Such data, of course, will lack the subtleties of response which are the aim of open ended questions – questions which ask the respondent to answer at greater length and in their own terms. The potential for richer and more varied information is possible with the latter type of questions since each answer is unique to the respondent. However, this quality and diversity of information is often at least partially compromised by the process of post coding. This is a procedure whereby, for purposes of assisting the quantification of the information, researchers look through the varied answers and construct a limited number of categories into which answers can then be pigeon holed for more statistical analysis.

Another approach sometimes employed within the social survey is the vignette technique. In this approach, hypothetical situations are presented to respondents to elicit their responses. The technique can be useful to measure attitudes toward various specified social situations. Such an approach was employed by Finch and Mason (1993) in their survey into family responsibilities. The following is an example from their research:

> Jane is a young woman with children aged 3 and 5. She has recently divorced. She wants to go back to work and she needs the money. But if she has a job she must find someone to mind the children after school. Her own family live far away but her former mother-in-law Ann Hill is at home all day and lives near by. Jane has always got on well with her former mother in law. Should Ann offer to look after Jane's children?

A further variation on the social survey is the focus group method. This method brings together small groups of participants who discuss issues within a framework clearly set by the researcher. It applies a higher observational element than the standard social survey. In using this approach, the aim of the researcher is to record the issues and group dynamics that emerge in a reflective group situation, information which would be absent in most standard survey interviewing. The focus group approach has been frequently utilised by political parties with the aim of obtaining a more in-depth understanding of the responses to political messages in social settings.

The social survey is a well-established research method. It has been applied in various ways across a broad range of topics. The most comprehensive survey in terms of numbers included is the government census which, once every ten years, aims to achieve a 100% response rate from the British population to provide information for government planning and social policy purposes. Poverty has been frequently studied through the social survey method, from the pioneering work of Charles Booth (accounts published 1889 - 1907) to more recent studies such as those undertaken by Mack and

Lansley (1985 and 1991). The study of social class has employed the survey method, as in Goldthorpe and Lockwood's (1969) research to test the embourgeoisement thesis. Young and Willmott (1957 and 1973) utilised the survey, amongst other methods, to study family and community life.

Social surveys usually take the form of cross sectional studies - one off pieces of research, gaining information at a particular point in time. Further surveys select new samples and take further snap shots of information. Whilst comparisons between survey findings can be made and social changes measured, there is no attempt with this approach to track a particular group of people over time. A good example of such a series of snap shot surveys is the study of voting behaviour in the British Election Studies dating from 1964. The alternative of longitudinal surveys will be reviewed later.

Supporters of the social survey point to statistical sampling, structuring, formality and standardisation as virtues of this method in the quest to obtain reliable and quantifiable information with the possibility of generalising research findings to a broader population. The procedure focuses on eliciting the precise information required. The wording of questions must be as clear and unbiased as possible, especially in the case of mail surveys where the respondent cannot ask the researcher for clarification. To assist this process, small-scale pilot surveys can be run in advance to provide feedback to improve the fine tuning of questions. Furthermore, it is normally expected that the style of interviewing should be non-directive - there should be no intimation of preferred answers. If guaranteed personal anonymity, respondents should then feel that they can answer honestly and impartially.

As a cautionary point, care should be taken not to over stereotype the survey approach. Surveys are likely, to a greater of lesser extent, to include ethnographic (study of everyday life) dimensions, especially if researchers live amongst the people that they are interviewing and conduct daily observations as part of their research. This was certainly the case in the above mentioned surveys carried out by Booth and Young and Willmott. However, overall, survey procedures are claimed to match up to traditional canons of scientific objectivity and tend to be preferred by positivist orientated sociologists.

From more interpretive perspectives, these features of the social survey can be viewed as a barrier to understanding the world of the subject since the interests and definitions of researchers are imposed on the interviewees or respondents. If interviewing is to be used, interpretive sociologists are likely to prefer to engage in **in-depth interviewing** which might be used alongside other methods as part of a broader ethnographic approach.

133

In-depth interviewing is far more time consuming per interviewee than formal style social survey interviewing. This is because the purpose of in-depth interviewing is to acquire greater insight into the world of the interviewee. To assist in the process, an attempt is made to create rapport between interviewer and interviewee. The interviewer allows the interviewee far more scope in the answering of questions. Furthermore, although the interviewer will have pre-specified areas of interest, the interview encounter will be less formal and less obviously pre-structured. Questions may well be formulated in advance of interviewing to assist research focus and achieve a degree of standardisation, but these may be referred to by the interviewer more as a guide than a rigid sequential list. The interviewee may be offered significant scope in answering questions in ways that they see fit and even some input into the direction of the interview. The interviewer will therefore need to remain alert to the emergence of unexpected information. At the extreme, in-depth interviewing may appear to be so unstructured to the interviewee that it is experienced as if it were a spontaneous conversation. In fact, strictly speaking, this will rarely be the case.

Although in-depth interviewing increases the potential for a rich flow of information, the interviewer can be faced with certain dilemmas in recording that information. Taking notes is likely to 1) interfere with the free flow of the interview and 2) lead to difficulty of keeping up with everything that is going on, with consequent loss of important detail. Making notes after the interview should overcome the first of these problems but would probably exacerbate the second due to selective memory recall. Using a recording device to capture the details may therefore be the preferred alternative. However, such devices are likely to be inhibiting for the interviewee who may take longer to feel relaxed, making a series of lengthy interviews necessary before much headway is possible. Covert recording of interviews is therefore justified by some sociologists. This approach will later be discussed under the broader method of participant observation.

Despite these dilemmas, research based on in-depth interviewing offers greater opportunity for the researcher to be open to unexpected insights. Thus, in her pioneering 1957 research into conjugal roles, in-depth interviewing in 20 London families led Elisabeth Bott to discover a relationship in her sample between conjugal role patterns and the different types of friendship networks engaged in by the partners.

A further advantage of in-depth interviewing is that it may be a more suitable way of engaging with groups who would shy away from more formal methods that could be suggestive of officialdom, a classic example being Howard Becker's 1963 study of 50 subjects who used marihuana as a recreational drug.

Other examples of research that has employed in-depth interviewing include Ann Oakley's research into household task allocation and Paul Willis' study of the culture of working class lads at school and on entering work. In Willis' research, to elicit more information the lads were often interviewed together.

Of course, in-depth interviewing may be used alongside other methods. This was effectively demonstrated by Young and Willmott, who, in their research into family life in the East End of London, used in-depth interviewing of a marriage sample from their broader survey sample to add a qualitative dimension to their research. Such sampling from within samples is referred to as multi-stage sampling.

A particular form of unstructured interviewing is taken in the form of **oral histories**. In this case, the interviewee is recounting past events such as the experience of emigrating and settling down in a new society or unofficial accounts of what life was like working within a particular institution. Oral histories are usually part of a broader approach referred to as **life histories** in which oral reflections are supplemented by personal and public documents as a check on the memory reliability of the interviewee or as a degree of safeguard against misrepresentation. The use of such documents will be considered in greater detail in a later section. Life history information is likely to be of a highly personal, descriptive and qualitative nature. Amongst the most comprehensive examples of this method is Thomas and Znaniecki's 1919 study of 'The Polish Peasant in Europe and America'.

The term **longitudinal research** refers to research which extends over a protracted period of time, often many years. It is perhaps not a method in its own right, but may be seen as a variant of the social survey when, through interviewing or other questionnaire approaches, the aim is to obtain quantifiable information from a large sample. However, whilst a cross sectional survey takes a snap shot of information from a particular sample at a particular point in time, a longitudinal survey periodically returns to the same people, in this case referred to as a cohort, over a protracted period of time to acquire more information from them. As such, the longitudinal method is seen as superior to a series of surveys in tracing processes that operate over lengthy time periods.

Longitudinal research sometimes takes the form of a 'panel survey'. Panel surveys originated in the study of political opinion, with the purpose of understanding why people change their attitudes over time or their vote from one election to another. For this research to be effective, the same people are interviewed periodically, for example at successive elections. Anthony Heath *et al* (1994) have conducted extensive panel studies of this type in Britain.

A further example of survey size longitudinal research is that conducted by the Office for National Statistics which, from 1971, took a 1% sample from census returns and followed up information on these people in subsequent censuses with the aim of studying the relationship between social class, illness and death rates.

As in the case of interviewing, longitudinal research does not necessarily have to be of social survey proportions but may adopt a small scale and qualitative approach to research which uses a more in-depth interviewing style. This was illustrated in '7 Up' – a television series commissioned in 1964. The study begun with 21 seven year old children from a broad cross-section of social backgrounds but only focussed on 14 who filmed well. This process of selection, of course, would not be acceptable for research purposes as those included were not likely to be a representative selection from the original 21. Returning to those participants who were prepared to remain in the project every seven years, the series traced, through the process of periodic open ended interviewing, their experiences, outlooks and fortunes against the backdrop of their varied life chances in an attempt to document the long term effects of social class background on their lives.

2 Primarily through observing behaviour

Methods which rely heavily on observation are limited, of necessity, to small scale research. The classic sociological observational method is **participant observation**. This method was first pioneered by anthropologists who found it necessary to live with primitive cultures to attune themselves to an understanding of their culture, rituals, beliefs and ways of life. It has been used in sociology in a variety of ways. For example, the role adopted by the researcher may be primarily that of an observer with little involvement in the activities of the group or a more fully participatory position may be adopted. The essential feature of this method, though, is that it attempts to study behaviour as it naturally takes place.

A number of key questions and difficulties arise regarding the use of participant observation. These include: how does the researcher enter a group? What stance or role can the researcher adopt? How is it possible to capture information which is constantly flowing? How can the researcher minimise the impact of their presence on the spontaneity of the behaviour observed? These issues will be touched on in this section.

In sociology, the method has been particularly useful, and sometimes the only realistic approach available, to study life within social groups that engage in law breaking activities or are viewed as deviant by mainstream society. It is likely that these groups would be defensive against being studied by such formal procedures as structured interviews and they may well deny access to the researcher. Furthermore, surveys have proved to be of limited worth in providing detailed ethnographic material or understanding behaviour. Because participant observation smacks less of officialdom, deviant groups may be prepared to allow research of this type to be overtly conducted. Where access to conduct research overtly is not likely to be forthcoming, an alternative strategy is to infiltrate the group and engage in undercover or covert research in which the participants are not aware of the researcher's role. The British Sociological Association's ethical guidelines tend to caution against such an approach which breaches the normal requirement of obtaining the informed consent of the subjects of research. Ultimately, the ethical decision lies with the researcher.

Whether conducted overtly or covertly, the aim of participant observation is to accurately portray the lives of people. There is debate as to whether this can be best achieved through the researcher retaining a degree of clinical distance from the members of the group, thereby implying a more observational stance, or whether a high level of subjective involvement in their lives is necessary. Those who advocate the latter argue that via a high level of immersion in the group, empathy with the participants can be maximised and insights generated, often through personal experiences as a group member, which may not be assessable by other methods.

However employed, participant observation is not usually as tightly a pre-structured method as more positivist approaches such as the social survey tend to be. Instead, the researcher may start quite open-mindedly and take time to formulate relevant questions and categories of analysis as he / she becomes sensitised to the life of the group. By this process, the research offers more opportunity of obtaining a grounding in the reality of the group than if a rigid but alien framework of researcher defined categories and structured analysis were imposed from the start. The fundamental aim of participant observation is to develop a sociological understanding of behaviour which the group members would themselves recognise as valid.

If observational research is overt, that is conducted openly, the researcher may occasionally resort to in-depth interviewing to acquire more precise information on areas of particular interest. For example, William Whyte (1955) would interview members of the street corner gang that he was studying to help clarify his understanding of their behaviour. However, if the covert approach is used, more focussed questioning may be difficult as anything approaching interviewing must be carefully disguised in a conversational style to avoid arousing the suspicion of group members.

Covert participant observation has been employed by journalists as well as sociologists. Although the method may be used in identical fashion, it is important to distinguish between the aims. The aim of pure sociological research is to advance understanding of society. Value judgements need to be avoided or held in check and the identity of participants will almost certainly not be revealed. By contrast, when journalists attempt to uncover the actions and identities of those engaging in deviant or illegal acts, it is likely to be for the purpose of raising moral questions, bringing about a public response or even the punishment of culprits. Journalistic approaches have included the covert recording of speeches by leading figures in the British National Party which were televised in the programme 'The Secret Agent' and used as prosecution material, and undercover research by carried out by Donal MacIntyre which contributed to the conviction of violent football hooligans.

Infiltration of such groups by covert means requires very careful preparation, and once in great care must be taken that one's cover is not blown. This need for painstaking preparation can be illustrated for MacIntyre's (1999) entry into the world of the Chelsea Headhunters. Police files were studied to obtain the names and pictures of those who were to be 'befriended'. Research of newspaper articles provided names and information relating to past cases of violence implicating members of the group. A general background on football hooligans was acquired through observations on the margins of their activities in bars and on the streets in the World Cup in France. MacIntyre needed to learn how to smoke convincingly and had to acquire a Chelsea tattoo. The history of Chelsea Football Club had to be carefully studied. Although he knew the locality of one of his key targets, MacIntyre had to hang around the streets to find out where he lived. He was able to move into the same block of flats and watch out for his target's routine. Designer clothes were worn, an expensive car was hired out and every effort was made to be seen. Eventually, first contact was made at a fast food outlet.

Attempts to track down another member of the group took MacIntyre to Reading where he trawled local newspapers for background information on cases against his target. This identified certain Reading pubs which were trawled but without success. However, a young accomplice who knew the target was befriended and further important information obtained.

Through such careful preparation, MacIntyre was able to enter the group, became accepted, and was able to record by using a covert camera, the stories and activities of the participants.

When conducting covert participant observation, it is likely that the researcher will need to think carefully about where to draw the line on the type of behaviour he / she is prepared to be involved in, especially if some form of initiation is necessary for acceptance into the group. If situations arise where non-involvement is decided upon, care must be taken to avoid arousing suspicion amongst group members. Great vigilance may be necessary to avoid one's cover being blown.

A major advantage of covert research is that the effect of the observer's presence on the natural behaviour of those under study can be minimal. To assist this, it is important that the role adopted by the researcher enables minimal interference through his / her actions or decisions. If research is taking place within a formal organisation, such as a psychiatric hospital or a benefit agency, an official role may be available under which the covert research can take place.

The main criticism of participant observation is likely to be that of its questionable reliability. How can studies be replicated and meaningful comparisons between them made when: 1) different sociologists may select different features from their observations which are important to them or 2) differ in terms of memory recall of events and 3) another researcher may have elicited different behaviour from the same group or interpreted the same behaviour differently?

Examples of participant observation range through the study of street corner gangs (W. Whyte, 1955, E. Liebow, 1967), organized football hooligans (D. MacIntyre BBC 1, 1999), violent gangs (J. Patrick, 1973), life on mental hospital wards (E. Goffman, 1968), religious groups (L. Festinger *et al*, 1956), life in a West Indian community (K. Pryce, 1979) and extremist political organisations (N. Fielding, 1993).

To uncover a detailed and accurate picture of life as it is, participant observation is a very time consuming method. Research employing this method is often of longitudinal dimensions, but is not of the normal longitudinal type. This is because involvement of the researcher with the group is a relatively continuous process rather than periodic.

A quite different approach to observation is used in the **experimental laboratory** method. In its most rigorous form, this approach, more often used by psychologists but in areas of topic interest to sociologists, claims scientific credentials through the setting up of a social equivalent to controlled scientific laboratory conditions. When used most simply, this method relies on matching two groups as closely as possible regarding their size and the characteristics of their members such as gender balance, age range, ethnic makeup, social class distribution etcetera at the start of the research. The environment that each of the groups is placed in is also closely controlled and matched. One factor (the independent variable), the influence of which is to be measured, is then introduced into the environment of one of the groups. This group is referred to as the experiment group. The other group, the control group, is not exposed to this influence. During and after the experiment, the behaviour or attitudes of members of the two groups is measured to detect any differences between the groups which are deduced to be attributable to the influence of the independent variable in the experiment group. By such means, the precise influence of a number of individual factors can be measured.

In one example of such tightly controlled laboratory experiments, Eysenck and Nias (1978) demonstrated that, compared to control groups, experiment groups that were exposed to television violence showed signs of aggression, from which the researchers deduced that similar effects may be taking place when people viewed television violence in the broader setting of their everyday lives.

Although experimental laboratory research should be easily replicable, knowledge of participation in the research is likely to affect the behaviour of the participants in ways that it is difficult to know or allow for. They may look for clues as to what the researchers deem to be preferred or acceptable behaviour – a phenomena referred to as demand characteristics. The artificiality of the situation also usually limits the potential for generalisation of the findings - it is questionable how far they can be applied to natural settings. For example, the time span over which influences are assessed is usually limited to a stimulus response framework which may reveal little about the effect of exposure to long term influences in the natural setting. Furthermore, the information obtained from such studies sometimes takes the form of quantified physiological data (for example change in heart rate, level of perspiration) which is difficult to translate unambiguously into the meaning behind it.

The degree of artificiality involved in laboratory experiments introduces the problem of uncertainty regarding the effect which knowledge of being observed can have on the behaviour of the participants. This contaminant is referred to as the Hawthorne effect, of which the name origin will shortly be explained. Some laboratory research attempts to get around this problem by use of unobtrusive observation. For example, attempts have been made to measure the impact of exposure to violence in the mass media under controlled laboratory conditions with the researchers observing behaviour through two-way mirrors.

In a more complicated version of the experimental laboratory approach, psychologists A. Bandura *et al*, (1965), studied levels of imitative aggression acted out by children who had been exposed to identical film of adult aggression toward a bobo doll. The control group were just shown the film, whereas one experiment group was also shown the adult being rewarded for the aggression and another group shown the adult being punished. Afterwards, the behaviour of each child toward toys including a bobo doll was observed and levels of aggressive behaviour recorded.

An alternative approach has been to introduce controlled intervention into more natural settings. This variation is referred to as the **field experiment**. A pioneering piece of research which adopted this method was conducted in the USA at the Hawthorne plant of the Western Electrical Company from 1924 to the early 1930s. The study attempted to measure the impact of changes in the work environment on the output levels of production line workers. By using an experiment and a control group, efficiency experts started by comparing the effect on the productivity of the experiment group of changing the level of illumination whilst leaving that of the control group the same. Elton Mayo was then brought in to test the effect on productivity of other changes imposed on the experiment group such as changing rest periods, the introduction of company lunches and shorter working weeks, etcetera. Surprisingly, during the research, the productivity levels of workers in both control and experiment groups increased. Indeed, even when changes were introduced into the environment of the experiment group which were anticipated to reduce productivity levels, output increased! The researchers realised that by knowing that they were being studied, the workers' behaviour was being affected. This phenomena – which confounded the original aims of the research - has subsequently become referred to as the Hawthorne effect.

To more fully utilise the benefits of the field experiment, some researchers have hidden or misrepresented the nature of their research to participants. For example, D. J. Smith (1977) set up a field experiment to measure the extent of racial discrimination in the labour market. Actors of different ethnic backgrounds but with otherwise matched CVs were used to apply for jobs. Measurements were taken of the responses by employers and where interviews were obtained covert recording took place. Clear evidence emerged that employers were discriminating against ethnic minority applicants.

Overall, there tends to be a trade off between the different uses of experimentation in the social sciences. The laboratory method is able to apply tight but artificial controls. Although logically the effects of variables can be isolated and precisely measured, there are likely to be major doubts about the affect of the artificial environment on behaviour and thus the validity of the findings and the possibility for their generalisation to natural settings. By contrast, in attempting to overcome these difficulties, the more naturalistic the field experiment becomes, the more difficult it is to impose tight controls.

A different approach to experiments is unique to ethnomethodologists and is referred to as **breaching experiments**. The theory behind this method will be explained in more detail in a later section. Essentially, the purpose of such experiments is to set up situations in which rules are broken to observe how participants go about rebuilding meaning and order. The intention is to show the extent to which everyday life is dependent on shared understandings which are taken for granted between participants. In one such experiment, Harold Garfinkle prepared some students to act like paying lodgers on their return home at vacation and to record the responses they received. The aim of the research was to lay bare the taken for granted rules concerning appropriate interaction within the family.

3 Primarily through utilising documents

Various types of document are available to sociologists, most of which is secondary research material. If official documents are utilised, the term **archive research** is usually applied. Such documents may include the reports of Royal Commissions and newspaper reports – two sources effectively used by Frederick Engels in his pioneering study of working class life in England in 1844 entitled 'The Condition of the Working Class in England'.

Sometimes, archive research relies more on historical archives. In this case, parish and census records may be useful. For example, Peter Laslett (1972) relied heavily on information gleaned from parish records in his study of family life before the Industrial Revolution. When, in the mid nineteenth century, Tocqueville studied the origins of the French Revolution of 1789, he relied quite heavily on gaining access to government archives. Although overstating his case, Tocqueville maintained that:

> 'in a country where a strong central administration has gained control of all the national archives there are few trends of thought, desires or grievances, few interests or propensities that do not sooner or later make themselves known to it, and in studying its records we can get a good idea not only of the way in which it functioned but of the mental climate of the country as a whole' (Tocqueville, 1966, The Ancien Regime and the French Revolution, pp. 24-25).

Archive sources may also be effectively used as a check on the accuracy of oral history accounts. For example, in the television series 'Nazis, a Warning From The Past', official letters were used to question the slant put on past events in interviews by those who had been officials in Nazi Germany

Life documents relate to more personal and intimate aspects of peoples' lives than archive sources. They may include diaries, letters, photographs, videos, and even autobiographies. As such, they will tend to supply detailed qualitative information and lend themselves to small-scale research or case studies. Such documents, along with oral histories, may form part of a broader life history approach. However, documents may also be the only source of information available if the person concerned is no longer alive.

Some life documents need to be reviewed with a degree of caution. A key factor here is whether the information was originally recorded on a strictly private basis, as in most personal diaries, or written with an audience in mind, as in the case of letters. In the latter form of document, the writer may well have chosen to put a particular angle on events to influence the recipient. Furthermore, letters and diaries of public figures may have originally been written with the expectation of future publication to a broader audience in mind. Autobiographies that select and sanitise this information therefore introduce at least two levels of distortion into the material. And it may not just be the small scale of the research through which we may question the representativeness of these materials, but also the fact that they focus on the lives of the more powerful, literate or articulate.

A form of primary research documentation is used to provide sociologists with **time budgeting** material. This method requires the participants to keep a detailed diary of activities or events for use as research material. A good example of the time budgeting method was employed in Young and Willmott's (1973) study of family life where participants were asked to keep a detailed record of the domestic activities and tasks that they engaged in.

Mainly applied to the study of the mass media, a **content analysis** approach studies the use of terms and phrases and the positioning of articles and pictures to measure bias, decode underlying messages, and identify intended reader manipulation. In its simplest form, the analysis of a message may be based on a count of words or phrases of key significance. However, approaches based on semiotics (the study of signs and codes) analyse communication with the purpose of revealing underlying or hidden meaning. This approach was applied in a broad range of research conducted by the Glasgow Media Group in the 1970s, including television coverage of strikes.

Content analysis has also been applied to the study of personal documents for the purpose of gaining insight into a person's frame of mind or their attempt to influence others.

A method which ranks amongst the largest and grandest in sociology is that of **comparative and historical research**. This method was comprehensively adopted by the founding fathers of sociology. It utilises information from historical events and therefore relies heavily on various sources of historical documentation. The method adopts a form of experimentation, but unlike the field experiment causes are not revealed through the manipulation of the situation but the deduction of causes is made by process of controlled comparisons. Through making systematic comparisons between societies or social groups, this method aims to tease out key causal influences on social change by identifying factors prominent in some societies or groups and not in others. For example, Durkheim used this method very effectively in his study of the social causes of suicide (1897) through painstaking comparative analysis of official statistics on suicide between and within European societies. Weber (1904 - 1905) also applied the comparative and historical method to reveal key influences contributing toward England being the first country to experience the transition to modern capitalism.

In a more recent piece of research, T. Skocpol (1979) engaged in a comparative analysis of the French, Russian and Chinese Revolutions in an attempt to develop a general theory of the origins of revolutions. This makes an interesting comparison with Tocqueville's research. However insightful, the latter was only based on the study of events leading up to the French Revolution. It was a large-scale case study (see below) and therefore, as it stood, Tocqueville's theory could only legitimately be applied to the French case. By engaging in comparative analysis, Skocpol could claim greater universality for her theory than Tocqueville.

The comparative and historical method has been used against the backdrop of nations as relatively separate societies. One may speculate that processes of globalisation cutting across national boundaries may at least complicate the way in which it can be used.

As noted above, a key source of information in Durkheim's study 'Suicide' was **official statistics**. Statistical information supplied by a variety of official bodies, such as the Office For National Statistics, and readily available in such publications as Social Trends, can be used by sociologists for statistical analysis. Official statistics are available on a broad range of phenomena including health, crime rates, strike activity, the distribution of wealth and income, student examination performance, church attendance, unemployment, births, deaths, marriages, and divorce rates.

Although convenient to use by sociologists, as this information has already been gathered by others, the data has well recognised limits. Firstly, both its reliability and validity may be an issue. Have there been changes over time in the categories used to compile the statistics? If so, questions of comparability arise. Are there social influences on the organisation providing the information, such as performance targets related to funding, which may distort the statistics provided? Do they really measure what they claim to measure?

Secondly, there may not be official statistics readily available in the form or from areas that the sociologist is interested in, such as regarding unofficial strikes, membership of religious sects, or marriages in a state of separation.

Thirdly, there are the criticisms of ethnomethodologists that the factual appearance of data in the form of official statistics will mask the fact that they rest on official interpretations and classifications of behaviour. Number crunching sociology based on such data is therefore seen from this perspective as a spurious science.

However, of all the documents so far mentioned, official statistics do offer one advantage over interviewing and observational methods – they are unobtrusive in terms of demand characteristics and the Hawthorne effect.

Under this section can also be included an approach which could be referred to as **library based research**. This approach may overlap with some of the others referred to above which use documents. However, what may distinguish it is the tendency to utilise academic sources for further theoretical analysis. As such, it may rely on the findings of research based on any of the methods mentioned above. Researchers who adopt this approach are sometimes referred to disparagingly as 'armchair theoreticians', but some of the greatest contributions to sociology, such as Durkheim's 1912 study of religion, have relied heavily on the study of other academic sources.

Finally, the **case study** approach is difficult to classify under any of the above sections in particular. The term simply refers to the detailed study of a single unit. That unit could be a person, a group, a community, an institution, or even a country. In a sense, rather than being a method in its own right, it makes use of any of the above methods as deemed appropriate. For example, J.Jacobs used participant observation to uncover the workings of a social welfare agency which lie below the bureaucratic façade of following the rules. By contrast, Tocqueville studied official documents in his case study of the French Revolution.

Although generalisation is not sustainable beyond the individual case, subsequent research may attempt to test case studies more broadly. Thus, Tocqueville's analysis of the French Revolution was more recently broadened into a theory of the social psychological causes of revolutions by J. Davies (1962) and T. Gurr (1980). Furthermore, researchers may bring together a range of case studies to develop a broader understanding of social phenomena. In his work 'Communities in Britain', Frankenberg (1973) drew on a range of community case studies to construct a rural and urban classificatory scale.

Founding perspectives relating to sociological research:

There has been much dispute during the twentieth century about the most appropriate methods and research strategies that sociologists can utilise to effectively study society. Disputes have often related to philosophies built into theoretical perspectives about the very nature of social phenomena and the appropriate approach to social 'science'. The following section builds on the distinction already made between positivist and interpretive approaches and indicates the main research methods associated with each perspective.

Positivism – methods which generate facts to test hypotheses

Early social theorists writing in the nineteenth century were often keen on gaining the same credentials as existed in the more established sciences for the emerging subject of sociology. To square with this quest, they tended to view society as operating in terms of causal processes from which laws of social change could be extracted. Comte and Marx were amongst the greatest exponents of this approach, both believing that they had discovered laws of change which were driving society in a predictable direction.

From his study of history, Comte believed that he had discovered laws of progress which demonstrated the spread of scientific thinking and methods from the physical to the social sciences. He was consequently able to predict that the understanding of social phenomena would be eventually rendered scientific. When this stage was reached, the study of society would be positivistic - social science would come to eclipse religion and philosophy and provide the rational means for both analysing and organising society.

Following in the tradition of Comte, Durkheim viewed the behaviour of individuals in society as largely constrained by external social forces such as customs, moral pressures and laws of the land. For Durkheim, society was more than an aggregate of free individuals, but a realm in itself which gives rise to patterned regularities in people's behaviour. These regularities could be measured and their broader social causes identified.

Both Comte and Durkheim were adopting a positivistic approach to the study of social phenomena. This approach tends to minimise the difference between causality in the realm of physical or natural and social phenomena. As science had proved to be the most productive way of explaining the physical world, a similar approach held the best prospect of explaining social behaviour. The main problem with the lesser progress of social as opposed to physical science was argued to relate to the greater complexity of the phenomena of the social realm.

What are the main implications for sociological research deriving from this positivist tradition? Regarding evidence, social phenomena must be reducible to factual information which can be precisely measured. Regarding research methods, those which provide data which can be quantified – hard data which can be statistically analysed to demonstrate levels of correlation (association) or, ideally, causality operating within society – are strongly preferred. Clear practical implications follow from this. Sociology can assist intervention to improve the social condition based on the solid foundation of scientific research.

From this perspective, social science progresses through endless cycles of research, referred to as the hypothetico-deductive process. In this process, the researcher adopts the stance of a distant and clinical analyst who observes social phenomena and develops ideas in the form of speculation and theory. Theory and research operate in a complementary way. Research findings help theories to become more clearly defined and clearly defined theory can precisely steer the research process. Clearly formulated theories should generate hypotheses in the form of statements making predictions of what is expected to be true and which can be precisely tested through research findings.

If analysis of the research information proves the hypothesis to be incorrect, theory and hypothesis must be modified to take on board the refuting evidence and new research set up to test it again. If analysis of the information leads to confirmation of the hypothesis, the theory is substantiated until further notice.

Through making predictions, gathering data, and taking measurements, knowledge is able to progress in scientific fashion as hypotheses and the theories from which they derive become increasingly attuned to the world of facts. These procedures enable positivist researchers to claim that their methods are highly reliable. They follow set procedures which can be replicated and the findings checked or compared with like research.

Favoured methods of those who identify with a positivist philosophy of social science include highly structured social surveys, the use of official statistics and the experimental laboratory approach.

Social action theory – a broad range of methods

Max Weber also believed that social action could ultimately be explained in causal terms. However, he viewed action in terms of agency, emphasising that it was meaning directed by wilful actors. Social action was seen less on the single dimension of people responding to social constraints. Instead, from this perspective, sociology had to more fully recognise that society was made up of people who interpret behaviour, learn from their experiences, modify their behaviour and attempt to influence their environment. From the social action perspective, it is individual consciousness which distinguishes human action from the causal processes operating in physical material and signifies the unique approach necessary in the social sciences. People act within the structural constraints of society, but they also react intentionally upon it. Any attempt, therefore, to explain social action without the sociologist uncovering the motivations and meanings fed into situations by individuals would be sterile and remain shallow and incomplete. Sociology could only become a complete science by combining an understanding of the micro with the macro, the qualitative with the quantitative, and the world of subjective meanings and intentions with that of objective constraining social forces. This perspective is therefore open to a very broad range of methods.

As sociology developed in the twentieth century, the early positivist emphasis was retained in functionalist and Marxist perspectives, if a little less naively. Other developments concentrated more exclusively on the micro and subjective dimension also emphasised by Weber. These interpretive approaches include symbolic interactionism, phenomenology, and ethnomethodology.

Interpretive perspectives:

Symbolic interactionism – methods that tell it like it is

Symbolic interactionism was pioneered as a social philosophy by a number of American theorists writing in the early decades of the twentieth century, a key figure amongst whom was G. H. Mead. The foundation of this perspective is that social co-operation and meaningful action can only be possible through the exchange of shared meanings contained in the symbols of language. Shared meanings provide expectations regarding the behaviour appropriate to people taking on particular social roles. These expectations are reciprocal and shape social interaction. However, individuals also engage in purposeful action. There is scope and choice available in terms of the roles that individuals can take on and the way that they manage their image and actions. Interactionists are therefore interested in studying how individual's actions are partially constrained by social meanings and roles, but also how they use roles and exchange meanings in small-scale social situations to negotiate self-image and intentions with others.

This perspective formed the main theoretical backdrop to the small scale ethnographic (studies of everyday life) work carried out by the Chicago school of sociology in the United States during the 1920s and 1930s.

Whilst maintaining that causal explanations of social interaction remained the aim of sociology, interactionists rejected the theoretical focus and research strategies adopted by positivists. For interactionists, positivists placed an excessive emphasis on the impact of the broader social structure on individual behaviour. Likewise, in positivist research, they criticised the tendency to impose researcher definitions early on in highly structured research programmes. This acted as a barrier to the understanding of social interaction as experienced by the participants. To overcome such research imposed distortion and achieve a close correspondence between the research findings and the world as viewed by the social participants, interactionists advocated the need for researchers to sensitise themselves to the world of social actors through lengthy processes of observation, in-depth interviewing, participation and the study of personal written materials.

Interactionist research strategies were therefore more flexible and cautious than those of positivists. The approaches adopted were often more suited to the generation of insights to help in the formation of hypotheses than hypothesis testing. However, the interpretive and descriptive nature of interactionist research tends to make it difficult to replicate and draw strict comparisons between the findings of different pieces of research, each unique and finely tuned to the situation studied. The small-scale case study approach also makes the findings difficult to quantify and generalise from. Positivists therefore criticise interactonist research for lacking the reliability necessary for scientific credibility.

However, for interactionists there is a more important criteria of rigor to address in the social sciences – that of validity – the certainty of measuring what one claims to be measuring with reference to the particular situation. Interactionists argue that their approach and methods enable a valid and detailed picture of society to be eventually developed from the bottom up through numerous micro studies rather than imposing a distorted picture from the top down by large scale positivist research.

Interpretive perspectives adopted a more radical criticism of positivism with the emergence of phenomenology and ethnomethodology.

Phenomenology and ethnomethodology – facts are provisional, the means by which they are constructed should be studied

The perspective of phenomenology was pioneered by Alfred Schutz between the 1930s and 1950s and provided the philosophical backdrop for the approach to sociological research later taken up by ethnomethodologists. Schutz attempted to systematically develop a theoretical approach to the study of subjective meaning.

For Schutz, people's natural attitude to life, for everyday practical purposes, is to take much for granted. Effective social action is dependent on taken for granted assumptions and people interact on this basis as they share a common pool of knowledge. Although shared meaning is the active product of interaction, when it is not disrupted it appears to exist independently as something solid and factual. For Phenomenologists, it is this appearance of factuality that positivists mistakenly take literally.

Taken for granted knowledge and assumptions which frame behaviour is provisional and will vary between societies, at different points in time, and between different groups within societies. The task of sociology to reveal how people rely upon a shared understanding in their everyday activities.

Although, like symbolic interactionism, the phenomenological perspective focuses on studying behaviour in terms of shared meaning, this perspective emphasises that individual action is often routine and unreflective. It can only be understood in relation to the universe of meaning which forms the interpretive context to behaviour rather than in terms of the subjective motives of individuals.

For phenomenologists, when people interpret and classify the behaviour of others, they are doing so in relation to provisional meaning systems. This applies equally to the person in the street and the official. All official statistics are therefore the consequence of official classifications based on a universe of meaning. Sociologists (especially positivists) who take such statistics as facts are simply reproducing everyday typifications. For phenomenologists, the role of sociology should not be the study of what people take for granted but the study of how meaning contexts lead people to this position. Likewise, sociologists should not treat social statistics as facts but study the meaning context behind which they are generated.

From these more philosophical origins, the closely linked sociological perspective of ethnomethodology developed during the 1960s and 1970s. The radicalism of this perspective takes the form of the questioning any certainty in sociological knowledge. This puts it at loggerheads with positivism and reflects the spirit of times when the authority and certainties of the 1950s came under great challenge in society. Although not itself a contemporary perspective, the attack launched by ethnomethodologists on the scientific orthodoxy of positivism with its claim to superior and reliable knowledge about society indicates some similarities with the more contemporary perspective of postmodernism.

For ethnomethodologists, knowledge and behaviour is understandable relative to its meaning context. The aim of sociology is to research into small-scale everyday social encounters to understand how people make sense of each other's actions. The methods applicable are therefore likely to be participant observation and in-depth inteveiweing.

Contrary to a more positivist approach which looks at small-scale situations as structured by broader social constraints, ethnomethodologists view such situations as social encounters which people navigate their way through, sometimes in an improvised way, based on and leading to the emergence of a level of mutual understanding. For ethnomethodologists, the focus of sociology should be exclusively on identifying the methods that people use to achieve the sense of shared meaning necessary to everyday life for purposeful action to take place.

The key research method developed to study the process of the construction of shared meaning is the breaching experiment. This method relies on the setting up of small-scale situations where the background expectations of actors are violated so that the methods used by the participants to develop a shared sense of meaning can be studied. An example from Garfinkle's research of a breaching experiment is referred to earlier in this chapter. Ultimately, through detailed analyses of such processes, ethnomethodologists intend to extract general rules on the methods that people use in social situations to develop a shared structured understanding. Identifying the rules of the construction, negotiation and imposition of meaning should be the goal of sociology, nothing more.

As conversation is a key means of communication, conversational analysis has been an important research method for ethnomethodologists. Conversations are viewed as improvised activities of reciprocal sense making. Detailed analysis of conversations has led ethnmethodlogists to identify how fit takes place as conversation progresses and to show that participants tend to share understanding of conversational rules and structures, such as the appropriate termination of a conversation.

What is so important about this seemingly trivial enterprise? The following points are worthy of mention. Firstly, ethnomethodology breaks down the barriers raised between the sociologist and the layperson that are erected in more positivist research. The traditional status and expertise of the specialist sociologist over the layperson is undermined as ethnomethodologists recognise that the sociologist is encapsulated in the world of everyday meanings which he / she is trying to understand just as much as the people whose interactions are the object of study. Even the activities of sociologists can be studied in the same way as other everyday social encounters. Sociology is thus 'disprivileged.'

Secondly, the perspective recognises that practical sociology is conducted all the time in the everyday encounters of ordinary people as they interpret meanings and rules.

Thirdly, the sociologist takes the lead from those being observed, rather than vice versa.

Fourthly, all social encounters are of equal worth for study – establishing the relative truth of different group's views is not the purpose of research, but simply the processes involved in the emergence of shared meaning.

Ethnomethodologists have pointed out fundamental weaknesses in the tendency of positivists to base causal explanations on the analysis of supposedly hard scientific data such as official statistics or that derived from interview surveys. For ethnomethodiolgists, official statistics are themselves the outcome of judgements, interpretations, definitions, stereotypes, etcetera made by officials. The task of sociology should therefore be to analyse the encounters and judgements through which interpretations of behaviour by officials are made. This would show that the resulting social statistics are highly provisional. When positivists base their research of the uncritical acceptance of official statistics which are viewed as if they are hard facts, the causal theories that they build on them are likely to distort social reality to reflect official viewpoints.

This perspective was applied by Cicourel in his 1976 study of juvenile delinquency in two American cities. Cicoural found that judgements made by officials - police and probation officers - were key to decisions over whether or not a person had officially engaged in delinquent behaviour. If a youngster who had engaged in anti-social behaviour exhibited those characteristics which officials stereotyped as associated with juvenile delinquency – eg. were black, or working class, or from run down areas – they were more likely to be viewed as delinquent than others from white middle class backgrounds who had engaged in similar behaviour. Theories of delinquency which are based on treating the resulting official figures as facts are reducing the study of reality to an uncritical reflection of stereotypes imposed on behaviour by officials. Instead, from an ethnomethodological perspective, studies of delinquency should be examining the different capacities which different groups have for imposing definitions and negotiating justice.

Likewise, in the case of social survey interviews, rather than trying to understand society in terms of the apparently hard data provided, the object of study should be the interview process itself to examine how this particular encounter is based on shared or constructed assumptions about how the process is conducted (for overview, see Box 1 opposite).

Box 1

Positivism and Ethnomethodology

Positivism

The study of 'facts' treated as hard data.

Upon such 'facts', causal theories are tested and developed.

'Facts' –

eg official statistics, survey data.....................↑.........................

Ethnomethodology

Research must simply look at the social processes behind the creation of 'facts'.

It stops at the point where positivist approaches start and shows that 'facts' are highly provisional as they are based on judgements and interpretations of behaviour which are themselves provisional.

Contemporary approaches to sociological research

Despite disputes between positivists and symbolic interactionists over the question of subjectivity and the actual research methods preferred, there tended to be agreement that a basis for truth could be established, that explanations in terms of causality should be aimed for, and that it was the role of the researcher to be a neutral analyst. What distinguishes some contemporary from more established approaches is the calling into question these fundamental canons of science. A departure from positivism has already been signalled in the approach of phenomenology and the practice of ethnomethodology. In this section, approaches will be introduced which radically challenge the assumptions of positivist sociology and may even question the possibility of achieving objective knowledge.

Critical theory and feminism – research and consciousness raising

Critical theory is based on insights derived from Marxism. It points to the political context of conventional social research. All research takes place within power structures and so, even from a position of methodological 'neutrality', the views of the powerless are unlikely to come through. To counter this, for Lee Harvey, the aim of critical methodology is to promote social improvement for oppressed groups by using research to reveal how they are oppressed in terms of broader social structures and through adopting dominant social values. Sociological theory and research can be used to encourage such groups to acquire new insights through which they may be able to improve their lives. Critical theorists agree with more established traditions that research can uncover the truth. However, they oppose established approaches by maintaining that the role of the researcher is not just that of revealing the truth but crucially also that of using research findings to encourage action amongst oppressed groups to improve their lives.

To some extent, critical methodology has affinities with interpretive approaches. It opposes the hierarchical nature of positivist research and engages the subjects of the research in discussions of findings to assist validity. Furthermore, research may often be small-scale, study the life of the underdog, and prefer to use qualitative methods. However, in the critical approach, the importance of the broader picture remains as findings and insights are aimed at developing a critical awareness of the repressive nature of the social structure and dominant values.

Feminist approaches to research can to some extent be viewed as a special case of critical methodology. Whilst feminists vary in the extent to which they recognise social class and ethnic factors as creating divisions between women, they focus on gender as the key category of social oppression. The feminist movement, especially radical feminists, aimed to raise consciousness of and challenge male dominance in society. Likewise, feminist sociologists challenged male dominance in sociology which reflected that in society. Sociology therefore also had an intellectual consciousness raising role to play.

Feminists tend to associate hierarchical and positivist approaches to research with male dominance. These approaches emphasise a clinical relationship between researcher as expert and the passive subjects of the research. This relationship is justified by positivists as protection against the intrusion of subjective bias into research. However, feminists like Oakley emphasise that this approach disempowers the subject and overrides opportunities for the feedback of insightful information and personal experiences which a more collaborative approach to research would give. The use of interpretive methods, such as in-depth interviewing, can improve the validity of information by establishing closeness and empathy between interviewer and interviewee. Communication at a more intimate level may help to overcome inhibitions and distortions introduced through more hierarchical approaches and participants can be consulted over the interpretation of the data. However, feminists often feel it legitimate to go beyond the stance of neutrality expected in most traditional approaches to research. Since their aim is that of consciousness raising to challenge patriarchal power, it is seen as valid that participants in the research be encouraged in their intellectual liberation.

Postmoderism – the end of social science

For many postmodernists, changes in contemporary society are so substantial that established judgements of truth and appropriate methods for establishing truth are under challenge and should be rejected. Established ideas of a knowable social structure and methods for gaining certain knowledge of it were part of the pattern of discourse of the modern metanarrative (an all-embracing story of how society operates). In the modern era, conventional sociological research operated against the premise that methods and procedures can be applied to provide information by which certain knowledge about how society works can be gained. The social policy dimension of this approach is that such knowledge can then be applied to improve society. Posmodernists emphasise that this approach is part of an Enlightenment metanarrative which put faith in the capacity of science to promote social progress and emancipate humankind from slavery to old dogmas and superstitions. In this tradition is positivism and the associated idea of social engineering in which it was believed that science based social intervention could remedy social ills such as poverty, misery and conflict. For postmodernists, the modern era has disappointed. Naïve faith in science and progress has been shattered by events of the twentieth century.

Different postmodernist writers emphasise different key aspects of the postmodern phase. This variety includes emphasis on post-industrialism, information society, post capitalism, postmodern capitalism, global media dominance, rapid fashion change, post-bureaucratic organisations and political revolutions ending communism *etcetera*. A common thread is that the postmodern environment exhibits, compared to modern society, a decline in social and moral unity and uniformity and a break down of rigid social structures. To claim that postmodern society is here or is emerging is to claim that a radically new social environment is unfolding. For example, the diversity of mass media imagery breaks down the collective identities of modern society. A radical position adopted by Baudrillard suggests that this produces a hyperreality in which media symbols, images and language are referenced by other media signs, symbols and language. Representations of reality thus become disconnected from the real world, the truth or underlying reality of which cannot be known.

Postmodernists are therefore highly critical of conventional sociological research methods and claims to truth. They see conventional research as part of the metanarrative of modernism which claims superiority for professional scientific knowledge. In postmodern societies, the modern matanarrative of truth based on rational thinking and scientific method collapses. Sociological research therefore loses its privileged status in understanding society. Social science is just one of a number of narratives for understanding society and there is no way that it can rightfully claim privilege to a singular truth. Society is diverse and all knowledge is tentative. There is no overriding criteria by which superiority for knowledge based on empirical research can be claimed.

Where then does this leave sociological research? Postmodernists often focus on the way that language is used to create the appearance of order and truth. They therefore argue that postmodern analysis should take the form of the scrutiny of texts written by others to bring out the techniques used to create the appearance of truth and to uncover contradictions. This is referred to as the deconstruction of texts.

A telling criticism of this activity is raised by Mats Alvesson who regards it as both negative and parasitic, pointing out that if all social theorists were to engage in such a venture, the study of the social realm would degenerate into a type of sociological literary criticism. There are surely more important and constructive concerns, such as attempting to understand the causes of war or poverty, which can make the above approach seem morally offensive.

7: Power and Politics

Abstract

There are various levels at which it is possible to view politics. One is that which focuses on political parties, governments and elections. Sociologically, this is a relatively restricted view. In this chapter, the reader is encouraged to adopt a broader approach to politics. This will be based on tracing the workings of power in social relationships. Definitions of some of the central concepts in politics are introduced to assist analysis.

A range of established sociological perspectives on power and politics are reviewed. These comprise functionalism, Marxism, the approach of Weber, elite theory and pluralism. Each of these theories apply sociological definitions of power systematically to social relationships. They offer differing analyses of the sources and distribution of power in society, who holds power and to whose benefit it is used.

A more restricted view of politics is adopted in the sections on voting behaviour. However, the approach remains sociological in the sense that attempts to understand changes in voting behaviour are related to broader social changes.

Contemporary perspectives on power and politics tend to emphasise the global dimensions of power and include postmodern and high modern approaches. These perspectives point to fundamental changes taking place in society. They raise challenging questions for both a sociological understanding of contemporary politics and, regarding high modernism, the guidance that the subject can give for the fashioning of political institutions appropriate for the current age.

The sociological challenge

At one level, politics can be seen to be about formal political party institutions and governments. This view focuses on the policies of political parties, general elections, Parliamentary processes and the policies and actions of government. Encouraged by certain sections of the mass media, our interest may also focus on the deeds of politicians in their professional capacities and private lives. Viewing politics at this level alone, our involvement is likely to be limited to participation in general elections when the aforementioned preoccupations become heightened.

Otherwise, we are often preoccupied with issues and problems of our immediate personal world. We may not consider these matters to be of a political nature and, as C. Wright Mills has maintained, we may tend to individualise problems rather than link them to broader public issues.

The study of politics in sociology requires us to break away from the vantage points identified above. In sociology, the study of politics is about the distribution and exercise of power at different levels within society, between societies and globally. Power, briefly defined, is to do with the capacity that some people have to exert their will over others. This concept of power can apply to any social situation. Based on this view of power, a focus on political parties, the formal institutions of government, and political personalities, is too restricted and may hide more about politics than it reveals. Instead, a sociological view can reveal the power and therefore political nature of organised groups such as trade unions or the capital of employers. Power can be exerted through military or paramilitary means. Playground bullying can be viewed as political as can the use of patriarchal (male over female) power in a variety of contexts. Even the language that people use in everyday social encounters to negotiate with others and attempt to persuade them or impose their meanings and viewpoints can be seen as political.

The tendency to individualise the relationships and problems of our personal lives is likely to blind us to their connections to the broader social structure. Immediate relationships themselves, of course, can be political in terms of the broader definition of politics identified above, even if we often do not see them in these terms. Furthermore, we should be prepared to recognise that the political influences acting on even our most immediate social relationships do not necessarily stop even at the recognised borders of nations! Decisions made by some to move investment and businesses across national boundaries can affect people's employment opportunities, standards of living, capacity to take political action, quality of life and relationships within families. Migration can bring about a range of different relationships between ethnic groups and cultures within a society. The fact that political issues can be global in origin takes us into the area of global political responses in terms of transnational pressure groups such as Greenpeace and supra-national governmental organisations like the European Union.

The difficulty that we may face in adopting a sociological view of politics can be in putting more conventional and limited preconceptions about the nature and scope of politics to one side. We will need to understand the precise use of sociological concepts and how applying them systematically may open up new vantage points on the nature and distribution of power. In so doing, it will become apparent that politics surrounds our daily lives. We may even gain insights which suggest why it is convenient to certain others that our view of politics should remain restricted.

Definition of main concepts

Establishing a clear meaning and use of key concepts is a necessary platform for developing a sociological approach to politics. So how does sociology approach politics? Politics is to do with the use of **power**. Power can be defined as the capacity that individuals or groups have to exert their will over others in social encounters. The inclination or capacity for resistance will depend on other features of the power relationship. If power is exerted in the form of **coercion**, it is experienced as an oppressive force exerted, from the viewpoint of the oppressed, without effective justification. In such situations, those with power are likely to be opposed by the oppressed should opportunities arise. However, if those exerting power are able to justify their use of it to others, they are able to claim **authority**. As the exercise of authority is backed up by justification, it is likely to realise a degree of willing compliance form those over whom it is exerted. In this case, the use of power is recognised as **legitimate**. However, the justifications upon which it is based may take the form of **ideology** – a term used in sociology to refer to the systematic distortion of reality for the purpose of gaining compliance. If ideology becomes so embraced that the way it defines the world is accepted as natural, it takes the form of **hegemony**.

Nations of the world are bounded territories governed by **states**. Institutions of the state include the government, regulatory apparatus such as the civil service, and the legal system. As traditionally defined, states hold **sovereign** power over national territories in their exclusive right to make and apply laws. In reality, contemporary societies have found it beneficial to relinquish some sovereignty to supra-state bodies such as the European Union for economic benefit, political allegiance and tackling a range of problems and risks which do not acknowledge national boundaries.

Citizenship denotes individual rights held by members of a society, but states hold a monopoly of the legitimate use of force within their territory and establish compliance through the courts, the police or the military. Welfare and educational institutions as well as local authorities also comprise part of the state apparatus.

Legitimacy may not always be easily maintained. If the behaviour of authorities falls conspicuously short of the values and standards by which it is justified, as, for example, if political corruption becomes evident, the authority of those in power, or even the entire social and political system, may face a loss of legitimacy. This can prove to be a fertile ground for the spread of counter ideologies and opposition movements. Under such circumstances, a government may be faced with a breakdown of social order and resort to coercive methods in an attempt to retain control.

Societies involve conflicts of interest. How these conflicts are managed by government will vary with the type of political institutions. In **authoritarian** states, power is imposed oppressively to limit the rights and freedoms of the subject population. If elections take place, it is with the purpose of legitimising single party rule.

In **representative democracies**, the population in the form of the electorate can periodically choose its government from rival political parties. Whilst the precise nature of political institutions and electoral systems varies from society to society, success in the electoral process gives government a **mandate** to introduce policies deriving from the manifesto that it was elected on without the need to regularly re-consult the electorate.

The matter of legitimacy is however not always straightforward in the real world. Governments in representative democracies legitimise their policies and actions through acquiring power by democratic means and as such hold authority. Consider the situation whereby through popular vote a government came to power pledged to nationalise certain industries. Whilst it would derive legitimacy and authority to do so from the electorate, implementing nationalisation could be viewed as a coercive act by private industry and therefore non-legitimate. The problem here would be a conflict of legitimacy based on the will of the electorate as opposed to the legitimacy of the ownership of private enterprise.

The term **fully participatory democracy** is reserved for systems in which those whom any decisions will effect must be consulted and allowed their input into the decision making process. Although arguably an unworkable form of democracy in complex modern societies, examples of participatory democracy on a smaller scale include Israeli kibbutzim as originally constituted and workers co-operatives.

The use of power may not be as transparent as these introductory definitions suggest. Various **faces of power** have been identified by Steven Lukes. At one level, a measure of power may simply be the ability some have to impose decisions on others. However, power can include the capacity that some groups have to avoid the raising of certain issues in the first place, thus precluding political debate and decisions in these areas. Lack of debate over the privileges of public schools may be an example of the use of this type of power. Furthermore, power can even involve the capacity that some have to persuade others to accept decisions which could otherwise be shown to be against their interests. The abandonment by workers of trade unions in Britain during the 1980s could be seen as an example of the use of this face of power.

Founding sociological perspectives on power and politics:

Sociological theory on politics attempts to address a variety of complex problems. Classical perspectives offer differing analyses of the origin and distribution of power in society, how it can best be measured, who holds it, and how they use it. These perspectives differ over the extent to which social relations are viewed as essentially harmonious or based on conflict, what the basis of harmony or conflict is, where lines of conflict are likely to occur, and how fluid they are. They also attempt to address such fundamental questions as the relationship between people's position in the social structure and their political consciousness and political action.

Despite fundamental differences between the classical perspectives, a key feature which they have in common is the tendency to view societies as if they are bounded entities. It will later be shown that contemporary approaches increasingly question the validity of this approach and, in some cases, even the degree to which political awareness still exists.

Functionalism – representative democracy and the use of power in the collective interest

The founding social context of functionalism can be traced back to the aftermath of the French Revolution and the writings of Auguste Comte. Developed by Comte as a reaction to the social instabilities in France following the Revolution, functionalism has retained an emphasis on gradual change, social order, hierarchy and stability as being both the natural and desirable social condition. Societies are seen as like systems or organisms. Although tending to self-regulate toward equilibrium, they can experience rapid and disturbing changes. For Comte, the forces of the French Revolution were rapid and fundamental in sweeping aside the institutions of feudalism, but left disarray in their wake. A new social and political order needed to be established, and Comte argued that this could be assisted by rational social analysis.

Following in this tradition, Durkheim maintained that a key practical aim of scientific sociology should be to assist in the fashioning of new social institutions to replace those that had been swept away with feudalism, for the purpose of assisting modern democratic societies to adjust to a new social stability.

Talcott Parsons developed the functionalist perspective in the modern American context. For Parsons, modern industrial societies are viewed as complex and highly differentiated social structures. For their efficient operation, and in contrast to traditional societies, positions of command must be allocated in terms of individual ability and expertise rather than through birthright. Modern capitalist society should operate as a meritocracy and to synchronise with this reality the values of a meritocracy would provide the most appropriate basis for social consensus. To motivate individual competition, a highly differentiated reward structure of occupations is necessary. Against the background of individual aspiration and materialistic values, high on the list of shared social goals by which governments can be judged is the enhancement of material living standards.

The institutions of representative democracy allow judgement of government to be expressed by the populace in the form of an electorate. Access to universal suffrage and choice between competing political parties enable the population to grant power on trust to the government to reflect collective sentiments, and pursue shared social goals. The winning party, legitimised through the electoral process to pursue common goals, will have to face future elections at which its performance will be again judged by the electorate, whose consent, if necessary, can be withdrawn.

As a consensus theory, functionalism focuses on the power 'of' society - led by government – measured in terms of its capacity for achieving common goals. The power of society can therefore grow with technological development, improved efficiency and minimal social conflict. From this healthy social condition, it is argued that members of society generally will benefit.

Marxism – representative democracy hiding the power of the capitalist class

A weakness of functionalism is clearly its inability to explain persisting levels of conflict and instability in capitalist societies. Most other sociological perspectives, and particularly Marxism, pay more attention to divisions and conflicting interests within society. However, the works of Marx and Engels are so extensive that different emphases have been detected in different works and varied interpretations of the role of the state have been proposed by Marxists.

The basic Marxist position is that social relations are fundamentally shaped by economic class relations. For Marx, political power derives from ownership of economic resources – especially the means of production. Power is firmly located in the employment relationship between employer and employee and this is a social class relationship. Political power is therefore as concentrated or distributed as is the ownership of the means of production. Under capitalism, economic and political power is concentrated in the hands of a minority capitalist class whose wealth depends on the employment of workers. This relationship is one of class exploitation.

Productivity, and the wealth it creates for the capitalist class, can only be fully effective if the working class is industrious and compliant. Since conflict of class interests is built into the capitalist system, how can such compliance be brought about?

Conflict of class interests is generated in the economic sphere. Marxists refer to this domain as the infrastructure. This conflict is managed by institutions and ideas, together referred to as the superstructure. The institutions are primarily those of state control. Coercive institutions, such as the legal system, the police and the military can suppress resistance. However, these institutions of control are vested in legitimacy and authority by appearing to represent the common good rather than primarily ruling class interests.

This takes the analysis on to another level of control. The willing compliance of the subject class can be most effectively furthered by the manipulation of their consciousness, referred to by Marx as the promotion of false consciousness based on a distorted (ideological) view of reality. For Marx, religion and the political institutions and values of liberal democracies were a potent means of such control. Marxists have since focussed more on the controlling impact of education and the mass media. All of these institutions and values are seen to play a political role in the broad sense of the term as defined at the beginning of this chapter – the capacity that some people have to exert their will over others. The focus here will be on what Marxists view as the real and broad political significance of the political institutions as narrowly defined – political parties, general elections and the policies and actions of elected governments.

The political institutions of capitalist representative democracies convey an image of accountability of political leaders to an electorate. Government, and the formal political system, are legitimised through giving citizens access to an electoral system in which they are free to choose between rival political parties by casting their vote at elections.

For Marxists, such legitimacy is based upon illusion. It serves the purpose of ideological control. The primary purpose of the political institutions of capitalist liberal democracies is to maintain the smooth working of the capitalist system. Whichever party wins has to govern within the constraints imposed by capitalism. Differences in the policy of different political parties therefore turn out to be quite limited when in government. From this position, it could be argued that changes in policy when New Labour replaced the Conservatives as the party of government in Britain from 1997 were not great and that the replacement of a discredited government by a fresh government with an electoral mandate was beneficial to British capitalism.

As power in capitalist societies actually originates in ownership of the means of production, the view that it rests with democratically elected governments fosters the illusion that the electorate has significant political power. From a Marxist perspective, whatever debate and acrimony takes place within Parliament, it is essentially a talking shop which restricts the image of politics to that of government and through the appearance of representation emasculates radicalism in society. Despite the veneer of democratic institutions, government is effectively little more than through a single party state, as whatever party governs will be more attuned to the power and interests of the 'hidden rulers' than that of the electorate.

The relationship between the state and the capitalist class is open to some debate within Marxist theory. An instrumentalist interpretation, advocated by Ralph Miliband, emphasises that the key positions of state are manned by a privileged group who share a common elite background and outlook. They can be relied on to run society in the interests of the capitalist class, even if the latter do not man the state directly.

Earlier in the twentieth century, Antonio Gramsci picked out a different emphasis from Marx's works. He argued that the state governed through the use of both force and ideology. If ideological manipulation becomes so all embracing that it encapsulates peoples' consciousness as the only possible outlook, it takes the form of ruling class hegemony. To achieve this, the state requires some autonomy from being used and seen as a direct instrument of the capitalist class. From this position, it has room to make occasional concessions to the working class and in so doing bolster its legitimacy by appearing to be a neutral arbiter in conflicts. By managing working class consent in this way, it works more effectively in the interests of capitalism.

A similar position to Gramsci's was put by structuralist Marxists Louis Althusser and Nicos Poulantzas. Here, in contrast to Milband's position, the social background and motives of state officials is of little importance. The structural position of the state imposes on officials service to the interests of capitalism, regardless of their social class background. A degree of autonomy between the ruling capitalist class and the governing political class enables more effective regulation of the system. It allows the state to occasionally act against particular capitalist interests (for example through anti monopoly legislation) or offer timely concessions to the working class (for example through welfare reforms) if to do so helps to promote the long-term interests of the capitalist system. Furthermore, by so doing, the appearance of the state as acting for the benefit of all can be more effectively conveyed.

For Marx, genuine democracy would only be possible with the diffusion of political power. However, as political power derives from economic power, this could only come from acquisition of the means of production into common ownership. As the capitalist class were unlikely to give up wealth and power without a struggle, meaningful democracy was only likely to be achieved through the revolutionary overthrow of capitalism.

For all of its valuable insights into power and control in capitalist societies, this perspective, developed around the middle of the nineteenth century, has faced a number of fundamental challenges in recent decades. Firstly, when communist societies did emerge, they took the form of repressive single party states, run by party elites, not the democratic societies that Marx predicted. Secondly, the collapse of Eastern Block communist systems between 1989 –1991 has led to the virtual global spread of capitalism – a trend operating in reverse to Marx's predictions. Thirdly, within capitalist societies, economic class as the key configuration of political divisions has arguably retreated rather than advanced. For example, in Britain although economic inequality has grown since the 1980s under both Conservative and Labour governments, class consciousness appears to have declined and interest group politics advanced. Fourthly, it is a new challenge for Marxists to show how their perspective can be applied to a modern service and information economy as opposed to industrial capitalism.

Weber – representative democracy versus bureaucracy

As explained in Chapter 5 on social stratification, for Weber social conflict is not essentially reducible to class conflict. Modern liberal democratic societies are arenas of conflicting status groups and interest groups as well as classes. Even in representative democracies, those who hold power usually attempt to retain it at the expense of others. To understand how power is legitimised to enable rulers to claim authority, Weber emphasised that legitimacy must be understood in the context of prevailing world views or social outlooks. Weber developed 'ideal types' to assist this understanding. Ideal types are intellectual models which highlight the essential features of a society. Their purpose is to assist in the understanding of highly complex phenomena in the real world and to classify different types of society. The essential types of authority that Weber identified were traditional, rational-legal and charismatic.

Traditional authority is prevalent in pre-industrial, particularly feudal societies. In these societies, life is largely tied to agriculture and the routines of the seasons. It is lived out in small communities which comprise well established hierarchies with people experiencing little geographical or social mobility. Religion and custom prevail. Tradition – the justification of present ways through reference to things having always been that way – tends to be accepted in its own right. In such a society, obedience to ones 'social betters' is often justified by recourse such ideas as superior social breeding – the notion that demonstration of a family lineage of leadership denotes inbred leadership qualities. The credibility of authority justified in this way can be related to social settings where people are familiar with livestock breeding.

For Weber, the advance of science and technology undermines tradition. Rational thinking is linked to the quest for efficiency which promotes the need for change. These forces prepare the way for industrial capitalism which comes to develop large scale and impersonal organisational structures. Life has become more freed from the routines of agriculture and is dominated by the routines of impersonal factories and offices, the latter referred to by Weber as bureaucracies. In such a society, authority in the workplace is justified by achievement and merit in a system of rules and laws that encourage impersonal competition for occupational position. The formation of government is based on political party competition within the rules of a democratic framework. Weber referred to this type of authority, based on standardised and formal procedures, as rational–legal.

Contrary to more recent organisational theorists, Weber maintained that bureaucracy is the most efficient form of social organisation. This efficiency stems from the top down imposition of authority through the machinery of a tiered formal organisational structure and the conformity of functionaries to orders, rules and regulations. Weber argued that competition between organisations and the drive for efficiency inclines modern complex industrial societies to become bureaucratised throughout. However, he was concerned that democratic accountability would become choked as in such a society decision making and power fall into the hands of un-elected bureaucrats and experts and that political participation of citizens may decline. Weber advocated that the best check against this risk is a well established multi-party representative democracy in which civil servants are accountable to politicians who themselves are accountable to the electorate.

For Weber, to overthrow capitalism and representative democracy by revolution and the acquisition of the means of production into public ownership would not lead to the fully participatory democracy that Marx had predicted. This is because, contrary to Marx, power does not flow exclusively from ownership of the means of production but can be concentrated in the means of state administration. State ownership would concentrate bureaucratic with economic power. Consequently, a revolution in which the means of production become commonly owned would lead to a single party state with little check on the advance of bureaucracy and the concentration of power in an unaccountable state apparatus.

Charismatic authority, Weber's third type, differs from the others in that it derives from the perceived exceptional qualities of an individual leader. Such leaders are most likely to come to power when people turn to them at times of social crisis. They are likely to engender strong emotional identification from followers and often adopt an authoritarian style of leadership. Napoleon, Stalin and Hitler each exemplify this type of rule arising from social crisis. However, charismatic authority is usually relatively short lived. Given its emotional intensity and personal nature, charismatic authority is likely to lapse with the fall of the leader.

Elite theory – representative democracy, fine as long as it does not amount to much!

Classical elite theorists, developing their ideas during the late nineteenth century, also strongly contested Marxist analysis. They agreed with Marxists only at the most general level – that power in society is concentrated in the hands of a small minority. For elite theorists, rule by a small superior minority is a necessary feature of all societies. That minority will comprise those who occupy key positions in society and especially the state including senior politicians, civil servants, ambassadors, judges, and high ranking military officials. It could include owners of the means of production, but not exclusively, and there is no reason why elite power should specially emanate from ownership of the means of production.

Classical elite theorists argue that a feature of societies throughout history is that their populations are divided into elites and masses. For Vilfredo Pareto, this universal feature is to do with the social distribution of personal or psychological qualities. Pareto adopted a view of the distribution of innate leadership qualities similar to that of psychologists who have came to use the bell curve to chart the distribution of innate intelligence in populations. Following his predecessor Niccolo Machiavelli, Pareto distinguished main two types of leadership quality: stealth and cunning and the ability to take decisive action. Pareto argued that people with these leadership capabilities will always be in short supply in any population. The majority, lacking the qualities necessary for political leadership, will need and even prefer to be led by others. On this basis, elite rule is inevitable and democratic accountability to the masses cannot be equated with progress.

It is in the interests of elites to act as cohesive groups to protect their interests and privileges. There can arise, however, threats to their prominence. Pareto recognised that the style of elite rule must be suited to the needs of the time. As social circumstances change, elites must either adapt so as to enable themselves to retain political control or they are likely to face a challenge from other aspiring elites more suited to rule. Such a challenge may take place through military coup or revolution, which if successful brings about a circulation of elites. Furthermore, although the masses are generally lacking in leadership qualities, an elite that becomes too socially closed off risks becoming decadent and vulnerable to challenge. Some degree of social mobility of the able few from the masses may therefore be desirable to replenish an elite and enhance its longevity.

Pareto's analysis of the distribution of power was similar to that of Gaetano Mosca, to whom he owed unacknowledged intellectual debt. However, Mosca did recognise that the qualities of elites may be acquired more through inherited social advantage than superior innate qualities. He also appreciated that elites that govern within the institutions of representative democracy can serve the general interest, especially if not drawn exclusively from privileged backgrounds. Mosca further recognised the importance of a growing sub-elite organisational stratum comprising, for example, managers, engineers and intellectuals, who contributed to the effective governing of modern society. However, both theorists held that the masses were generally unworthy of exercising power and should be excluded from doing so. And, even further, for Pareto in particular, it is in the best interests of society that in a representative democracy elites can effectively manipulate the masses into believing that they are being consulted rather than meaningfully consulting them.

Robert Michels, in his work 'Political Parties', reached a similar position to that of Pareto and Mosca but based his analysis on society's organisational requirements. Like Weber, he argued that bureaucracy, a top down form of organisation, was necessary for any large organisation or modern society to operate efficiently. Hierarchical organisation inevitably leads to rule by the few – otherwise known as oligarchy. Representative democracy equates to the political organisation of large populations who are consulted, but it is impossible for them to be regularly involved in the decision making process (a situation akin to fully participatory democracy). Instead, full-time bureaucrats and political leaders are required to take key decisions and implement policy. However radically democratic the original policies of an opposition party may have been, once established into power, political leaders acquire privileges and a vested interest in protecting their own position more than representing the populace. They therefore become an elite. Even in representative democracies, oligarchical structures headed by elites are inevitable – a process for which Michels coined the phrase the 'iron law of oligarchy'.

From the classical elite theory perspective, Marxism is not the scientific theory of social change that it claims to be, but just a utopian ideology. As an ideology, it is a system of thinking which distorts reality and can itself be used by an aspiring elite to manipulate the masses in its support against a ruling elite. It is utopian because the fully participatory democracy that it promises for the future cannot be realised. Any revolutionary party that gains power will need to govern a modern and complex society. In such a society, participatory democracy, if attempted, would lead to massive inefficiency associated with the necessity for regular consultation. To tackle this, direct leadership would need to be asserted. Thus, even out of communist revolution, a new oligarchical structure will have emerged with leaders becoming increasingly detached from the lives of the led. A revolutionary party gives rise to a new elite which will protect its power and privileges by controlling the masses through both coercive means and the ideology rather than the impossible reality of communism.

If Michels is correct, in the interests of efficiency, fully participatory democracy is an unworkable type of political system, and even representative democracy will amount to little in terms of meaningful consultation. Governments in representative democracies, of course, have to periodically face the electorate. Whether a particular change of government is a change of elite or a change within an elite is a matter of analysis. However, oligarchical structures remain. Oligarchical tendencies can become particularly evident when governments that have been in power for a long time display a tendency when facing the potential accountability of media questions to frequently not have ministers available for comment.

Other sociologists have taken elite theory in a radical direction. From this position, elite rule is not regarded as preferable or inevitable. Instead, it is lamentable that many modern societies that masquerade as democracies can be better understood as being controlled by elites who are by and large un-elected. An early exponent of this position was C. Wright Mills who argued in the 1950s that America was dominated by a single and largely unaccountable power elite with contacts across the upper reaches of business corporations, the military and the governmental apparatus.

Sociologists adopting this general position raise the following points. There are certain key occupations in society, positions at the top of which confer great power, status and privilege on their occupants. These include the armed forces, the church, the legal profession, the civil service, government and large business corporations. The top positions in these institutions tend to be occupied by people of similar privileged background. People in these positions often know each other and share a similar elitist social outlook and membership of exclusive clubs. There is much movement across the top. For example, business people may move into top governmental positions or vice versa and individual politicians may hold interlocking directorships (be directors of a number of companies). All of this helps illustrate what John Scott calls a 'web of connections' at the top of society. At the same time, it has been argued that, through consumerism and growing affluence, general populations have become depoliticised and politically apathetic.

The evidence available may suggest a modest long-term decline in the proportion of MPs with a public school educational background, but that substantial differences remain between the main political parties. For example, figures provided by Bilton *et al* (1985) indicated that in 1966, 76.6% of Conservative MPs in Parliament came from a public school background as opposed to 19.5% of Labour MPs. At the pinnacle of government power, it was found that in the 1963 Conservative cabinet, 63.6% of members had attended one of the top six public schools, and the figure for the Labour cabinet for 1967 was 15.8%. Research by Criddle indicated that in 2001 the proportions of MPs with public school background had declined to 64% of Conservatives and 17% of New Labour members. Two out of 412 Labour MPs had attended Eton whereas 14 out of 166 Conservative MPs had. However, New Labour achieved a large majority in the 2001 general election. With such marked differences in access to privileged education between the parties, the overall proportion of public school and top public school educated MPs would almost certainly increase if the Conservatives were to win a general election, bucking the more modest downward long-term trend.

Pluralism – representative democracy as a balancing of diverse interests

Even if it can be demonstrated that privileged and self-recruiting elites exist, this is not in itself proof of the effective exercise of self-interested power by a single and unified elite. Pluralists strongly reject both Marxist and elite theory models of the concentration of power in capitalist liberal democracies. In contrast to the classical elite view of oligarchical organisation and unified elites, classical pluralism emphasises that in modern liberal democracies power has many competing centres. To express this, Robert Dahl uses the term 'polyarchy'. In liberal democracies, it is argued that power is diffused down to individuals and organised groups, who, so long as they act within the law, are free and empowered to compete to influence the governmental decision making process.

From this perspective, representative democracies are complex societies which comprise a broad spectrum of interests. Individuals have their own range of interests which they may want to pursue. People are free to voice and pursue their interests through pressure group activity and so can come together with other individuals in different groups to do so. In the competitive process of influencing political decisions, all interests can have an input, although the involvement and influence of groups will vary from issue to issue. In support of this model, Dahl (1961) used empirical evidence from his study of New Haven to show that across a range of issues the decisions arrived at in this local government gave no single interest group a monopoly of influence.

For pluralists, a cornerstone of representative democracy is the competition between political parties by which, at elections, voters periodically hold governments accountable. To attract the support of voters, political parties must keep a careful eye on the state of popular opinion. To this end, voter opinion surveys are regularly conducted and parties may need to change their policies or political position. The power of the vote therefore gives the electorate the power to shape policy and to replace political parties in government. It could therefore be emphasised from a pluralist position, in contrast to a Marxist interpretation, that it was not the constraints of the capitalist system which forced the British Labour Party to 'modernise' between 1983 and 1997, but the opinion of the electorate which they had to satisfy.

Pluralists emphasise that whilst voters are free to vote for a party which most closely reflects their range of interests, pressure groups, as organisations of individuals with shared interests and aims, enable people to fine tune their influence on decision makers on an ongoing basis. Government is therefore about responding to the pressure of different organised interests and seeking compromise. By such means, in representative democracies the process of democratic accountability is deepened.

Where, then, lie the boundaries of legitimate pressure group activity? Pluralists tend to have in mind hierarchical organisations whose representatives have regular contact with local and central government decision makers. These have been referred to by Wyn Grant as 'insider' or conventional pressure groups. In Britain, such groups may include the Confederation of British Industry, Age Concern and the Automobile Association. In relation to these groups, the state acts as a referee and honest broker between the competing interests, each operating within the law and the rules of the political game. It also relies on them for information and expertise in helping to shape policy in their specific areas.

Other pressure groups may employ the tactic of rapid response and direct action and operate on the margins of or outside the law. These are sometimes referred to as 'outsider' groups. Within this category would be included the Animal Liberation Front, Fathers for Justice, and some environmental pressure groups. Against such groups, pluralists argue that state power may need to be rallied to ensure that the law is not subverted and, in the extreme, the very institutions which safeguard the freedoms of law abiding individuals are not threatened.

A further influence open to people is the use of their consumer spending power. Contrary to Marxism, which emphasises the relative powerlessness of the employee, pluralism focuses on the power of the consumer. Classical pluralists argue that in a system of private enterprise and competition in the pursuit of profit, businesses must respond to consumer demand in order to flourish or even survive. As well as the need to satisfy customers with particular goods and services, businesses, along with political regimes, will be concerned about their ethical image since if viewed as disreputable they may face concerted action in the form of consumer boycotts. Consumer action against the apartheid regime in South Africa in the 1980s and more recent boycotting of genetically modified crops offer good examples of the potential impact of such movements.

To sum up, classical pluralism is distinguishable form functionalism in that although it recognises the importance of commonly agreed values, these are more of a backdrop to social diversity and particular conflicts of interest which should be followed within the rules of the political game. For pluralists, the needs of all can never be met all of the time but can best be responded to through democratic institutions enabling compromises to result from the active pursuit of individual and sectional interests. Unlike classical elite theory, classical pluralism does not maintain that liberal democracies are or should be governed by a single ruling elite, nor does it emphasise the passivity of the masses. Power is diffused down to an active citizenship. In contesting the Marxist position, classical pluralism argues that in contemporary complex societies divisions of interest break up the formation of any significant cross cutting common class interest. Neither, with the growth of interventionist legislation, the spread of business ownership via shareholding down to a larger section of society, and the power of the consumer, is power monopolised in the hands of a narrow capitalist ruling class. Instead, labour and capital form part of a number of interests which feed their influence into the political system.

Elite pluralism or fragmented elites?

Pluralism, a particularly influential theory in the United States, is, indeed, a highly self-congratulatory view of the distribution of power in capitalist liberal democracies, but just how accurate is this model? A number of questions, including the following, have been frequently raised. Are all sections of society adequately represented? Are some groups substantially over-represented? Are pressure groups themselves always internally democratic? Answers to these questions have led some writers such as J. K. Galbraith to a refocusing of pluralism in the direction of elite pluralism (sometimes referred to as neo-pluralism). Although retaining the pluralist perspective as a touchstone, advocates of this modified position acknowledge that some groups in society, in particular large business interests, are likely to have a disproportionate influence on political decisions, especially in the economic sphere, whilst the needs of others, such as the homeless, tend to get overlooked. It is also often now emphasised that there has been a degree of reconfiguration of pressure group activity away from a focus on national governments as political problems and the means of tackling them have become more globalised. Furthermore, as organisational hierarchies, conventional pressure groups are often not very open to democratic influence by members from within but are effectively run and represented by elites. Power may not therefore be as evenly spread, focussed on national government, or as diffused down to active participants as classical pluralism once maintained. From this modified perspective, liberal democracies are sometimes referred to as 'deformed polyarchies'.

From the other end of the scale, there have also been criticisms and modifications of the classical elite theory position. The idea of fragmented elites, adopted by Ian Budge *et al*, argues that rather than a single cohesive elite operating with a unified purpose and sense of direction, there exists different interests which elites strive to pursue. The interests of business elites may diverge with that of government elites, for example over taxation and anti-monopoly legislation. The elite of the judiciary can come into conflict with government elites over sentencing policy. There may even be fragmentation within each of these elites. For example, it is doubtful, other than at a very general level, whether there is a single business community interest, and within government different spending departments often have to compete for limited resources. However, although fragmented, from the above perspective these elites may share a similar general background and outlook and experience little popular control.

A summary of elite theory and pluralist positions can be represented as follows:

Continuum of Elite Theory and Pluralist Perspectives				
Classical Elite	**Fragmented Elite**		**Elite Pluralism**	**Classical Pluralism**
Single power elite exists with a shared interest. This is necessary, beneficial and inevitable. Masses need to be led.	Elites rule, but not as a single cohesive group. Different elite interests divide them.		Popular participation in interest groups may be limited as leaders represent their interests.	Diversity of pressure groups involves members in active and effective participation in pursuit of their interests.

The vote – more an index of power than power itself?

Universal franchise – the extension of the vote to all people over a certain age bar limited prescribed sections of the population – is a fundamental feature of contemporary representative democracies. Having access to the vote opens up a degree of choice and political power to the electorate; just how much choice and power is open to debate and is an issue which is disputed from various theoretical perspectives such as those introduced above. Furthermore, viewed sociologically, power, as previously defined, is potentially an element of all social relationships. Prior to the study of voting behaviour, it is therefore important to appreciate that the acquisition of universal suffrage can itself be placed in the context of political struggles between groups within society for a say in the formation of governments. In this context, the restriction and extension of the vote itself provides a barometer of changing power relationships within society.

Groups that have used their power to acquire access to the vote have sometimes attempted to exclude its extension to others. By so doing, they promote social closure. In Britain in the early 1830s, the extension of the vote to a broader category of male property owners reflected the growing social power of the middle classes following the Industrial Revolution. At the time, the exclusion of non-property owners was justified on the ideological basis that a more open social structure had emerged in which property acquisition by the self made man was proof of industriousness and the capacity to make sound judgements.

At various times and in different societies, other ideological justifications, including those based on racism and sexism, have been used by some groups to exclude other sections of the population from acquiring full access to the vote. Thus, although universal suffrage is the hallmark of modern liberal democracies, it has been fought for by chartists, suffragists, supporters of civil rights, and anti-apartheid movements, etcetera.

In Britain, through legislative reforms responding to the growing organisation and power of the industrial working class and the women's movement, all males over 21 had gained access to the vote in 1918, and females, on an equal basis to males, in 1928. Legislation passed in 1969 brought the minimum voting age down to 18 and there has recently been talk of a possible further reduction to the age of 16.

Sociological approach to voting behaviour

Academic sociology is parcelled into different topic areas to assist in the focus of analysis. Politics, and more specifically voting behaviour, is part of this process of academic specialisation. However, the real world is interconnected. To reflect this, sociologists need to be able to make interconnections within their subject. Hence, to understand voting behaviour sociologically requires a sociological understanding of surrounding social conditions and changes within which evidence of patterns of voting behaviour can be interpreted. The reader is therefore encouraged to relate an understanding of voting behaviour to sociological analysis in other chapters, especially that on social stratification.

A post war baseline - voting behaviour and social class

During the post war years and up to the early 1970s, voting in Britain appeared to exhibit quite a stable pattern. Voters tended to retain loyalty to their chosen political party from one general election to another. Swings in party support between elections were modest. The beneficiaries of this stability were the Labour and Conservative Parties, who between them regularly obtained over 80% of the vote and took their turns in government.

Explanations of this stability tend to emphasise the long term and cumulative effect on people of political socialisation within a relatively stable social structure. Such explanations have been referred to as 'primacy' explanations. At this period in time, social class appeared to be the primacy influence of overriding importance. It was argued that social class was the basis of partisan identification and alignment in voting behaviour. Partisan identification refers to a high level of voter commitment and loyalty to a particular party, often based on commitment to a set of ideological values and the pursuit of a cause. Partisanship therefore entails a high degree of emotional commitment from the voter. Class alignment emphasises a link between a person's social class and the tendency to vote for a party which is perceived to represent that class interest. Seen as combined, this influence is referred to as partisan alignment. In a stable class structure, with limited opportunities for social mobility, the impact of family socialisation and class identification – reinforced, according to Butler and Stokes, by the type of neighbourhood lived in, school attended and work environment – provided a class differentiated pattern of socialisation which produced a strong predisposition toward class based voting behaviour. According to this explanation, a strong bond existed between being manual working class and voting for the Labour Party and being white collar middle class and voting for the Conservatives. Social class alone provided the best indicator and predictor of voting behaviour.

Detailed evidence to support this interpretation was not abundant, since sophisticated electoral surveys in the form of exit polls only date from 1964. However, supporting circumstantial evidence was strong. This included low levels of voter volatility between elections, comparatively high electoral turnout of around 75%, and the dominance in politics of two major parties, Labour and the Conservatives, reflecting a society of two main social classes.

However, evidence also indicated that a significant proportion of voters in each class did not conform to the dominant voting pattern. For example, research conducted by Ivor Crewe (1983) established that in the 1959 general election approximately 1/5 of non-manual workers voted Labour and about 1/3 of manual workers voted Conservative. An important concern during the 1960s and 1970s was therefore to explain the reasons behind these levels of 'deviant voting' or 'class defection'. Some of these explanations are briefly summarised below.

Firstly, social classes are not uniform blocks; different occupational sectors exist within social classes which may encourage different political outlooks. Within the working class, Goldthorpe and Lockwood argued that agricultural labourers and coal miners tended to adopt opposing political attitudes which were based on their differing views of the social structure. Such differences were related to distinctive occupational and community influences. For example, the dangers of coal mining required high levels of co-operation between workers who also lived in tightly knit community networks around the pits. This life encouraged a view of the social structure as divided between 'us and them' – a view which promoted strong identification toward Labour as the party of the working class. By contrast, agricultural workers, who worked and lived in smaller groups and communities and had more regular contact with their employers, were more likely to view the social hierarchy as a justifiable order. Associated traditional attitudes of deference to social superiors would incline many of these workers toward voting Conservative as the party of natural leaders.

Secondly, there is the question of how social class is defined and measured and who is defining and measuring it. If people are designated to a social class by sociologists through the use of traditional occupational scales alone, their own subjective interpretations of their social class position are being ignored. Butler and Stokes found that where people's subjective judgement of their social class did not agree with that allocated to them by researchers, they were more likely to be deviant voters in terms of sociologist's class definitions, whereas if their subjective views correlated with sociologist's definition of their class they were very likely to be class conformist in their voting. Personal perception of their class was therefore of some importance to a person's voting decisions and could help to explain levels of so called deviant voting.

Thirdly, voters experiencing cross class social mobility may, through the continuing effect of earlier political socialisation, remain loyal to the party of their class of origin, thus becoming deviant voters in their class of destination. The upwardly mobile may therefore remain loyal to Labour – as discovered by Goldthorpe and Lockwood in the case of the sons of affluent blue collar workers who became white collar workers. Likewise, the downwardly mobile may retain adherence to the Conservative Party.

Fourthly, although the impact of social class was arguably very powerful, other social factors can cut across and to some extent break up its overriding influence. For example, Anthony Heath has shown that within the working class, private home owners were more likely to vote Conservative than council house occupants.

Another cross cutting influence is that of religion. Catholics tend to vote Labour whereas those who identify with the Church of England (the religion of the establishment) are more likely to vote Conservative (seeing it as the party of the establishment). For example, Heath found in 1992 that of middle class voters who identified with the Church of England, 72% voted Conservative, whereas only 47% of middle class voters who held no religious beliefs voted Conservative. Furthermore, the intensity of the impact of religion is likely to vary alongside levels of religious identification in different parts of the country. Since locality, gender, ethnicity and age all show some influence on voting behaviour, they also provide potential for breaking up the influence of social class.

However, even during the 1960s, there was evidence emerging of a changing relationship between the electorate and the parties they supported. For example, Goldthorpe and Lockwood found that although 80% of affluent blue collar workers in their research had voted Labour at the 1959 general election, their identification was based less on strong party loyalty and an ideological commitment than was thought to traditionally be the case for working class Labour voters. Although these affluent voters still tended to see themselves as working class, their greater affluence and home centeredness encouraged a more instrumental attitude toward trade unions and political parties, support for which became more contingent on the furtherance of their standard of living. As affluent workers comprised an expanding section of the working class, there was a possibility of potential desertion from voting Labour by a growing section of blue collar workers in the future.

Some similarity to the above trend but with reference to the nature of attachment to voting Conservative was argued by McKenzie and Silver. Whilst Goldthorpe and Lockwood, and before them Walter Bagehot, had argued that a substantial proportion of Conservative support, including that from working class voters, was based on a deferential social outlook, McKenzie and Silver argued that of increasing importance in voting Conservative was a secular outlook which focussed more on party policy and the assessed implications for a voter's standard of living.

From the mid 1950s, a number of changes were affecting working class community life. These included: the start of a long term decline in employment in traditional industries such as steel working, shipbuilding, and dock work, followed by a later dramatic decline in coal mining, and with this a decline in the possibility of working class nepotism; geographical movement required with the demolition of slums and re-housing or the search for new types of work; and some improvement in opportunities for social mobility. In these developments can be seen the undermining of community life and a thinning out of the boundaries of class formation which were likely to diminish the impact of social class on working class social and political outlook and voting behaviour.

Whatever attachment was to remain between social class and voting behaviour, if, as Dahrendorf has argued, class decomposition was taking place, it should be expected that likewise a pattern of decomposition in voting behaviour would follow. This and the decline of the traditional working class already signalled long-term problems for the Labour Party it if relied on appealing to the working class voter.

The decline of social class based voting?

Signs of how these underlying social changes were having a significant effect on voting behaviour were first observed in the February 1974 general election. In this election, the Liberal vote increased substantially to 19.3% from a 1951 low of 2.6% and a level of still only 7.5% in the 1970 election. This increase was at the expense of the combined Labour and Conservative vote which fell from 89.4% in the 1970 election to 74.9% in February 1974. After falling back a little in the 1979 election, the 'Liberal' vote surged again in 1983 when the Liberal SDP Alliance polled 25.4% of the vote; only about 2% behind the Labour vote. This decline in the two party monopoly, at least as far as proportion of the vote is concerned, suggested a significant move away from the two party partisan identification and class alignment model of voting behaviour. Of much debate since has been the question of how fundamental this change has become and what other social factors may be emerging to influence voting behaviour at the expense of social class.

Of some significance to the debate has not just been the increase in the 'Liberal' vote (the parties of the Liberal SDP Alliance merged in 1988 and eventually settled on the new name of Liberal Democrats), but also the nature of its support. Until well into the 1990s, the Liberal Democrats had retained the Liberal tradition of being fairly centrally positioned between the Labour and Conservative Parties. Their supporters have been amongst the most fickle section of the electorate, with only a minority remaining loyal over two consecutive elections. Instability in voting behaviour, although not only concentrated here, appears to have become an increasing feature of British general elections. There is also clear evidence of a significant decline in voter turnout in recent general elections: 77.7% in 1992, 71.4% in 1997, just below 60% in 2001and just above 60% in 2005. This trend would appear to offer evidence of declining partisan identification by the electorate.

It is against the backdrop of such evidence that arguments over dealignment in terms of both party loyalty and class identification have emerged. An early advocate of the interpretation that a fundamental dealignment was taking place in voting behaviour was Ivor Crewe. He argued that voting was becoming less based on feelings of loyalty to a particular political party – a process referred to as partisan dealignment. An effective way to measure this is to look at the strength with which voters identify with political parties. To this end, research conducted by Crewe and Thompson found that whilst 44% of voters identified very strongly with a political party in 1966, this figure had fallen to 16% by 1997.

Furthermore, evidence suggested that social class, based on occupation, was becoming a poorer indicator of voting behaviour – suggesting that class dealignment was also taking place. General election figures provided by David Saunders show that during the1960s, Labour and the Conservatives held steady class based monopolies of the vote at the expanse of the Liberals. The Liberals then made some inroads in 1974. Over the four elections between 1979 and 1992, Labour were the main casualties of dealignment with the Conservatives regularly polling between 35 and 36% of the manual vote. However, in 1997, dealignment worked against the Conservatives with Labour becoming New Labour and capturing 40% of the non-manual vote.

Anthony Heath had been initially more sceptical of the long-term impact of dealignment. He acknowledged that there was research evidence indicating a decline in partisan voting, but cast doubt on the extent and lasting effect of class dealignment. Much depends on how social class is defined. Heath made more specific distinctions than between middle class and working class and when focussing on the voting behaviour of powerless blue collar workers, found an unchanging pattern of support for Labour through the 1960s and into the 1980s. Overall, for Heath, changing patterns of voting behaviour were tending to reflect changes in the class structure itself with a declining size of the working class disadvantaging Labour. However, Heath argued that growing inequality under the Conservatives could reverse any class dealignment and lead to the re-emergence of class as the major social factor in voting behaviour.

The problem regarding this last point is that as inequality was increasing under the Conservatives, class consciousness may have been simultaneously declining. A more individualistic culture had been promoted by the new right. Many blue collar workers were turning away from trade unions who were blighted with unpopularity following the 'winter of discontent' and were looking toward the potential individual benefits from Conservative reforms such as the promotion of home ownership. There is therefore not necessarily a straightforward causal relationship between occupation and economic factors and class consciousness.

Could patterns of voting behaviour still be explained in primacy terms? Could they be better explained by reference to an overriding social factor other than social class? Dunleavy and Husbands (1985) thought so in their sectoral politics model. Central to this explanation is the view that a closer fit with voting behaviour than social class division appears in the division between the public and private sector. This model predicted that the more that people were involved in the public sector in their employment position, consumer capacity and housing situation, the more likely they were to vote Labour whatever their occupational class, whereas the more they were implicated in the private sector, the greater likelihood that they would vote Conservative, again largely irrespective of social class. In terms of consumer capacity and use of services, important areas of the pubic and private divide would include housing, educational provision, health provision and pensions. Given the changing balance in these provisions and the declining numbers employed in the public sector during the 1980s, each brought about by Conservative reforms, it is clear that if this analysis is correct, the Conservatives were building a substantial social basis of long term support that Labour would need to respond to.

Another possibility is that no single primacy or structural factor can any longer adequately explain voting behaviour, but that a fluid combination of influences may be coming into play. Religion, region and neighbourhood, age, gender and ethnicity all show some impact on voting behaviour. However, it may be suspected that higher levels of volatility are associated with the impact of more short-term influences. These have been referred to as 'recency' influences and tend to be associated with a more instrumental approach to voting in which individuals make rational decisions based on the calculated impact of policy on their personal well being, especially on their standard of living. Amongst these influences may be leadership image, the econometric or 'feel good' factor and the impact of the mass media. Indeed, as the latter enables the electorate to acquire up to date intelligence on the state of the parties through the findings of opinion polls, effective tactical voting (usually taking the form of switching to a party which has a perceived better chance of defeating a disliked party than voting for one's party of first choice in a constituency) becomes more of a possibility. This arguably both presupposes and promotes a decline in partisan voting and further assists volatility.

A further aspect of voting behaviour relates to the ideological and policy positioning of political parties themselves. For example, in the 1983 general election, there was clear polarisation between the Labour Party and the Conservatives both ideologically and on a range of issues including privatisation and nuclear disarmament. The Conservatives won the election and attracted the vote of 35% of voters in manual occupations. The wide gap in the middle of the political spectrum enabled the Liberal / SDP Alliance to occupy a position from which their percentage of the vote peaked. Labour has since become New labour and in distancing itself from its historical connections with trade unions and the imagery of being the party of the working class, and accepted many of the Conservative reforms, has moved into the political middle ground. In doing so, New Labour successfully managed to broaden its appeal across society to the extent that in the 1997 general election it obtained about 40% of the middle class vote.

The classical sociological perspectives differ in their evaluation of the impact that the electorate can have on political decision making. This should be quite apparent in a comparison of classical pluralist and Marxist perspectives on the sources and distribution of power in capitalist democracies. For Marxists, the electorate can only appear (but for the main beneficiaries of capitalism it is important that this appearance is kept up) to have significant say in the complexion of government in capitalist societies. In reality, much of the power to influence policy is concentrated in the hands of a capitalist class and serves the interests of capital. The pluralist model, by contrast, has been argued to effectively explain the impact of recency influences and instrumental attitudes toward voting. This model, put forward for example by Himmelweit, suggests that social class and party ideology have little impact on the decision making of voters because they adopt a pragmatic consumer based approach to voting. They shop around and rationally compare the benefit to themselves of the policies on offer before casting their vote. Political parties must compete in packaging their policies to attract the votes of political consumers who are thus able to shape party policy.

A growing concern of the political parties, though, is that an increasing proportion of the electorate do not appear to be buying into party politics, if the turnout at recent general elections is anything to go by. It is with this concern in mind that various alternatives to people having to turn out to the voting booth, such as the expansion of postal, electronic and telephone voting, are being considered. In the next section, it will be suggested that the process of globalisation appears to be having a significant effect on national and electoral politics.

Contemporary sociological perspectives on power and politics:

Important contemporary developments in power and politics involve debates concerning the nature and extent of globalisation and the responses advocated, on whether contemporary societies can best be explained in terms of postmodern or high modern conditions, and what the social implications of these analyses are. A central issue in this is how power in the contemporary world may be becoming reconfigured and what the opportunities are for new types of political action and control.

Globalisation – the erosion of the power of national government?

Globalisation is defined in terms of processes taking place whereby nations become increasingly intermeshed into networks of information, economic relations and power that cut across national boundaries. A driving force of this change is global capitalism and new technology, but as well as economic, the effects are social, cultural and political. Satellite, internet, and mobile phone technology allow instantaneous communication around the world. Masses of information can be exchanged. Global financial movements can instantly take place based on access to the latest financial information. Businesses can readily move their production between countries to take advantage of cheaper labour and / or more profitable activity.

A number of issues and questions, including the following, can be raised with reference to globalisation and politics. How fundamental and wide ranging is the impact of globalisation? What are its consequences for national governments? What are the benefits and risks involved? What responses are emerging to globalisation, and what alternative political institutions may be necessary? To what extent are national governments losing power to the forces of international capitalism? To what extent are governments able to retain a monopoly in the use of power in their prescribed territories? And to what extent is it necessary, or possible, for national governments to beneficially reconfigure their use of power by a degree of devolution downwards to regional and local levels and passing power upwards to supra-state organisations?

A variety of positions on globalisation can be identified. For purposes of classification, the author will be guided by a system devised by David Held. One position is labelled traditionalist. This emphasises that the impact of globalisation has been overstated and that states remain strong and powerful political entities. Toward the other extreme, a second position emphasises that the forces of globalisation are profound and irresistible, fundamentally weakening the power of the state. This position can be sub-divided into opposing camps. The first of these, sometimes referred to as hyper-globalisation, adopts a positive and optimistic view of the benefits of global free enterprise. The second adopts a negative and pessimistic view of the ravages of global capitalism. In between the traditionalist and globalist positions lies the transformationist position. Transformationists agree that profound forces of globalisation are at work and that they bring both benefits and risks. This stance is cautiously optimistic. For transformationists, it is possible and necessary to steer the globalisation process through appropriate forms of global governance so as to enhance benefits and minimise risks.

The arguments of Hirst and Thompson tend to reflect the traditionalist position. They maintain that the differences between the level of global interconnectedness in the contemporary world and that which existed in previous conditions of colonialism and world trade around the turn of the twentieth century are not that great. International trade was then well advanced and national economies have not since become disembedded and integrated into a single global economy dominated by highly mobile transnational corporations. Instead, they are integrated into an international economy, with some divisions into trading blocks, and where multinationals with headquarters in national economies are the key business organisations. Hirst and Thompson tend to adopt the 'state as container' view of politics which maintains that states retain a very powerful political influence in the world.

The above position now tends to be a minority one. Most analysts recognise that modern technology has compressed time, sped up the pace of change and reduced the barriers of distance. For example, continuity of access to information is part of the new global environment. As communication is global and instantaneous, events happening in different parts of the world and communicated globally are received in countries at their own local time. Long gone seem the days (the early 1980s) when most people in Britain had access to only three television channels, each of which went off the air late at night, with the BBC airing the national anthem.

The effects of globalisation are arguably varied and penetrating. Change and innovation are vital to the survival of businesses in a competitive global environment. National governments are likely to find it increasingly difficult to operate as bounded sovereign entities in the face of world financial markets, business investment decisions and flows of information. Faced with these dynamics, workers have to be prepared to retrain or relocate and governments need to support this process, as well as keeping down rates of corporation tax, if they are to attract and retain inward investment. As countries open up to attract investment from overseas, they tend to also be open to its potential withdrawal. Viewed in this light, the impact of global capitalism equates to the impact of highly mobile capital over less mobile labour with governments relatively powerless but to support the latter in adjusting to the needs of the former.

Kenichi Ohmae argues that the forces of free enterprise global capitalism are irresistible and beneficial. This is the above mentioned hyper-globalist position. Left to itself in a free market globalised world, business finds the most advantageous places for operation. Such freely operating globalised business and trade enhances overall prosperity and should therefore be embraced. In complete opposition to the 'state as container' view, Ohmae argues that national governments will lose power as the forces of globalisation bring about a 'borderless world'. Attempts to erect national trade barriers or introduce subsidies would be counterproductive and governments can best help by promoting conditions of flexibility and free market conditions for both businesses and workers. Power becomes increasingly transferred to consumers who benefit from massive diversity and choice in global markets. From this perspective, there would be little role for supra-national government apart from guaranteeing a framework for the operation of global free enterprise. Ohmae claims a further benefit of globalisation to be a reduced risk of war between nations. This is because the capital of organisations is increasingly global and conflict would destroy abroad the resources of home based businesses.

Critics have suggested that Ohmae's position is reminiscent of the ideological arguments adopted by mid nineteenth century liberal economists on the civilising and wealth creating benefits of free trade. As such, it attempts to justify those processes which primarily benefit a few by emphasising that the benefits are widespread.

If national governments are weakened by powerful forces of globalisation, it may be very difficult to resist pressures toward a deterioration in some workers' terms and conditions of employment when coupled with the threat of unemployment that highly mobile transnational companies can bring. How can workers combat undesirable working terms and conditions imposed by a transnational business which can withdraw operations at short notice? Governments that try to restrict such practices are likely to find it difficult to attract inward investment in the first place and traditional trade union action is likely to be ineffective or even counterproductive as businesses are able to utilise cheap labour in developing countries.

Leslie Sklair adopts an opposing stance on globalisation to that of Ohmae. He takes evidence of the growth of transnational corporations as an index of globalisation. Sklair argues that the driving force for expansion of these organisations is the maximisation of shareholder profit. It is not the consumer with whom power lies under global capitalism but via the indoctrination of people through the mass media into the ideology of consumerism, the real beneficiaries are the corporations and their shareholders. Otherwise, the effects of global capitalism are largely negative in two interconnected areas. Firstly, it is claimed that globalisation brings about growing inequality between and within nations, and secondly it is ecologically destructive. Driven by consumerism and the quest for profits, transnational corporations hold little concern for the sustainability of resources.

Held and McGrew favour a transformationist interpretation of globalisation. Although recognising that states in a globalised world are losing some power, they can remain effective by working in conjunction with other political bodies to steer globalisation to maximise beneficial outcomes. This position will be scrutinised in more detail in a later section as it tends to be aligned with high modernist analysis.

Postmodernism – the illusion of politics

The effects of globalisation, especially with reference to the mass media, are an integral part of postmodern theory. For postmodernists, the positive connotation of modernity associated with the eighteenth century Enlightenment was the idea of progressive human liberation from control by fear and superstition through the application of science and rational thinking. Faith in the application of science to society brought the prospect of improvement social through social engineering. For Bauman, this metanarrative (all embracing system of beliefs) became associated in the twentieth century with the political metanarratives and collectivist ideologies of fascism and communism which were adopted by totalitarian regimes through which states controlled their populations through fear and repression. In Britain, the post war creation of the welfare state was seen by Bauman as another example from the modern period of the state attempting to engineer policy to conform to truth based on a single set of ideals.

Postmodernists maintain that the crisis that confronted modernity was the abject failure of social engineering based on political metanarratives to deliver the progress that it promised. With this failure collapsed the modernist metanarrative and from it postmodern society, devoid of an overarching metanarrative, and experiencing a fragmentation of state power, was emerging. Arguably, the watershed of this change in Britain was the emergence of new right anti-collectivist politics during the 1980s when the promise of improvement for the poor through social engineering gave way to policy of general improvement through free market forces. Abroad, the failure of social engineering was dramatically evidenced in the collapse of the Eastern Block regimes from the late 1980s. For Bauman, in the postmodern global environment, collective projects and actions collapse and the state retreats from being a focal point of both power and political protest. The politics of control by or fear of the state give way to a new type of fear that people experience in having to make choices in situations of individual autonomy.

Postmodern societies are media, information and high tech societies. In such societies, according to Lyotard, knowledge loses its monopoly as an all embracing truth, used by the state to engineer social control. Instead, people apply knowledge for its usefulness in a society of diverse interests. Through this relativistic and pragmatic use of knowledge, power becomes dispersed down from the state to various pressure groups and businesses who use information to advance their different interests.

Baudrillard takes the postmodernist position further and argues that in a media dominated society, politics recedes to the manipulation of symbols to convey political messages which have no necessary connection to any underlying political events. As political messages rely on endlessly back referenced media images, neither truth nor authentic reality can be substantiated and politics collapses into the realm of illusion.

High modernism – transformationism and the reconfiguration of political power

Social theorists who adopt what can generally be called a high modernist position argue that postmodernists go too far in their analysis of the decline of politics. Whilst it is recognised that globalisation has led to fundamental social changes, high modernists argue that the modernist task of rational understanding as the basis for social intervention should not be abandoned. They tend to adopt what Held refers to as a transformationist approach toward globalisation. This position shares some common ground with globalists in opposing the 'state as container' view held by traditionalists and acknowledges that global processes are intruding into national politics. However, for transformationists, unlike hyper-globalists, this does not mean that state power is in fundamental decline. They argue that governments can and have to respond to the impact of globalisation through reconfiguring their power and legitimacy alongside other institutions. This provides the governance to enhance globalisation by steering the process at appropriate levels. For transformationists, national governments must therefore be prepared to share some sovereignty with international (for example the United Nations), transnational (for example the European Union) and sub-state organisations (for example non-governmental organisations).

Both Anthony Giddens and Ulrich Beck draw attention to new levels of risk which emerge with globalisation. The risks themselves are manufactured rather than natural risks – they are a product of technological advances which were aimed to control other risks. Manufactured risks are often of global magnitude and include environmental damage, the consequences of global warming, reliance on internet computer systems which are vulnerable to computer virus, possible economic destabilisation through rapid and vast currency movements, polarisation of rich and poor nations, and international crime and terrorism.

Giddens points out that people in mature democracies appear to be losing faith in the capacity or will of national governments to tackle global problems as they can see global forces cutting across domestic democratic politics. In Britain, for example, a steady decline in turnout at recent general elections may reflect a growing lack of confidence that national government has the political purchase on events in a globalised world that it once had. Furthermore, faith in politicians can be undermined as more open information societies are likely to provide information on misdeeds and corruption in politics.

On the other hand, there is evidence of increasing involvement, especially by young people, in global pressure groups on issues such as world trade, poverty and the environment. These movements are usually less hierarchical than more traditional pressure groups and utilise modern technology for people to communicate and organise quickly, sometimes at a global level. Government, which tends to operate top down, can be slow footed compared to such groups which may even coalesce, as in the varied causes which came together under the umbrella of anti-capitalist demonstrations.

For high modernists, new and more appropriate institutions, guided by contemporary theory, need to be developed to help obtain political purchase on events in the face of new global risks. It is argued that we cannot be resigned to the intellectual anarchy of the postmodernists and the economic anarchy of the global free marketers. Instead, guided by the insights of a transformationist and high modernist analysis, political institutions need to be refashioned and sufficiently sophisticated to respond to new challenges. This relates particularly to the need to develop supra-national institutions which can operate to combat global problems and risks more effectively than states can individually.

What practical guidance can theory provide to improve governance in a globalising world? In Runaway World, Giddens argues that democratic political institutions are the only ones which are sensitive enough to respond to a dynamic global environment. Democracy therefore needs to be enhanced. For Giddens, improved responsiveness to people and processes requires a deepening of democracy. The following dimensions are emphasised:

1 Democratic institutions need to be devolved below state level to regions, localities and pressure groups which national governments should work closely with.

2 The expansion of voluntary and self-help groups requires the nurturing of a civil culture of responsibility. Free market reforms are not enough. They can damage the social fabric by leaving a void between the individual and the state, as experienced in the reforms introduced in Russia following the collapse of the Soviet Union.

3 The development of a range of democratic institutions above the state are essential to cope with global matters. These may include international organisations such as the United Nations, which have limited power over the sovereignty of state members, or transnational organisations such as the European Union, whose member states pool a degree of their sovereignty to engage more effectively at a transnational level. In organisations of the former type, it may be beneficial for member states to cede more sovereignty, whilst in the case of the European Union, an argument is put for greater democratisation.

A number of criticisms have been frequently made against supra-national organisations. Some organisations, such as the World Bank and the World Trade Organisation, were set up to promote the development of poor countries. A strong criticism is that grants, loans and debt cancellation usually have attached to them the requirement of liberal market reforms which arguably have often worsened the life of the poor in the recipient countries.

A related criticism is that wealthy nations are the main beneficiaries of free trade, yet they have the power to oppose free trade agreements when it suits them. An example here is the deadlock faced in free trade negotiations following the 2001 World Trade Organisation meeting on such sticking points as the subsidies paid to farmers in the United States.

Both the World Trade Organisation and the G8, which represents the world's leading eight industrial nations, have often been perceived as being only concerned with the interests of powerful capitalist nations. As a result, the meetings of both organisations have encountered massive protests, the most notorious being at the WTO meeting in

Seattle in 1999. A related issue is that these organisations are also sometimes seen as out of step with issues of concern to their own populations. For example, at the 2006 G8 meeting at St. Petersberg, attention was focussed on co-operation on energy and combating global terrorism, whilst opinion polls conducted amongst people in the member states indicated that they wanted issues of global poverty, human rights and combating infectious diseases discussed.

A further issue is that some supra-national organisations, such as the United Nations, lack binding controls over member states. For example, although the UN General Assembly can pass resolutions, these are not legally binding and cannot override national sovereignty. Furthermore, national sovereignty again prevails vis-à-vis the UN International Court of Justice in relation to which only about a third of member states, notably excluding the United States, accept its jurisdiction.

Against the backdrop of such criticisms, several pointers toward institutional reform of supra-national organisations have been suggested by J. Lloyd in 'The Protest Ethic'. Firstly, he argues that global institutions need to be based on a broadly agreed global ethical basis without appearing to be an imposition of the west. Secondly, it is likely that new and more powerful supra-national organisations and agreements will need to be established to form a binding obligation between nations if some of the most pressing global problems are to be tackled. Thirdly, institutions need to be established in a form which is more responsive to challenges than traditional bureaucratic hierarchies. Fourthly, these institutions must not be too remote but need to be in touch with issues of concern to citizens. Fifthly, governments will often find it beneficial to set up cross-national organisations sharing surveillance and intelligence to deal with problems such as the global dimension of criminal activity and terrorism.

High modernism, transformationism and third way politics

Anthony Giddens offers a broad analytic basis for New Labour politics and has been open in his intellectual association with 'the third way' approach in his text of that title. Applied in the context of British politics, he argued that the politics of the traditional Labour left and the old new right Conservatives have failed and are increasingly inappropriate approaches for the current age of globalisation. By demonstrating the intellectual foundations of third way politics, Giddens argues that the radical nature of this centre ground position will become clearer.

The politics of the old left regarded the motives and actions of private enterprise as suspect and in need of regulation. The traditional left distrusted the free market as a means of allocating goods and services. Instead, faith was put in state bureaucratic centralisation, in economic planning and the nationalisation of strategic industries.

Egalitarianism was to be promoted through redistributive taxation and welfare services delivered through the public sector. Top down planning was imposed to control the anarchic features of free enterprise capitalism. Politics following this model was adopted by the post war Labour government and, the author of this text would add, more reluctantly by post war Conservative governments.

The economic failures of the 1970s led to a resurgence of free enterprise thinking and the coming to power of the new right Conservatives in 1979. State regulation and an over bloated public sector were blamed for the economic sclerosis and social breakdown of the 1970s. The response of the new right was to cut down bureaucracy, pursue privatisation and reinvigorate the free market. With successive election victories in 1983, 1987 and 1992, anti-collectivist policies were followed.

For Giddens, the fluidity and interconnectedness of the new global world has rendered both positions inappropriate. On the one hand, the central control and planning approach of the old left is too top down and not responsive enough to the needs of quickly changing contemporary global markets. The suspicion of and restrictions on private enterprise are not necessarily well founded and would be counterproductive to investment and employment in a global environment of mobile capital. On the other hand, it is argued that relinquishing social responsibilities and allowing free market forces to rule is very dangerous to social stability in the fluid conditions of global capitalism.

So what is the alternative? For Giddens, the high modernist approach coupled with a transformationist view of globalisation leads to third way politics. This is not just about politics in Britain but, as part of a modernising response to globalisation, Giddens argues that it is necessary for all governments to take heed of contemporary challenges and cooperate in developing supra-national guidelines and institutions. Although sovereign powers of nation states remain, there needs to be some pooling of sovereignty for the benefit of all nations.

Capitalist markets cannot be banned or overregulated. At one extreme, the collapse of the old Eastern Block command economies shows that such central planning cannot cope with globalisation. At the other extreme, however, left to their own devices, free markets will wreak havoc. Giddens suggests that markets need to be improved by governmental action, but not a centralist approach. Instead, more institutions both above and below the state need to be developed to improve the workings of the market and offer safeguards against its negative effects. For example, the world economy is now so integrated that the impact of financial crises could be swift, major and extensive. This does not mean turning away from global capitalism but setting up institutions for both surveillance and fast response.

Man's impact on the environment is bringing global changes. This again does not mean turning away from modernisation and shackling businesses. Often technology provides solutions. Thus, waste is now increasingly becoming a resource and the knowledge economy produces more with less resources. However, the increasingly global nature of risk does mean that globally agreed political responses with teeth and based on science need to foster ecological responsibility in both producers and consumers.

New Labour – the radical centre?

There has been much debate over the policies and ideology of New Labour. Has it betrayed the values and goals of the old Labour Party? Is it bereft of ideological guiding principles and preoccupied with pragmatic decision making? Is it little different from new right Conservatism but with a limited social dimension? In this section, a brief account of New Labour policy and its intellectual basis will be offered.

The 'third way' tag and official re-branding of Labour as New Labour emphasises a break from the old ideologies of the post war political left (collectivism) and more recent new right approach to conservatism (anti-collectivism). Respectively, these ideological positions prioritised the state and public sector or the deregulated private sector as superior models for organising society and delivering services. Unlike the new right, New Labour retains the view that there is such a thing as the common good, but just what this common good is and how it can best be achieved mark New Labour off from traditional Labour.

Given the high tech nature of the contemporary economy, the break up of the old class structure and the decline of class politics, New Labour has not put itself forward as a party of the working class. Rather, it has managed to broaden its appeal to attract electoral support from across a broad range of occupations.

Reform of the public services has been central to Labour's modernisation agenda and exemplifies its third way approach. It is argued that whilst the goal of providing good quality public services remains, the means of achieving this must be more flexible. The old model of state provided and top down planned public service provision is argued to be insufficiently responsive to user needs and modernisation. By contrast, an emphasis on the free market, privatisation and contracting out has arguably damaged public services. New Labour's position is less ideologically fundamentalist than either of these approaches. It relies on breaking down boundaries and the ideological divide between public sector provision and private sector provision. It may be that in a number of cases, the resources for public services can be maximised by public and private partnership arrangements. The exact configuration for the provision of different public service projects will be a matter of analysis in each case.

New right reforms placed emphasis on the individual and tended to neglect 'society'. A criticism of this emphasis is that a social void tended to be left between the state and the free market. Reminiscent of Durkheim's earlier suggestions for engineering a more integrated society, an emphasis is placed by New Labour on the need for more intermediate level institutions such as voluntary groups to help bind civil society and encourage people in civic responsibilities.

For New Labour, it is the role of government to help create the conditions for both business and workers to adapt to global change. Given the enhanced challenges of global competition, the government has attempted to work with the grain of capitalism by promoting a flexible labour market underpinned by retraining to encourage economic competitiveness and inward investment. This is referred to as the creation of a 'magnet economy' of skilled labour in which the government attempts to combine the economic competitiveness of a market economy with social justice goals of fairness through such safeguards as the minimum wage.

New Labour has attempted to enhance opportunity of the many by maximising opportunities for participation in work to those who may otherwise have been excluded (for example the unskilled and single parents). In doing so, it has balanced the left derived principle of rights with the right orientated principle of obligations. This means that the government provides schemes, including retraining and child care, to help people to become self-supporting, but emphasises that it is their responsibility to take advantage of such opportunities.

On the question of equality, New Labour dismisses the conception of equality of outcome as a relic of old Labour which would be completely inappropriate in a market driven global world. Instead, equality should be seen primarily in terms of opportunity. There are problems here however, which tend to get side stepped. For example, Giddens points out that the diverse outcomes of equality of opportunity for one generation can lead to inequality of opportunity for the next generation. Little is said by Giddens or New Labour on whether or how this can be countered. Furthermore, society has itself by some measures become increasingly unequal in the distribution of income, not just during the period of new right government but also since New Labour has come to power. In this context, the Labour government has been remarkably quiet on the issue of executive and director pay packages and massive city bonuses, all of which are way above the settlements that lower paid workers have had to accept.

It could be argued that those who oppose the third way and criticise it as an amorphous compromise with no real compass bearing tend to do so if they are rooted in the old left or right ideological opposition and models of the past. For Giddens, by abandoning these redundant positions, it can be appreciated that politics of the third way has a dynamic cutting edge necessary for coming to terms with and managing the challenges of globalisation where past approaches would fail.

If the logic of Giddens' position is sound and heeded, we should expect a degree of convergence to take place in both national and supra-national politics around social democratic third way politics. The powerful intellectual underpinning of New Labour's position and their achievements up to 2008 of continuous economic growth and the creation of employment throws down a major challenge to the British Conservative Party. Although under David Cameron's leadership they have promoted a more caring and modernising image, there at present remains some doubt over the substance of their position. How far will they be prepared to abandon their new right past and move onto the ground already occupied by New Labour?

8: Sociology of Religion

Abstract

In this chapter, the reader is alerted to the need to suspend personal religious or anti-religious beliefs so as to approach the study of religion dispassionately and sociologically. Sociology does not attempt to answer questions about the existence of a god but analyses religions as belief systems and how they operate within society. To do so, the reader will need to be prepared to consider different ways of defining religion, some of which go beyond religion as conventionally defined.

Some of the key terminology utilised in the sociology of religion is explained, followed by a study of the role of religion in society from the vantage point of the modern sociological perspectives of functionalism, Marxism, phenomenology and social action theory.

The question of secularisation is addressed. Secularisation is defined as the declining importance of religion which is associated with the process of modernisation. The secularisation debate is introduced in the context of the Enlightenment which pitted rational scientific thinking against religious belief systems. The question of secularisation is also discussed in terms of the reliability and validity of data and touches on methodological disputes between positivists and phenomenologists. The issue of secularisation is later returned to, less as a methodological dispute within sociology but more in terms of the possible resurgence of religion in the context of globalisation. Fundamentalism is defined and related to this context.

The apparent divide between science and religion is examined in this chapter with reference to the positivist theory of Comte. This examination is used to illustrate that social scientific theory can also have religious significance.

Contemporary disputes within the church in terms of tradition versus reform reflect debates within society. Those raised here will be the issues of gender equality (the ordination of women priests) and sexuality (the ordination of gay priests).

Postmodernist and high modernist theoretical perspectives on religion are finally considered. Postmodern theory characterises contemporary society in terms of diversity of belief systems which consumers are free to choose from and move between as lifestyle options. For some high modernists, a world of diversity, rapid change, and uncertainty holds the risk of attraction to the certainty of religious fundamentalism.

The sociological challenge

Religion can be one of the most sensitive of topics to approach sociologically. Its study raises a number of obvious and less obvious problems for the layman to confront. An obvious problem is that the study of religion can tap a person's profound beliefs, feelings, emotions and deeply held convictions. The individual may not even be that aware of holding such beliefs, but if so, perhaps the greater is the risk of value judgements intruding into analysis. Measuring the extent of religious belief in society is itself a complex issue. However, given their own beliefs, people may be predisposed to viewing evidence differently. Thus, the response to evidence of decline in religious belief from a believer may be to dismiss it or lament a presumed associated decline in moral standards. Alternatively, to an atheist, such evidence may be welcomed as indicating progress from the grip of dogma and superstition. Arguably, atheism is just as much a belief system as religion. The challenge for the sociologist is to step back and attempt to suspend such judgements.

As sociologists, we must also be prepared to break away from pursuing the theological question of the existence of god(s). This is not a question tackled directly in sociology but one for theologians and philosophers. Sociological analysis is on a different plane; religions are viewed as systems of belief which serve human and social purposes. Sociologists are thus interested in studying how religion sanctifies moral values which influence and guide behaviour. This secular approach can lead to an expansiveness in the definition of religion, since belief systems not conventionally viewed as religions, for example political ideologies, may perform similar functions. These belief systems are often referred to as 'quasi religions', a definition which the believer may find difficult to accept.

Neither is it the role of sociology to compare the plausibility of different systems of religious belief. If sociologists are to compare religions, it is in terms of their impact on behaviour and society. From this vantage point, key questions include the following: to what extent do religions tend to promote social harmony or conflict? In what ways do they primarily support tradition or help bring about social change? What opportunities do they offer or exclude to different social groups? What is the relationship between religion and politics in terms of controlling peoples' lives?

A further issue relates to disagreements within sociology over the extent to which science can lay claim to a different and superior way of establishing the truth than religion. This would lead to the need to be prepared to examine certain assumptions about the nature and practice of science.

Religious belief systems also raise the question of ethnocentricity. Socialisation into a particular religious tradition through family or broader cultural influences may incline the believer to view the religions of other cultures as strange or incredible, bizarre or inferior. But this outlook is likely to be reciprocated – a similar view is likely to be applied by those of other religious and cultural traditions to our beliefs. The sociologist must be prepared to step back from such ethnocentricity and partisanship and examine the relationship between religious belief systems and the different ways of life that they sanction.

Definition of main concepts

A **belief system** comprises an integrated and self-contained set of ideas which give a community of adherents a shared understanding of the world. The interconnection of ideas can make belief systems resistant to criticism and change. Ultimately, they rely on followers retaining faith in the basic principles upon which the system is based. Religions are classic cases of belief systems, but there is debate in sociology as to how different they are to other systems of thinking such as the sciences.

Defining **religion** is problematic and disputes within sociology regarding the pervasiveness of religion in society and its effects partly relate to the application of different definitions. Attempts to provide a definition of religion may vary in emphasising the importance of such different aspects as religious institutions, rituals, beliefs, sacred texts, or supernatural beings. For example, it has been suggested that a universally applicable feature of all religions is their claim that supernatural beings have a governing effect over events on earth. This definition derives from the work of Ronald Robertson. Anthony Giddens adopts what shall be seen later as a more Durkheimian definition of religion. He regards its universal features to include: the existence of sacred symbols which elicit a feeling of reverence from a believer; engagement in ritual activities by a community of believers; and places separated from everyday activities in which ceremonies can take place.

Some definitions can be criticised as being too exclusive – being rather narrow, they would exclude some phenomena which are broadly agreed to be religions. Robertson's definition of religion, for example, would exclude Confucianism. By contrast, other definitions may be so broad and inclusive that they could include as religions some phenomena which many would discount. For example, if religion includes any system of beliefs through which followers acquire an answer to ultimate questions of life, Marxism could possibly be included as a religion. It is important to be aware in this chapter of the variable scope of definitions applied by different sociologists.

It is not always easy to distinguish whether certain beliefs or activities should be referred to as religion or magic. In principle, religion tends to refer to matters of public well being and the engagement in ritual to these ends by a community of believers. In usually recognising the existence of supernatural powers or beings, then the attitude of believers is likely to be one of conciliation and humility toward these powers as benign in the hope of intervention bringing beneficial outcomes.

By contrast, **magic** tends to be practiced in small groups or by individuals. It can include the belief that occult forces can be manipulated by a specialist, such as a magician, to cast a spell on certain others, usually to perform harm. Voodoo or vengeance magic would come under this category. It may also include individual acts of ritual which are thought to bring good luck or the belief in fortune telling. The rituals that some sports people engage in, in the hope of continuing their success, may therefore be examples of magical superstition. The evolutionary anthropologist E.B Tylor referred to the existence of such rituals and beliefs in the contemporary context as 'survivals'; they survive as a relic of more primitive times.

Distinguishing between religion and magic is not always a clear-cut matter and can be fraught with the problem of pejorative judgement.

As well as in the form of belief systems and ritual, religion can be studied sociologically in terms of organisational types. At a general level, the classification of **religious organisations** includes church, denomination and sect. A **church** is a large and formal religious organisation, run by a hierarchy of professional specialists. It is usually closely allied to the policies of the state and, being part of the establishment, is closely identified with by the upper echelons of society. Church membership is relatively open and conducive to full participation in broader social life. The Catholic Church in the Middle Ages can be seen as a strong example of this organisational type, whereas in more pluralistic contemporary societies some organisations loosely referred to as 'churches' may have some of the characteristics of denominations.

A **denomination** is an intermediate level of religious organisation, between that of church and sect. It does not have the extent of universal appeal within society as does a church. It is likely to be more removed from close identification with state policies than a church and less supported by the upper classes. It does not tend to place heavy prescriptions on the way that members should live their lives and is conducive to their full participation in mainstream society. As in the case of nineteenth century

Methodism, a denomination may grow out of a smaller and more radical group, a sect, which has broken away from an established church but 'cooled down' in fervour, compromised its strictures and grown.

Sects are small and often intensive belief groups, forming religious communities which originate as dissenting groups from churches that they condemn as having compromised their teachings. Sects may attract larger proportions of members who oppose the state and the ways and values of mainstream society. Quakers and the early Wesleyan Methodists are examples of religious sects. The expectation of deep commitment may mean, in certain types of sect, that membership requires the withdrawal from participation in mainstream society and living a highly prescribed way of life. Proof of conversion experience and the undergoing of initiation ceremonies may be necessary for entry into a sect.

Even within sociology one can find definitional and classificatory inconsistencies in the use of the terms sect and cult. Both exist on a similar small-scale and may reject the ways of mainstream society. The main distinction usually made is that a **cult** is a new religion, not, as in the case of a sect, a breakaway from an existing church, but this is not always an easy distinction to apply. For example, should Transcendental Meditation, a derivative of Hindu religious beliefs, be referred to as a sect or a cult? Cults tend to be more deviant from orthodox religions. They may to be highly ritualistic and through their own signs and symbols contain esoteric knowledge which they attempt to keep secret to their followers. A diversity of belief systems and degrees of organisational intensity, ranging from an interest in astrology toward the one extreme to membership of the Heaven's Gate movement at the other, have been referred to as cults. Furthermore, if a cult claims to be able to cultivate supernatural powers, offered in service to individual customers, as in the case of spiritualism, this may be classified as magic rather than religion.

Millenarian movements are groups who anticipate fundamental world change through supernatural intervention. Such intervention invariably offers salvation to followers and punishment to the corrupt. Millenarian movements therefore tend to appeal to people who have been marginalized in mainstream society and who feel oppressed or have experienced painful social change. Millenarian religions may predict a specific date of reckoning or read into signs foretelling apocalyptic events. Millinarian movements usually take the form of sects or cults, although more mainstream religions may also include millenarian beliefs.

The term **new religious movements** refers to a diversity of small-scale alternatives to established religion. A classificatory scheme for these has been devised by Roy Wallis. He identifies **world rejecting** religions as those which are highly critical of the beliefs and ways of broader society. Such movements usually establish a clear psychological and sometimes spatial divide between themselves and mainstream society through their own intensive community life. Members are often expected to renounce contact with broader society, including family, and undergo a process of conversion to the ideas and life of the movement. This can include the giving up of past identity and the acquisition of new names and uniforms. World rejecting religious communities may take the form of total institutions which impose intense control over all details of the lives of members through charismatic leaders. In such extreme cases as the Heaven's Gate cult (see box section below), intense control combined with millenarian beliefs has led to mass suicides. These groups commonly experience much social hostility.

The Heaven's Gate religious cult – a case study of a world rejecting cult

Leaders

Heaven's Gate was a world rejecting cult community. It was established by Marshall Applewhite and Bonnie Nettles in 1975. Within the group, Applewhite took the name of 'Do' and Nettles the name of 'Ti'. When Ti died, Do became the exclusive group leader.

Claims

Do claimed that he had been sent to earth on a mission from the 'next level', as had Jesus, to save souls. The purpose was to save those who could be saved from base human ways, since the day of reckoning was at hand when those who adhered to such base ways would be 'recycled'.

Belief system and opportunity

The belief system was explained through a gardening analogy. Do explained that from the level above human, occasional contact with humans was made. On such occasions, souls from the level above human enter pre-prepared human bodies. Do and Ti were themselves incarnated into human bodies to spread the message – an identical process and purpose to that of Jesus 2000 years ago.

At the time of contact, only some individuals receive souls. This gives them an initial capacity for growth to a higher level, but only under the guidance of the incarnated representative, Do. Do's purpose was to nurture souls, taking followers on a difficult path of renouncing base human ways, a path which only some would be able to follow.

According to Do, each 2000 years, base humans, like weeds, are 'spaded under' and a new cycle of human existence starts. The purpose of the human

---

body in this is to grow souls. Those who are able to follow the rigors of working toward this new level of knowledge and consciousness will ascend to the next level at the day of reckoning. This point in time is immanent and joining the group offers a window of opportunity.

Lifestyle

The group took the form of a highly controlled total institution in which salvation could only be possible through following the tutorship of Do. All members were given new names. Since the next level to which members were aspiring to graduate was sexless, within the cult sex was banned and sexual thoughts had to be guarded against as forms of base human ways. Females had their hair cropped, unisex clothing was worn and some males were castrated. The higher level was able to add to its members through the process of metamorphosis which members were being guided to achieve. Any slippage toward sexuality had to be admitted.

A list of regulations prescribed behaviour in great detail. Exact recipes and procedures had to be followed in the cooking of meals. Occasional fasting was required to cleanse the body. Even the process of shaving had to follow specific instructions. Members were watched over by check partners.

Since Do was convinced that the cult were being watched by the authorities, he devised deception techniques. The community were often on the move, and where they were settled, only a limited number of members were allowed outside the building in an attempt to deceive the authorities as to the size of the gathering.

Behind such controls there was always the threat that the cult offered members their last chance of salvation, to which Do was the only one who held the key.

Science

The imagery of science took numerous forms. It was claimed that Do and Ti had arrived on earth in UFOs. A group member explained that to rise to the next level of consciousness was just like reprogramming a human computer brain with next level knowledge. Web sites were frequently used to propagate the cult's message. The appearance of the Hale-Bopp comet was taken by Do as a sign from Ti that a spaceship was arriving to evacuate the group who would be saved from the spading under process. Even the costumes that group members wore on the goodbye video had space insignia on them.

Evacuation

On 22 March, 1997, in preparation for evacuation, the 39 group members took their lives, mainly through the ingestion of pain killer mixed in apple sauce. The scene of the mass suicide showed the bodies laid out in a highly organised fashion in an attitude of serene countenance.

By contrast, **world affirming** religions focus on developing the spiritual powers of individuals to cope within society. They therefore enable followers to positively embrace mainstream society and are far less intrusive into their lives than world rejecting religions tend to be. These religions sometimes appeal to high profile celebrity figures, as in the case of the attraction of the Beatles to Transcendental Meditation and Tom Cruise to Scientology, as they offer means of happiness and coping within the world rather than change of it. They actively market themselves, sell their services and seek widespread participation.

World accommodating religions can be distinguished from each of the above types in that they are not driven by criticism of broader society or the enhancement of success within it. They tend to become established through process of breakaway from churches or denominations and therefore in line with the earlier definition will be sects. The usual cause of their breakaway is the quest for religious and spiritual purity (as, for example, with Neo-Pentecostalism) which it is believed the parent organisation has compromised. Such religions are therefore more preoccupied with issues of doctrine and make little imposition into the everyday lives of their followers.

Despite evidence of the growth of new and non-western religions in western societies in recent times, an enduring debate in sociology surrounds the question of **secularisation**. Secularisation is the view that the process of modernisation brings with it a decline in the significance of religion. Its advance is often related to the progress of scientific knowledge and industrialisation which are accompanied by rational explanation of and control over the world. It is argued that the advance of rational thinking inclines behaviour toward efficiency and change and undermines tradition and religious beliefs. All this suggests that science and religion are opposed ways of thinking and are inversely related – the more there is of one, the less there is of the other. Most sociological theorists involved in establishing the foundations of the discipline during the modern period were convinced that forces of secularisation were powerfully at work, although some contemporary theorists have been more cautious.

Founding sociological perspectives on religion:

Functionalism – the social utility of religion

Functionalism is a theory of social utility. In the case of religion, it therefore focuses on how religion benefits society or promotes social well being. This perspective adopts a holistic approach; religion is seen as giving sanction to a single body of values that provide constrains on individual behaviour, thereby integrating society.

Early functionalist approaches to religion were heavily influenced by the social destabilisation of the French Revolution of 1789. Auguste Comte, writing between the 1820s and 1850s, was pained by what he saw as the anarchy of the times, but believed that a new stable social order was on the horizon. From the perspective developed by Comte, the condition of society is largely determined by the prevailing condition of knowledge about society. For example, the Catholic Church had provided social stability through the Middle Ages because Catholicism was a coherent doctrine that bound the individual to society in a series of religiously sanctioned duties which provided powerful moral constraints on behaviour. However, throughout the eighteenth century, Enlightenment writers were attacking the dogmatic teachings of the Catholic Church with rational, scientific and atheistic critiques which promoted ideas of individual rights as opposed to religious duties. According to Comte, this intellectual attack on the integrated belief system of Catholicism undermined the religious consensus which had upheld the old social order of feudalism and helped to precipitate the French Revolution which was followed by a protracted period of social destabilisation.

Comte argued that the re-establishment of a stable social order required a new and positive coherent social doctrine to bind people to society. He maintained that as knowledge progresses, science must replace religion in this constructive role. In this future 'positivist' society, experts would use social science to analyse and organise society and science would operate as an integrating body of beliefs for the populace as religion once had.

What was the basis of Comte's certainty about the future? For Comte, the driving force for social change was change in dominant systems of thinking. He believed that he had uncovered laws of progress in human thinking from which he was able to anticipate the immanence of the positivist society. These laws he referred to as the law of the three stages and the hierarchy of the sciences.

The law of the three stages posited that all areas of knowledge progress sequentially through three different types of thinking: the theological, the metaphysical and the scientific. In theological thinking, the behaviour of phenomena is explained in terms

201

of the volition of divinities. Metaphysical thinking explains phenomena in terms of mysterious forces inherent in the phenomena. Eventually, through rigorous observation, notions of mysterious forces give way to the establishment of concrete scientific laws which explain the behaviour of phenomena in terms of causes.

Comte maintained that all phenomena actually operated according to scientific laws which were of different levels of complexity depending on the phenomena concerned. The hierarchy of the sciences represented this ascending order of complexity. The complexity of the phenomena affected the pace at which scientific knowledge could be established in different subject areas. For example, our knowledge of the physical realm could be more easily and quickly reduced to scientific and mathematical laws. The metaphysical beliefs of astrology and alchemy could therefore make the transition to the sciences of astronomy and chemistry respectively, but the understanding of the most complex area to explain in scientific terms – society – had for the longest remained at the theological level. However, the study of society had progressed to the metaphysical stage during the Enlightenment where critical philosophy had undermined religion. It was now necessary and inevitable that social scientific understanding would form the basis of a new stable social order.

Comte's attitude toward the Enlightenment was ambivalent. Although as a rationalist, he acknowledged the great divide between religious and scientific thinking, he argued that the social purpose of each was much the same. The certainty involved in a coherent scientific understanding of society would form the basis of social regulation by leaders and a climate of faith for the masses appropriate to the modern age.

Following in the tradition of Comte, Durkheim's functionalist approach studies religion in terms of its social utility. However, he maintained that as societies evolve in terms of size and complexity, the essence of religion from a sociological viewpoint can get lost. Durkheim argued that to understand the fundamental nature of religion, it should be studied in its most primitive still existing form. For this purpose, Durkheim based his study of the essence of religion on Australian Aboriginal clan society.

In Aboriginal society, clans were social groups which claimed common ancestry. However, bands comprised the smaller social units in which people lived out their daily lives. Each clan was distinguished by its symbol which took the form of a plant or animal. These distinguishing symbols operated as totems – sacred symbols demanding respect and veneration from clan members and acting as rallying points for bands to come together and participate in collective ritual and worship. When engaging in ritual, individuals often experienced religious ecstasy and felt themselves to be in contact with a superior force. Durkheim wanted to examine what was the social function of these activities and experiences.

He argued that the purpose of religion is to assert the primacy of the collective conscience over self-interest for the benefit of society. This requires symbols representing the group to have sacred significance. As such, the individual conscience is impressed through the experience of ritual participation with respect for the community whose codes of conduct are given sacred sanction.

What fundamental truth about religion did Durkheim claim this analysis revealed? For Durkheim, religion acts as a unifying social force. All that can be rationally established is that when worshipping what they experienced as the superior force of a god, group members are in effect worshipping the personification of the superior force of society imposing itself over the interest of individual members.

Sociologically, the question of the truth of peoples' religious beliefs is of little importance. Conscience is a social product. Through socialisation, backed up by powerful sacred symbols, the individual internalises social guidelines demarcating acceptable and non-acceptable behaviour.

From the study of religion in primitive social groups, Durkheim claimed to have identified a universal and indispensable function of religion, equally applicable therefore to religion in the contemporary world. What, then, if the advance of rational thinking undermines faith in the supernatural and adherence to religion thus defined declines? Durkheim argued that a religious type function is indispensable to any society. As secularisation takes place, new belief systems with their symbols of allegiance are necessary to keep the collective conscience alive. Such belief systems can include nationalism and patriotism. Symbols associated with these belief systems, in the form of national flags and anthems, are kept alive in the minds of individuals at such occasions as political and state ceremonies and national sporting events which convey common feelings of national identity. These belief systems have been subsequently referred to as quasi religions – they are not strictly religions but perform a similar and necessary social function.

Writing in the context of a more individualistic culture of the United States, Talcott Parsons placed less emphasis on collective ritual in his explanation of the functions of religion. For Parsons, religion offers an umbrella of abstract beliefs and meanings that translate into more specific guidelines and recipes for behaviour which are shared by a community. It promotes the constraint and controlling of behaviour and an ordered society through applying ethical standards with sacred backing against which behaviour can be judged. These standards are reflected and further backed up by corresponding social norms and laws.

As well as constraining individual behaviour, Parsons emphasises that religion supports individuals by helping them come to terms with such experiences as illness or death which when viewed rationally may seem unjust. Serving such profound individual needs furthers social stability.

Marxism – religion as political control

The term 'economic determinism' is often applied to Marxist theory. This means that social ideas and institutions and the consciousness of members of society are shaped by economic forces. For Marxists, the most important economic factors are the means of production – the means through which production takes place. Where these are privately owned, a system of social class dominance inevitably exists. To perpetuate class inequalities for the benefit of the class owning the means of production, the ruling class, ideas that explain social reality also systematically distort it. In this context, religion acts as a highly conservative force. It distorts reality so as to encourage in the exploited class, who work in the employment of the owners of the means of production, an attitude of application to work and acceptance of its position in the social structure.

Important to understanding religion from a Marxist perspective is the concept of alienation. From this perspective, alienation is experienced under capitalism in the form of powerlessness, meaninglessness and lack of fulfilment which accompanies the use of one's labour as an object of others' profit in the productive process. Religion provides a belief system which fills this meaning vacuum. For exploited workers, it offers solace to a hard life but also promotes resignation to it. For example, Christianity creates the image of paradise in an afterlife which awaits the righteous (or eternal suffering for the wicked). Some austere ascetic sects even elevate worldly suffering to a virtue. Millenarian religions prophesy the world being put to rights only by process of future supernatural intervention. Religious teachings, therefore, tend to give supernatural sanctity to the prevailing social structure. Furthermore, religion has often sided with the forces of order and repression. When it teaches that human nature is essentially sinful or wicked, repression can be justified as necessary for the maintenance of social order. In various ways, then, religion stupefies the believer and distracts the attention of the exploited from the socially created situation of their exploitation and the need or possibility of improving life in this world through direct political action. It acts as the opium of the masses.

Marxism challenges religion as taking the form of highly 'conservative' ideology. It adopts a view derived from the Enlightenment that the condition of human nature is in fact not fixed, but is a product of the social environment. Human wickedness or 'sinfulness' is itself a product of the social conditions of oppression and exploitation rather than a fixed condition. It is therefore by recognising and eradicating the conditions of exploitation that we can improve social conditions to the benefit of human nature and strive to realise utopia on earth in the form of communism.

Within the Marxist perspective, belief in supernatural forces guiding events on earth is viewed as false consciousness. Notions such as 'divine providence' draw a veil of mystery over the real laws of social change. For Marx, social change can be understood scientifically by adopting a materialist view of history. From this viewpoint, the driving force for change is the development and ownership of the means of production and class relationships. To believe in god is to remain in an infantile state of believing in a benign supernatural power when the alternative of social scientific knowledge in the form of Marxist analysis is available to guide mature and responsible action to bring about the full realisation of Christian values on earth through direct political action. The creation of an environment in which the potential for good in human nature can be fully realised will be a society in which the need for religious distortion of reality will be redundant along with the exploitation that it perpetuates. Communism is therefore the true realisation of Christian values.

To sum up, Marxists agree with functionalists that religion tends to integrate society, but thereafter their analysis is diametrically opposed. Whilst Comte argued that the driving force for social change and economic development was the progress of systems of thinking, Marx argued that systems of thinking are determined by the economic system. Whilst functionalists relate religion to the promotion of social integration for the benefit of all, Marxists view religion as propping up exploitative social systems for the benefit of a minority. Whilst Durkheim related religion to the positive integrative function of promoting the collective conscience, Marx referred to the containing effect on class conflict of religion through promoting false consciousness. Although both perspectives explain forces of secularisation, for Marx, religion will only be redundant with the advent of communism, whereas functionalists argue that 'religion' will always be of functional necessity even thought the form it takes is likely to become increasingly secular. Consequently, even atheistic communist societies would require their own totems (as in statues of leaders) and celebrations which integrate society and operate as quasi religions.

Weber – religion and western capitalism

The social action approach adopted by Weber emphasised that action could only be understood with reference to peoples' motives. To understand motives for action, the world views or meaning systems that they relate to and how they interpret them must be studied. Amongst the most potent of world views for orientating action can be systems of religious belief. However, for Weber, in contrast to Marx, systems of meaning do not necessarily just emerge from economic systems. Meaning systems can have their own dynamics and can be important in their influence on economic change. Weber was therefore countering what he believed to be the excessive economic determinism and materialism in Marxist theory.

Of special interest to Weber was the relationship between religion and social change. As a result of comparative and historical studies of world religions, Weber felt that he was able to demonstrate that a relationship existed between religious belief systems and propensity for social modernisation or relative stagnation. In particular, he was interested in explaining why England was the first country to industrialise and what shaped the value system of western capitalism. Through comparative analysis, he believed that he had identified a key influence in the form of a religious ethic which was present in England prior to industrialisation but relatively absent in many other countries. This was seventeenth century Calvinism – a puritanical and ascetic protestant belief system which came to instil in believers a powerful work ethic.

Calvinism was a salvation religion. For Calvinists, only an 'elect' few are chosen by god to enter heaven. Although this choice was predetermined and fixed by god, individuals could not know whether they were one of the elect. Weber argued that seeking an answer to this uncertainty created anxiety for the believer. This drove believers to attempt to resolve the following tensions. Actions on earth could not change predestination. Yet believers questioned whether god could have predestined an elect who disobeyed his commandments. Conversely, it was thought to be likely that he would have chosen the elect as those who live by his commandments. From this, for the believer, following an upright life of sober dedication could be taken as a sign of being one of the elect. The asceticism (industriousness and single minded application to hard work and a simple life of moral rectitude) of Calvinism guided the believer in the resolution of salvation anxiety and the resultant achievement was industrial worldly success.

Weber argued that there was a conspicuous similarity between this religious ethic and the values of western capitalism – the one was conducive to the emergence of the other. Driven by their religious beliefs and anxieties, many Calvinists were enterprising in their values and behaviour in a pre-capitalist age. Calvinism was therefore a religious belief system originating in pre-capitalist society which promoted action conducive to capitalist modernisation. Worldly success could be measured in terms of profit derived from application. Profit maximisation required abstinence from luxury and focus on application. To the believer, time and money should not be wasted on idle pursuits, but profit should be relentlessly ploughed back into one's business. Calvinist salvation religion was therefore a powerful driving force for believers to live a simple, dedicated and industrious lifestyle. Furthermore, Calvinism tended to promote rational based and innovative decision making at the expense of following tradition for its own sake since profit maximisation required careful calculation of the comparative returns from different courses of action.

A number of important points emerge from this perspective:

1 Weber was able to show that a religious belief system was an important factor in the process of modernisation along the lines of western capitalism. Ascetic protestant beliefs sanctioned dynamic action and domination of the environment as a route to individual salvation. By contrast, eastern religions tended to emphasise in the believer escapism to spiritual experience, contemplation and harmony with the environment. Some of these societies, many of which were once scientifically and technologically advanced compared to the west, did not generate an internal dynamic of capitalist modernisation.

2 Comparing western societies, the prominence of Catholicism in a society did not seem to be conducive to early capitalist modernisation. Catholicism did not readily provide an ascetic based work ethic. The church conveyed an image of splendour and luxury, fostering the view that it was acceptable to idle one's time in comfort. Furthermore, it offered an outlet to the continuous anxiety regarding individual salvation through the confessional, something absent in Calvinism, and also encouraged monastic retreat.

3 Although indicating their great potential influence, Weber did not regard religious belief systems as a single determinant of social change or stagnation. Maintaining a multifactoral view of change, Weber recognised that religious belief systems would be one of a number of factors of varying importance in different societies at different times in history. For example, another favourable factor to the creation of industrial wealth in England was that as part of an island, less wealth creation was diverted to supporting standing armies than was necessary in a number of European countries that shared borders with potential enemies. Capitalist modernisation was influenced by a contingent mixture of circumstances, an important one of which was a Calvinist belief system.

4 For Marx, the economic arrangements of capitalism preceded and determined the nature of religion which acted as a conservative social force. Weber challenged this economic determinism and materialist approach to religion. In his study of the emergence of capitalism in England, he argued that conducive religious beliefs tended to precede the economic arrangements of capitalism and promoted the dynamic action which helped bring it about. But Weber did not challenge the materialism of Marxism with a similarly one-sided idealist account which would emphasise that ideas always determine economic matters. For Weber, the question of causality was always open to detailed analysis.

5 Weber argued that over time Calvinism proved to be a religious ethic that undermined religion. The rationality and quest for profit maximisation that Calvinism helped set in

train, even though driven by the quest for salvation, had focussed action on worldly business endeavour. Over time, the values and organisation of modern capitalism that had been set in motion were able to become self-sustaining, enabling rational based action to increasingly became a secular orientated end in itself rather than a means to an end in an afterlife. The forces of modernisation which Calvinism helped to unleash were creating an increasingly spiritless and disenchanted world which was dominated by the achievements of scientific and rational thinking and efficient bureaucratic organisations. Weber therefore proposed a powerful theory of secularisation.

Phenomenology – religion and ontological security

For phenomenologists, religion relates to the crucial importance to humankind of the creation of meaning. From this perspective, Peter Berger explains that religion operates as a sacred canopy of protection against the terror of chaos which would accompany meaninglessness – it provides ontological security.

Central to the phenomenological perspective is the distinction, raised in chapter one of this text, between the human and animal condition. Unlike animals, human behaviour is not highly pre-ordered by biology. However, human intelligence includes the capacity and desire to impose meaning on the world. Society is the product of this active creation of shared meaning and provides the civilising influence of the ordering of behaviour. Berger identifies the main components of this process as externalisation, objectivation and internalisation. Externalisation refers to the projection of meaning onto reality. The communication of shared meaning and understanding provides a social environment of belief systems and institutions which is experienced as an external objective reality – the process of objectivation. This shared social world becomes internalised into the subjective consciousness of individuals. As a result, actions of individuals take place within the constraints of society. The creation of meaning and the imposition of order thus acts as a shield against the terror of chaos that would otherwise be experienced by the lack of biological ordering of behaviour which is part of the human condition.

Religion plays a key strategic part in maintaining order. This is because it offers an ultimate legitimisation of social meanings and institutions by providing sacred sanction and locating them within a cosmic frame of reference. Religion assists human activity to operate within humanly constructed social constraints which nevertheless appear to have inevitability and provide a necessary framework of security.

Modernism and the secularisation debate

In sociology, secularisation refers to the undermining of religion by forces of modernisation. Key features of modernisation include the advance of scientific and rational thinking and their application to understanding an increasing range of phenomena, the development of industry, and the ability of humankind to predict and control its environment. Rationalists tend most strongly to support such changes. Dating from the eighteenth century Enlightenment, the rationalist tradition viewed science as a progressive force toward the establishment of truth in the face of religious faith, dogma, and superstition. The emergence of such thinking opened up a 'great divide' between religion and scientific method as the means to achieve certain knowledge.

To rationalists, science and religion are opposed ways of thinking and the two are essentially inversely related – the more there is of one, the less there is of the other. Therefore, as science, which employs logical method and fact based explanations, provides demonstrable knowledge of a growing area of reality, its progress tends to erode understanding based on religious faith. Furthermore, it can be argued that as the spread of science are technological advances enhances the ability of humankind to exert increasing prediction and control over the world, the need to resort to supernatural explanations of events or to appeal to supernatural forces for benign intervention decreases.

Rationalism and the Enlightenment were a powerful influence on the emergence of sociological thinking in the nineteenth century. Advances in the physical sciences held the prospect and kudos of the extension and application of science to the understanding of society. This was the aim of positivism – the understanding of society through observation, measurement and the rational analysis of data. It is not the purpose of the sociological study of religion to enter into theological disputes but to attempt to explain the purpose of religion in society and measure its influence. It is to the study of the latter that we now turn.

In the study of religion, the positivist tradition in sociology looks for hard evidence in the form of measurable behaviour as indicators of religious belief. An obvious source of such evidence is the availability of statistics on levels of involvement in religious institutions. Those who work in the positivist tradition tend to regard this evidence as reliable (it is standardised) and valid (it is relevant) evidence on the question of secularisation. For purpose of analysis, official statistics, particularly on church attendance and membership, are readily available. In Britain, the sources of statistics on church attendance in a broad range of Christian 'churches' include the 1851 Census on Religion and more recent church censuses. Overall, these statistics indicate a long-term decline in regular Sunday attendance from almost 40% of adults in 1851 to now below 10%. Statistics for church membership closely follow this trend although remain two or three percentage points higher. Baptisms and church weddings have also significantly declined throughout the twentieth century.

However, some exceptions to these general trends can be revealed when looking at the figures in a little more detail. For example, in Northern Ireland, figures on attendance and membership have held up at a remarkably high level. Over 70% of the adult population were members of Anglican, Roman Catholic or Presbyterian churches in 1995, with total membership figures slightly up from those of 1980.

Non-trinitarian churches can be distinguished from the above on the theological ground that they do not believe in the unity of the father, son and holy spirit in one god. Although the profile of change in non-trinitarian church membership shows variation between different religions, the overall pattern is one of over a 50% increase between 1980 and 2000. Survey figures provided by Brierley show that Jehovah's Witnesses and Mormons have the largest membership in this category of religions in Britain and their growth is above the average increase whilst some other religions are experiencing declining membership. However, the smaller Church of Scientology (also classifiable as a world affirming new religious movement), has seen its membership increase almost five fold over this time period. In total, membership of non-trinitarian churches as a proportion of all Christian church membership is relatively small but growing, the figures for 1995 and 2000 being approximately 8% and 9% respectively.

Membership of religions other than Christian has likewise shown a variable pattern of change but an overall increase, in this case of over 70% between 1980 and 1995. The greatest increase in membership has been amongst Muslims and Sikhs, together roughly doubling their membership between 1980 and 1995. In terms of the more general measure of percentage of the population, current estimates put followers of non-Christian religions at about 6% of the population. However, attendance and membership figures for these religions tend to be a higher proportion than those of the main Christian religions.

The term 'new religious movements' refers to a diversity of very small religious sects and cults. These groups often eclectically utilise ideas from a diversity of eastern religions. When applied in this restricted way, although they have increased their following in recent decades, estimates still place their membership at below 1% of all church membership. However, the term new religious movements is sometimes applied a little more broadly to include somewhat larger groups such as The Church of Scientology.

Overall, the figures indicate a decline in religion if religion is measured in terms of church attendance and membership. However, they also indicate a changing balance in which the monopoly of the main Christian churches has given some ground to a greater diversity of religions. This partly reflects the growing ethnic diversity of Britain's cosmopolitan population. The case made for secularisation therefore also accompanies evidence of divergent patterns and greater religious pluralism. Bryan Wilson has explained this combination in terms of the tendency of religion to be consigned to the margins of mainstream secular society.

Although the secularisation thesis is well established in the tradition of sociology and the above evidence appears to strongly support it, there are various reasons why caution may be necessary in this assessment.

Firstly, both the reliability and the validity of survey and official church statistics have been questioned, as has the preoccupation (by positivists) on measuring religion in terms of institutional participation. Different churches use different attendance and membership criteria upon which to construct their statistics. There may also be distortions in the statistics resulting from the vested interests of those who produce them. Fears of church closure may encourage the inflation of Anglican Church attendance figures whereas the payment of taxation based on congregation size is likely to have the opposite effect on Catholic figures. Furthermore, different religions vary in their emphasis on the need for regular institutional participation. In its emphasis on church hierarchy and ritual, the Catholic Church arguably places greater importance on attendance than the more liberal protestant tradition of the Anglican Church. And given the growing diversity of religious life, it is important to question the different emphasis on attendance or what membership actually means between the different religions. Does attendance and membership therefore really provide a comparable statistical basis of measurement between the religions?

Secondly, disagreements over measurement of religion can relate to differences over emphasis in definitions of religion between different theoretical approaches. Those who incline toward a positivist approach are likely to emphasise the importance of defining and measuring religion in terms of institutional participation because it is observable and reducible to hard data from which statistics and trends can be derived. By contrast, phenomenologists emphasise that establishing the extent of religious belief is more important than measuring action, and the assumption that belief correlates highly with participation has been questioned. From this position, David Martin has argued that the relatively high rates of church attendance recorded in the nineteenth century were partly attributable to the quest for social status which attendance gave at this time. As more people were attending church for social status reasons, the validity of the figures in terms of profound religious belief must be questioned and with it the extent of secularisation since then if based on a decline from these figures.

There remains some doubt about the validity of church attendance figures in contemporary times. For example, parents have been known to attend church to exaggerate their show of religious commitment for the benefit of gaining their children access to faith schools.

Thirdly, social surveys have been conducted which offer quantitative evidence on religious belief. They regularly indicate that religious belief is far more widespread than implied by measurements of institutional involvement. For example, a 1991 British Social Attitudes Survey found that 62% of respondents could be classified within three belief categories ranging from having no doubt about the existence of god to believing at some times but not others. However, such surveys may offer more of a challenge to the validity of measuring religious belief through church attendance rates than to questioning secularisation itself. Comparing the findings of a number of surveys dating back to the late 1950s, Steve Bruce found that there was evidence from this approach of a decline in religious belief. This trend has appeared to continue as the Social Attitudes Survey of 1998 found that only 58% of respondents fell into the same categories of believers as identified above in the 1991 survey. Furthermore, the decline was concentrated in the two strongest belief categories.

Fourthly, there is evidence to show that 'church' attendance rates in the United States are as high as about 40%. This evidence would appear to pose a fundamental inconsistency regarding the secularisation debate. Since secularisation is supposed to be intimately connected to the forces of modernisation, how is it that the most industrially and technologically advanced nation shows such a high measure of religiosity in terms of church attendance compared to Britain and other European societies? The answer given by Herberg in 1960 was that religion itself took a more secular emphasis in the United States and so, compared to the retention of old medieval dogmas and beliefs in European churches, was able to retain greater plausibility in a highly secular society. From the present viewpoint, perhaps this explanation overstates the differences to attempt to iron out the inconsistency.

Looking beyond the question of church attendance, there is little doubt that, over the long term, the involvement of the church in different areas of society has declined. This process is sometimes referred to by the term disengagement. In this sense, compared to the extent of its involvement in society during the Middle Ages, the church in modern society has retreated from many areas of daily life, including the provision of welfare for the poor, education, and as a major patron of the arts. The modern state has taken over as a main provider of these services. This process has arguably been accompanied by a degree of separation of church from the state and a cooling of relations between these institutions.

However, even general agreement on the process of disengagement has led to different interpretations regarding the secularisation debate. For Steve Bruce, through disengagement, the influence of the church and religion in society has declined. Secular state provision in peoples' lives has expanded and church provision declined. The secular state has grown in power and largely sidelined the church from the process of political decision making. By contrast, for David Martin, the distancing of church from state may have assisted the cause of religion. This is because in the Middle Ages, the church could be more easily corrupted by its involvement in politics. Detachment from politics has enabled the church to specialise in more purely religious issues and enhance its social status.

Parsons, from a functionalist perspective, came to a similar conclusion to that of Martin. For Parsons, structural differentiation was a key process of modernisation. This refers to a process whereby as societies grow and modernise, new institutions develop to perform increasingly specialised social functions. Old institutions, which once covered a broad range of functions, will lose some of these functions to emergent specialist institutions. Religious institutions are no exception as they are left to increasingly specialise in the promotion of religious based social values.

Modern liberal democracies are societies of diversity. In terms of religion, a single church cannot expect to be able to claim a monopoly of truth such as did the Catholic Church in a number of medieval European societies. Instead, alongside established churches has developed a proliferation of denominations and sects. This diversity has stemmed from various sources such as schisms from established churches, new religions and a growth in following of religious beliefs introduced by immigrants. But what does the growth of religious pluralism mean in terms of the secularisation debate? One interpretation, for example that of Bruce, is that a truly religious society will be a society of a single dominant faith. In such a society, religious beliefs can better perform a positive function of promoting social integration. The advance of religious pluralism would therefore tend to undermine communal integration and individuals would recognise that faith is a matter of personal choice. As mainstream religion declines, sects and cults, often critical of mainstream society, grow at its periphery. Sociologists such as Peter Berger and Bryan Wilson see such change as evidence of secularisation as individuals have to seek out more marginalised forms of religion on the periphery of a secular mainstream society.

Others argue that religious pluralism is compatible with a religious society. For example, Greeley points out that as some sects and cults require a higher level of commitment, intensity of belief and sacrifice from their members than is usually necessary with churches, sects and cults may be deepening religion. Furthermore, it should be noted that religiosity, measured in terms of attendance rates, is very high in the United States – the most religiously pluralistic society - compared to other western societies.

Social science and religion

Phenomenologists such as Peter Berger question the divide between religion and science that rationalists claim exists. They emphasise that in their everyday lives people need to create an ordered reality – they devise meaning systems which give them certainty within which to operate. This is referred to as the need for 'ontological security' and could include attaching oneself to a political ideology, support for a football team or following a particular genre of pop music. Whether or not meaning systems derive from religion as conventionally defined, it is argued that they still perform a necessary and similar purpose to that of religion in enabling people to make sense of the world.

From this perspective, Comte's desire for the establishment of a positivist society - the need for society based on the values and regulations of social science - can be seen in historical context as a response to a period of breakdown in society and established religious dogma. Comte's mission was for positivism to provide ontological security equivalent to religion of the old society but in a form appropriate to the modern world.

Contemporary developments with reference to religion:

1 Tradition and reform

In this section, a brief consideration of tradition and reform will relate to issues of gender and sexuality. Contemporary society has witnessed reform toward gender equality in the workplace, improved educational opportunity and achievement levels for females, and changing conjugal roles. Compared to these advances, there is substantial evidence available to those who regard religion as an essentially conservative force which perpetuates traditional gender inequalities. In most religions, male figures or symbolism tend to predominate. Within most religious institutional hierarchies, women have traditionally been excluded from power by being confined to low level roles. Furthermore, religion has often supported the subordinate position of women to men in the family and society. In recent decades, though, opposition has arisen between liberals and traditionalists on the question of the ordination of women in the Anglican Church. From the late 1980s, the Church sanctioned the opportunity for women to become deaconesses and later opened up access to the priesthood. Further reforms are likely to lead to women gaining access to the bishopric. The response of a number of male and female traditionalists has been to convert to the Catholic Church which had remained staunch in its opposition to such reforms.

On the issue of sexuality, homosexuality has ceased to be a criminal offence in Britain since 1967 and from December 2005 secular ceremonies allowed same sex couples to enter into civil partnerships. An issue which has recently ignited much feeling and debate within the Anglican Church is that of the ordination of gay priests. In England, Jeffrey John, a priest who admitted to having a past gay relationship, stood down from his appointment as Bishop of Reading in the face of much opposition from within the church. The ordination of Gene Robinson, a practicing gay, as Bishop of New Hampshire in the United States, has been the focus of much attention in the Anglican Church throughout the world. Opponents have been forthright in quoting from the scriptures, whereas supporters have looked to such reforms in terms of promoting a feeling of inclusivity for all members of the Church.

2 Secularisation revisited

Up to the 1970s, the secularisation debate within sociology was mainly a methodological one between supporters of rival camps of positivists and phenomenologists in which positivists were the main providers of powerful arguments and evidence demonstrating the process of secularisation and phenomenologists raising cautionary arguments. However, world events in recent decades have arguably heightened scepticism against the once persuasive case for the relentless march of secularisation. The changes which have raised caution have also moved the debate on from being of largely academic and methodological interest within sociology to matters of more practical and political concern at a global level.

From the late 1980s, the atheistic regimes of the Eastern Block communist states were collapsing. In many of these states, the church had been highly influential in pre-communist times. During the decades of communist rule, religion had been largely driven underground. However, as these regimes came under challenge from reform movements during the 1980s, churches were allying themselves with the forces of change. A good example of this was the growing prominence of the Catholic Church in Poland during the growth of the free trade union movement 'Solidarity'. As communist regimes collapsed, many societies witnessed a revived influence of Catholic and Orthodox religions.

These changes offer a fundamental challenge to the secularisation thesis, but the extent of religious revival and desecularisation are difficult to ascertain. This is because although religion may have re-emerged, there remains uncertainty about the extent of secret religious belief and practice under the old communist regimes.

Fundamentalists of any religion maintain that there is only one correct view on religious matters, which is the one that they adhere to. Basic teachings and principles, usually deriving from a sacred religious text, must be returned to. These principles cannot be compromised and must be applied as strict guidelines for behaviour in all areas of life. The rise of Christian right fundamentalism in some parts of the United States from the

1980s is a case in point. Christian fundamentalists believed that Christian teachings had liberalised too far and in so doing compromised from correct moral and religious strictures which derive from a literal interpretation of the Bible. The issues that they raised shared some common ground with the political right which was prominent in the United States (and Britain) during the 1980s – in particular, the need to return to such basics as the sanctity of family life and sexual restraint outside of marriage. The measures that some have been prepared to take have included direct action in the form of threats and extreme violence against practitioners at abortion clinics.

The actual impact of Christian fundamentalism on mainstream culture in the United States has been open to debate. For example, for Bruce, the prominence that it has acquired is out of proportion to its more restricted appeal and should be seen as a measure of religion standing out against the background of a largely secular society.

In Britain, 'back to basics' during the 1980s and early 1990s was more a political than religious campaign. However, more recently, controversy has been sparked by the inclusion of teaching of creationism, applying literal interpretations of the Bible to explain creation, in a small number of mainly independent Christian schools. Furthermore, New Labour policy has encouraged the establishment of faith schools, even though they require more liberal entrance criteria on religious grounds than some religious organisations would prefer.

The emergence of Islamic fundamentalism can be viewed as an attempt to return to literal and uncompromising teachings from the Koran in the broader historical context of the perceived corruption of an Islamic culture in retreat to the influence of westernism – especially the United States - and Christianity. A momentous example of this religious and cultural re-purification process was the Iranian Revolution of 1979 which overthrew the modernising and pro-Western Shah of Iran. The emerging state was effectively a theocracy – a society ruled by religious clerics in strict accordance with religious strictures. The rule of the Taliban in Afghanistan between 1996 and 2001 provides another example of rule according to fundamental Islamic principles.

The impact of Islamic fundamentalism was brought home most dramatically by the 11 September 2001 attack on the twin towers in the United States. These events, the reasons behind them and the response of the west may be opening up fault lines between Christian and Islamic civilisation and heightening religious awareness at a global level.

Contemporary sociological perspectives on religion:

In light of the issues raised in the above section, contemporary social theorists are often more cautious on the question of secularisation than the founding theorists were.

In fact, there is a tendency in much contemporary theory to acknowledge the growing impact of religion. How is this change explained?

Globalisation – religious cosmopolitanism or fundamentalism?

There is much debate about the exact nature and impact of globalisation, but to many the world can now be less understood in terms of unit nation states with distinct boundaries. Societies are increasingly intertwined as forces such as international investment and high tech communications operate across national boundaries. It is possible that these processes can generate greater understanding through growing contact between people of different societies and cultures. Both Giddens and Beck consider this optimistic possibility to which they apply the term 'global cosmopolitanism'.

However, it is also possible that globalisation may bring about new conflicts and global reconfigurations. For example, the growth of global capitalism can lead to western (particularly American) values, culture and ways tending to impose themselves on the cultural traditions of the societies that they 'invade'. The term 'cultural imperialism' identifies this process. As a reaction, in some cases a rise in nationalism and religious fundamentalism can result. Thus, the 1979 Iranian Revolution was both Islamic fundamentalist and a reaction against western influence.

Taking a broader perspective, Karen Armstrong views Islamic fundamentalism as a reaction to forces of rapid social and economic modernisation experienced in a number of Muslim countries. She argues that these strains tend to undermine moderate religious traditions and give rise to fundamentalism - a response which blames the west (often especially the USA) as the cause of changes which it reacts against. Hatred of America by radical groups is based on its perceived arrogance as a superpower and supporter of corrupt feudal oil rich dynasties which they oppose. In this context, terrorist sacrifices against America and the west can come to be raised to that of religious duty. Furthermore, the mass media now offers these groups the impact of a global theatre for sensational actions.

However, evidence of growing religious fundamentalism is not confined to that of the Islamic religion. At times in recent decades there has been evidence of a rise in Christian fundamentalism in the United States and Zionism in Israel. America is seen in many Islamic states as biased in its dealings toward the state of Israel, an enemy occupying Muslim land. For its part, following the Islamic Revolution in Iran and later the collapse of the Soviet Block, the United States has come to view Islamic fundamentalism as the new religiously inspired ideological threat to the west.

For S. P. Huntington (1993), enhanced civilization consciousness is providing such new fault lines of conflict. The cultures of civilisations are closely linked to the religious traditions of the major world religions. Civilization consciousness and religious fundamentalism are important ingredients in the heightened tensions which have emerged between Islamic and Christian civilization. This new global configuration, it is argued, is taking the form of a 'clash of civilisations'.

Relating the above comments to issues raised in the politics chapter, it could be argued that the forces of globalisation which promoted rapid change and helped undermine the command economies of the old eastern block have also been responsible for the emergence of new fault lines running along religious civilisations. As the fault lines have shifted from the ideological opposition of capitalism and communism to divisions between regions of Islamic and Christian influence, a process of desecularisation has been taking place at a global level.

The processes and features of modernisation identified by the founding sociological theorists include the spread of rational thinking and science, and the associated belief in the certainty of its explanations and solutions. A rational and scientific based society would be the end point of historical progress. However, a number of more contemporary sociologists argue that advanced societies are undergoing a fundamental transition to a type of society where these certainties become undermined. In such a society, scientific certainty is giving way to a growing diversity of belief systems, including sciences and religions, the superiority of any one of which cannot be absolutely established. Against this backdrop, there is dispute between supporters of high modernist and postmodernist positions as to the exact nature of life in contemporary society and how fundamental this change from the modern period has been.

Postmodernism – religious and cultural diversity

In his postmodernist writings, Zygmunt Bauman claims that advanced contemporary societies have reached a stage which is fundamentally different from modern society. In this postmodern society, individuals are free from the imposition of traditional or modern metanarratives (all encompassing belief systems) which offered all embracing truths as well as guidelines and constraints on behaviour. Dominant religious metanarratives in traditional society (for example, feudal society of the Middle Ages) engulfed thinking in religious dogma and superstition which provided an essentially non-optional ready recipe of moral guidance.

The modern period (industrial) witnessed the emergence of a new metanarrative of rational and scientific truth which promised liberation from the constraints of religion and the guidance of behaviour through rational intellect. However, Bauman argues that the modern metanarrative has enabled individuals to evade moral responsibility in their choice of action through the justification of rational and institutional based behaviour to achieve ends. This has led to many of the disasters of the modern era.

For postmodernists, what is distinct about the postmodern world is the collapse of metanarrative and with it a collapse in the perception that there are universal truths. Individuals are therefore free to search for intellectual and moral guidance from a diversity of belief systems and lifestyles, offering bewildering choice in a market in which they are the consumer. Change is relentless and choice of beliefs may take more the form of fashion or status statements as people freely move through different belief systems and lifestyles. In such a society, culture is fragmented and new types of religion will emerge as recipes for living which will replace the discredited metanarrative of rational and scientific certainty.

There is arguably some evidence to support this process of fragmentation in the form of a growing diversity of 'new religions'. Such religions may appeal to those turning away from institutional religion in a search for greater spiritual meaning in more intimate settings. They may also be chosen as fashion accessories and status symbols, something which could be referred to as spirituality shopping. In Britain, although in aggregate following new religions are growing, they still appear to have a very minimal following, but do offer evidence of growing diversity and choice in religious beliefs as adherence to mainstream Christian religions appears to be declining.

For Bauman, individuals in the postmodern world have to act more autonomously. They have to seek self-determination and self-construction in a social world without clearly prescribed models. People have to relate to a rapidly changing environment 'reflexively' – they have to engage in constant self-reflection and self-evaluation, processes which enhance moral self-awareness. Consequently, ethical debate becomes heightened and religious type agencies specialising in moral values may gain attractiveness. Ultimately, diversity places moral responsibility in the hands of the individual.

High modernism – fundamentalism as an escape from reflexivity

Anthony Giddens prefers to refer to contemporary societies as having entered a high modern stage. Unlike postmodernists who view society as collapsing into a state of moral and intellectual relativism, Giddens argues that rational criteria can still be applied to establish the superiority of intellectual and belief systems. However, societies face new challenges in retaining a grip of rational understanding in an increasingly complex and rapidly changing globalised world which generates a new environment of manufactured risks which offer unprecedented challenges. These include the consequences of global warming or the possibility of economic meltdown.

As well as new risks and uncertainties, high modern societies offer choice of belief systems. Individuals are required to relate to life reflexively – they need to constantly examine their beliefs and strategies.

In 'Runaway World', Giddens expresses concern that against the experience of openness in a risk society, some will feel the need to retreat to tradition or oppose with religious fundamentalism a response of tradition and certainty against a world of rationalism and uncertainty. Furthermore, what certain manufactured risks associated with high modernism and globalisation have in common is their cataclysmic nature. As such imagery is also common to religions, the experience that the world is running out of control can encourage responses in the form of religious revivalism.

For Giddens, the test of our time is to develop new forms of rational analysis appropriate to this complex world which will enable enough purchase to be possible so as to steer the juggernaut of change.

9: Contemporary Sociological Theory

Abstract

The purpose of the final chapter is to pull together ideas on contemporary theory which were introduced in the second chapter and built upon at the end of subsequent topic area chapters. These ideas are then taken a little further.

The emergence of contemporary sociological theory is related to conditions of social change, for example technological advance and the role of information and the mass media in society. It is emphasised that such changes bring about new opportunities and problems and with them a desire for the development of new theory to assist in their understanding. Key conceptualisation and theories through which sociology is attempting to understand the contemporary world include globalisation, postmodernism and high modernism.

A definition of globalisation is built up and technological, economic, cultural and political dimensions are brought out. Explanation of different positions on globalisation, based on the writings of David Held - globalist, traditionalist and transformationist - is then undertaken.

Linked with the question of globalisation is the emergence of postmodern and high modern perspectives. Some of the features of postmodern theory are explained and related to the social conditions behind its emergence. It is shown that whilst postmodernism offers little hope of certain knowledge and positive rational intervention in society, high modernist approaches retain faith in our potential to understand new challenges that confront us and the capacity of sociological theory to assist in rising to these challenges.

In trying to explain a rapidly changing world of extensive and immediate communication, some of the theory touched on in this chapter is at a relatively formative stage of development. The reader may therefore find it more useful in terms of the questions and insights that it raises rather than the more firmed up analysis of the founding perspectives.

Introduction – a rapidly changing world

In chapter two, it was shown that sociology emerged as a response to the fundamental social changes which formed the transformation from traditional pre-industrial to modern industrial societies. Theories were developed to explain the characteristics of the main social types and the processes, dynamics and direction of change. These theories explained how traditional societies, characterised by local communities and rural life, relatively closed social hierarchies, and the prevalence of religious thinking, were giving way to urban development, more open social hierarchies, greater geographical mobility and the advance of science. The development of social theory can be viewed in terms of a response to the need for 'ontological security' – the need to structure understanding of society brought about by times of fundamental change.

To many contemporary observers, it appears that fundamental changes at least as profound as those involved in the emergence of modern industrial society are again afoot in the world. These changes are posing new challenges to our understanding of society. Sociologists who adopt this view are arguing that new forms of conceptualising society are needed. There is, however, much debate on the nature of this society and how it can best be conceptualised, with the most radical positions asserting that society no longer exists.

Recent decades have been marked by the development and mass uptake of new technologies. Most notable of these are satellite television, computers, the internet and mobile phones. Computers have rapidly advanced in their speed of operation, capacity and their mobility - the latter in the form of lap tops. Mobile phones can now have internet facilities and the capacity to take and send pictures. Video conferencing enables the supplementation or replacement of face-to-face meetings by 'bringing together' participants who remain spatially separated and the possibilities of holographic technology to transport talking images of people has been demonstrated. In schools, the internet is now both an educational aid and its use an essential skill for the workplace. We are living in a world in which, through the medium of advanced technology, it is increasingly commonplace that communication is both becoming instant and overcoming past barriers of distance.

How is the use of new technology affecting peoples' lives? It can help to provide more efficient private and public services. However, our reliance on modern technology is particularly evident when systems struggle to cope with the job for which they were designed. This was evident in the case of problems encountered with computer systems installed for the London Ambulance Service and Air Traffic Control.

Modern technology also gives organisations access to information on us as consumers and citizens and the authorities are equipped with improved surveillance techniques. There is more information stored on us than ever before. On the other hand, advances in technology have also enhanced peoples' capacity to organise direct political action by establishing networks of rapid and flexible communication. In the case of the direct action taken by farmers and lorry drivers in Britain in response to high fuel duty prices in 2000, the use of internet and mobile phone facilities initially seemed to catch the government on the back foot. Other forms of direct political action made possible by the use of modern communications technology have included more global based protests such as those timed to coincide with G8 summit meetings.

New technology may be used as a weapon of sabotage through sending computer viruses and by terrorist groups recruiting and organising through the internet. Mobile phones have been used both to detonate explosives on a public transport system and also to track terrorists.

For all of its promise, modern technology introduces new risks into our lives. Such risks include the uncertain but potentially catastrophic effects of global warming and concerns regarding the introduction of genetically modified crops. Against these challenges, a key question is the extent to which technology may both help provide solutions and introduce further problems and risks.

From this brief introduction, the broader question to be considered in this chapter is the effect that recent changes are having on both society and peoples' lives. Whilst sociology can help to address these questions, it should also become evident that to do so sociologists must reflect on the theories and concepts that have been inherited from the period of the inception of the subject and be prepared to develop theories and concepts better able to shed light on contemporary conditions. It is in this context that some of the debates surrounding globalisation, postmodernism and high modernism will be reviewed in this chapter.

Conceptualising globalisation

Globalisation is a term that has become commonplace very quickly. However, it is sometimes used loosely and applied uncritically. It is therefore particularly important that both the term is defined and the processes examined as carefully as possible.

The writings of David Held offer a valuable starting point. Held has identified the key features of globalisation as the stretching of social relations, the intensification of flows, increasing interpenetration and the emergence of global infrastructure.

Social relations are stretched when they are able to cut across and transcend prescribed national boundaries or geographical regions. Stretching can be evidenced by an increasing range of migration and labour movement and the improved retention of communication that people have with their area of origin.

Flow refers to extent and intensity of communication which increases the volume of stretched interaction. It may involve the volume of migration flows or information flows as communication (relationships?) can be detached from the limits of geographical space by high tech communication.

Interpenetration refers to the complex relationship between the global and the local which can promote on the one hand global uniformity and on the other local diversity. The impact of global uniformity can be illustrated by 'McDonaldism' – the setting up of McDonalds fast food outlets with their uniform products and symbolism across the world. However, also through globalisation, consumers are provided with access to a growing diversity of foodstuffs, products, restaurants etcetera in their localities.

Finally, global infrastructure refers to the emergence of networks and institutions which may effect the policy options available the state. This infrastructure could involve the power of transnational corporations to influence labour relations policy, the emergence of super national organisations of global governance designed to tackle new global problems, or the influence of non-governmental organisations such as Amnesty International to monitor globally abuses of human rights.

For Anthony Giddens, the world is becoming more interdependent. A key feature of globalisation is time-space distanciation. Through the speed and reach of contemporary communications technology and transportation systems, past barriers of time and distance fall down and the world is experienced as if shrinking. There is little doubt that we are becoming socialised into seeing the world as a much smaller place than people just two generations ago would have, let alone those who lived in pre-industrial times. An important consequence changing time-space distanciation is that decisions directly effecting people, for example corporate investment decisions, can be made at ever increasing distance. The impact of such decisions can sometimes be destructive of local culture and opportunities, a process referred to by Giddens as 'dismembering'.

Analysing globalisation is a very complex process. As a preliminary exercise, different dimensions of the social - the technological, the economic, the cultural and the political - will be separated out for purposes of definition and illustration. In the real world, of course, these categories overlap. These dimensions will then be reviewed in the context of a classificatory system of rival interpretations of globalisation developed by Held.

Dimensions of globalisation

A key aspect of globalisation is the advance of **technology**. Technological advance has enabled the high-speed transfer of information within and across national boundaries. This makes it possible for financial institutions which are globally linked to transfer money from place to place instantaneously. It allows news events to be instantly communicated globally and other mass media information to be broadly disseminated. Modern technology has enabled call centres, servicing people in western countries, to be set up in countries such as India where the advantages of cheap labour can be utilised. In developed and even increasingly in developing countries, the technology of the internet is a commonly used means of access to information and communication. Rapid means of personal transportation over great distances are now accessible to more people, as witnessed in pressures for airport growth.

A measure of **economic** globalisation is the emergence of industrial and service enterprises, often giants, with a base in more than one country in the form of multinationals and transnational corporations. Following definitions employed by Hirst and Thompson, multinationals are international organisations with a home based headquarters and are thus subject to regulation by their home government. Transnational corporations differ from multinationals in that they can move their operations and even headquarters anywhere in search of the most favourable conditions of operation. They are relatively light and nimble footed and this can make them more difficult for governments to impose controls upon. For Hirst and Thompson, whilst multinational corporations point to an international economy, it is the activities of transnational corporations which are more indicative of truly globalised economic relationships. In reality, though, the difference is more a matter of degree. However classified, corporations such as Toyota, Coca-Cola and General Motors operate as global organisations.

Global communications enable businesses to utilise up to date intelligence on the state of markets and adapt innovatively to changing conditions and opportunities. In this environment, they tend to employ flexible production techniques in which they can change specialist runs of products based on the latest consumer demands. Employees therefore have to be increasingly prepared to respond to change in the form of retraining and new working practices as well as the possible threat of redundancy or unemployment.

In sociology, **culture** refers to an environment of meaning. It is conveyed through language and symbols and can be located in local environments and communicated by process of face-to-face contact. Culture is the means of conveying national traditions and heritage and it shapes peoples' values and understanding of the world. However, culture also arguably has an increasingly technologically related aspect to its formation through the output of the mass media. A key question here is the degree and nature of the impact of a mass media of global range on national or local culture. Is it likely to erode national cultural differences? May it help to promote an enhanced cosmopolitan outlook and tolerance throughout the world? Or may it promote cultural reactions in the form of assertions of national traditions or even the appeal of fundamentalism?

Politics is about the institutions of government but it is also about the distribution and use of power locally, nationally and globally. Traditionally, the key institutions of government have been associated with the nation and the state. The sovereignty of the state gives governments the right to legislate and form policy at national level. A number of questions bearing on sovereignty arise with reference to globalisation. To what extent may governments have to modify policy to accommodate the wishes of global corporations? How can governments respond to international crime and terrorism? How can governments respond to global environmental issues? In a globalised world, there are many pressures on governments to compromise a degree of national sovereignty for the mutual benefit of their societies. What is the playing field upon which compromise is or should be based?

Held's classification of approaches to globalisation

Analyses of the nature and extent of globalisation are varied. Following a review of a broad range of sociological contributions on the subject, David Held has devised a classification system of positions adopted. This classification system will be followed here and reference made to the above dimensions of globalisation.

Held applies the term **globalists** to those who view the process of globalisation as inevitable. Globalisation can be measured in terms of the growing extent and frequency of flows of information, communication, trade, capital etcetera. From the perspective of globalists, this has an eroding effect on national boundaries and the sovereign power of the state.

Those who adopt a globalist position can be differentiated into optimistic and pessimistic camps. An optimistic position is taken by Kenichi Ohmae who advocates the merits of global free enterprise capitalism based on the complete opening up of national borders to trade and finance. By such means, businesses and consumers can take maximum advantage of local specialisation in the production of goods and services and the total global creation of wealth can be maximised. Ohmae argues that in an increasingly borderless world economy, governments need to go with the grain of global capitalism, enhancing the competitive edge of their workforce by encouraging employee flexibility and retraining. It is argued that wealth will in time trickle down to poorer sections of society and to the poorest countries so long as free market reforms are embraced. This is quite an extreme globalist position which Held has referred to as 'hyperglobalist'.

A less predominant and more pessimistic globalist position tends to be adopted by globalists taking a neo-Marxist slant. Here, globalism is viewed in terms of the imposition of the interests of western capitalism throughout the world. The result is a deterioration in the terms and conditions of workers in the face of profit maximising mobile capital and increasing polarisation within society and between the richer and poorer nations.

At the cultural level, the massive expansion of commercially funded satellite and cable television and the internet can be taken as a measure of globalisation. A positive slant was put on the emergence of a global media by Marshall McLuhan as far back as the 1960s. McLuhan emphasised that communications revolutions are the driving force for social change and that the electronic media revolution held the potential for bringing the world together in a 'global village' of shared information to which our sensory perceptions would adjust. More recently, Ohmae sees the emergence of a common global enterprise culture accompanying the triumph of global free enterprise capitalism as positive change.

More pessimistically, neo-Marxists such as Tunstall tend to view global media in terms of the cultural imposition of western capitalist values on developing countries. From this perspective, the mass media has the power to impress on populations an external culture of consumerism against which an indigenous culture has little defence. This process of dominance is sometimes referred to as 'cultural imperialism'.

In the realm of politics, the forces of globalisation, as argued by Ohmae, render national governments relatively powerless to control their own economies. The mobility of capital tends to pressure states toward open market friendly policies so as to attract inward investment. For Ohmae, government intervention in the form of protectionist barriers in a globalising world would be damaging to the process of wealth creation.

Traditionalists adopt a sceptical position on the extent of globalisation. Hirst and Thompson, for example, maintain that the case for globalisation has been overstated. They argue that state power and national culture within national boundaries remains substantial. In terms of economics, they point out that there is little new in the nature and extent of international trade. For example, Thompson offers evidence that the trade to GDP ratio for many countries in 1995 was little changed from that of 1913. Furthermore, he maintains that most international corporations are multinationals. With their headquarters fixed in one country, these organisations can be controlled by national governments. Very few businesses are strictly transnational corporations that can move freely between countries and call the shots – the true index of globalisation.

A traditionalist position on culture emphasises that national cultures are rooted and quite resistant to the more ephemeral effects of the global media. Information crossing national boundaries is mediated through the prism of a national media, especially where public service channels such as the BBC operate.

For traditionalists, the focus of political power remains with national governments. Governments retain the ability to pass legislation, control their own economic and social policy and, where inclined, to defend the welfare state. They retain their own armies, police and intelligence services. Arguably, the development of modern technology in the form of information gathering and surveillance techniques has actually enhanced the power of the state.

Transformationists adopt a position somewhere in between that of globalists and traditionalists, perhaps a little closer to the former. They maintain that profound globalising changes have been taking place but, unlike globalists, they see no single and inevitable direction to these changes which are very complex and can work themselves out differently in economic, cultural and political spheres. For writers such as Giddens and Beck, although the challenges and risks associated with globalisation are great, sometimes new, and solutions uncertain, global governance is emerging and needs to be developed to manage these problems. The state remains a powerful entity but must increasingly work alongside a plethora of global, regional and local institutions to go with the grain of globalisation but also to tame its excesses.

Transformationists recognise some of the economic changes that have been highlighted by globalists, but do not view them in terms of unmitigated success or disaster as optimistic and pessimistic globalists respectively tend to. Although the global economy is capable of producing great wealth, it is argued that if left unchecked it could lead to a further polarisation between winners and losers within and between nations. Writers in this tradition tend to emphasise that it is possible and necessary to rationally intervene to tame global capitalism in such a way that international and national security and justice can complement economic efficiency.

For transformationists, the impact of globalisation on culture is complex. Unlike neo-Marxists, transformationists argue that cultural flows from the mass media are not simply one-way influences which are passively absorbed by populations. Different readings of standard media output are likely to form in the context of different cultures. Thus, although 'Dallas' achieved massive worldwide coverage, it was read differently by audiences in different cultures. Detailed research is necessary to establish the dynamics involved in the different readings of media output in different cultural contexts.

Transformationists such as Giddens strongly emphasise the need to develop new institutions of global governance to tackle problems of global dimension such as the distribution of wealth, international crime, the risk of global economic collapse and environmental damage. Governments must be prepared to cede some national sovereignty for the common benefit. Giddens sees the EU as an important model in the direction of global governance.

Reviewing the above typology, it is possible to extract from the different positions different consequences for the nature and role of sociology. For globlists, there is little that planned intervention can, or in the case of positive globalists, should, do to stem the headlong process of global capitalism. From this position, sociology would be reduced to little more than the handmaiden of free market economics. For traditionalists, a sociology similar to that of the founding theories which conceptualises society in terms of national boundaries remains relatively valid. For transformationists, there is both the possibility of and need for enlightened human agency to influence social changes. Sociological theories and concepts are needed to guide human action, but the new conditions require a creative reworking rather than the retention of ideas fashioned in a different age. We will review this position in more detail in a later section.

Toward contemporary theory

In this section, consideration will be given to some key insights into social change that would later be taken to a new level in postmodern and high modern social theory. The first is Daniel Bell's anticipation of a post-industrial society. For Bell, writing from the 1960s, capitalism was in the process of changing from a manufacturing to a predominantly service orientated, white collar professional middle class society. He predicted that service and information sectors would need highly skilled management to head flexible organisational structures. A managerial revolution would separate ownership from control of business, with decision making power resting more in the hands of those with knowledge and expertise than those who owned capital. Technological advances would allow the length of the working week to decrease and in this post-industrial consumer and leisure society, the importance of social class, class conflict and the appeal of ideology, all linked to earlier industrial capitalism, would decline. Likewise, the Calvinist self-restraint and work ethic of early capitalism would give way to present time orientation and instant gratification through the availability of instant credit and mass consumption. In effect, post-industrial society would deliver affluence to depoliticised consumers.

A further aspect of social change has been referred to as the transition from Fordist to post-Fordist production techniques. Michael Piore was one of the earliest exponents of this change. The argument here is that the fluid conditions of globalisation require highly flexible and responsive production techniques, more collaborative styles of management and highly skilled workforces – the features of post-Fordism. This is in contrast to the top down management and assembly lines typical of the Ford era of mass production in which standardised goods were turned out by workers engaging in low skilled and repetitious tasks. In the globalised world, rapidly changing consumer demand requires the quick response of flexible production methods. Workers must therefore be more highly skilled, prepared to retrain and be flexible. Governments and employers must provide education and training programmes for the benefit of organisations and in the national interest – a message clearly embraced by Britain's New Labour government.

Some accounts of change have adopted a neo-Marxist analysis which maintained that consumer capitalism had become the dominant means of social control and de-politicisation. For Guy Debord, a key figure in the French Situationist International movement of the 1950s and 1960s, modern technology, the media and advertising created product 'spectacles' which enticed consumers into a fantasy world of artificially created needs for the latest goods which were associated with images of happiness.

Situationists argued that in modern consumer capitalism, the world is fabricated by advertisements and images which entice people to live their lives through the objects of consumption. Goods are desired and acquired for their status value. Identification with stars and celebrities, who themselves help give spectacle to consumer goods, offers some compensation for the very shallowness of these consumer orientated lives.

From this theoretical position, peoples' awareness of the class divided nature of capitalist society, which emanates from work based relations, becomes hidden behind consumerism which addresses all equally. The image of happiness associated with luxuries and the latest goods is open to all. By such means, social control is raised to a new level. Aiming for such happiness fantasies, workers become trapped into working harder to spend. Through the 'false consciousness' of achieving happiness through consumption, workers are not just exploited in the workplace but as consumers they are also the ultimate payers of the cost of media advertising. A further tie and burden is that of the cost of consumer debt. This pervasive form of domination renders workers de-politicised. As consumers, they abandon the trade union for the shopping mall.

In contrast to the classical Marxist position, this and other schools of post war Marxism tend to recognise a greater potency of the superstructure, especially in the form of mass media advertising, to encourage workers, as consumers, to embrace capitalism. Thus, although retaining a Marxist perspective, such writers are often less certain that Marx was regarding the immanent demise of capitalism. Postmodernists have since taken on board and developed further such insights into the effect of the media on society but have largely abandoned the Marxist framework of analysis.

Postmodernity or high modernity?

There has been much recent dispute over the nature of contemporary society resulting from the types of changes identified in the first half of this chapter. A key line of demarcation is between those who maintain that modern society is being replaced by conditions of postmodernity and others who refer to change to 'high modernity', 'second modernity' or 'liquid modernity'. Although there is some commonality between the two main approaches which emphasise the fluidity and uncertainty of contemporary life, there is one fundamental difference: whilst those who refer to conditions of advanced modernism believe that even in a complex and fluid contemporary global world it is possible to still rationally analyse social conditions with the assistance of sociological theory and beneficially intervene in society, ultimately, postmodernists (although some are less radical) claim that truth statements about contemporary social reality are not possible, that authentic society ceases to exist, and that sociology as a rational quest for truth about society and as a guide to intervention is now redundant.

Postmodernism and the periodisation of history

Before the social condition advanced by a diverse body of thinkers commonly bracketed as postmodernists is outlined, it is necessary to review how they periodise history leading up to the postmodern stage. The stages they identify are traditional, modern and postmodern.

An early exponent of postmodernism was Jean-Francois Lyotard. Lyotard emphasised the importance of understanding the world through narratives. A narrative is a story conveyed by a narrator and social dominance is acquired through the ability to impose a form of discourse. The nature of narratives defines historical stages. In traditional societies, narratives took the form of fables, religious stories and legends etcetera. The acceptance of narrative explanations legitimised the status of the storyteller elders and reinforced positions within a closed social structure.

The transition to modern society was paved particularly by Enlightenment thinking of the late seventeenth and the eighteenth century which applied rational criticism to attack traditional thinking. Particularly important were French Enlightenment thinkers who applied reason to undermine religious dogma (for example Diderot and d'Alembert) and the veneration of antiquity and its thinkers (for example Fontonelle). For Enlightenment thinkers, reason held the prospect of liberation from the clutches of religious dogma and superstition and could be applied to establish universal truths, organise society and promote progress. Such thinking assisted the transition to modern societies by helping cerate the conditions for scientific progress and political and industrial revolutions.

Postmodernists refer to the dominant system of thinking accompanying the modern era as a metanarrative. A metanarrative is an all-embracing system of thinking. The modern metanarrative, derived from the Enlightenment, asserted that the establishment of scientific truth was superior to all other knowledge, possible, applicable to all areas of understanding, and beneficial. It accompanied a more open social structure in which statements could be judged according to the impersonal criteria of scientific truth rather than from a person's privileged position in the social structure. Scientific understanding could now be applied to all realms of the world, including society, and those with scientific and professional expertise acquired the power and status to control peoples' lives. This is the social context of the birth of sociology in its positivist (pretensions to science) form in the writings of Comte, Marx and Durkheim.

For Lyotard, the dominance of the metanarrative of science in the modern era failed to achieve the promised liberation. Instead, it created a sterile world of clinical efficiency, deficient of emotional intelligence and moral guidance. Technological advances accompanied by social disasters undermined faith in the superiority of scientifically established truth and spawned the conditions for the collapse of the scientific metanarrative as the context for superior knowledge and the transition to the postmodern world. Zygmunt Bauman, during his phase of postmodern writing, pointed out that the metanarrative of rational thinking, emphasising organisational efficiency, is by itself devoid of moral guidance. Associated with the modern propensity to try and create utopia through social engineering, it has been put to use by totalitarian communist and fascist regimes with disastrous consequences.

According to postmodernists, the scientific metanarrative is collapsing and leading to 'societies' (the reason for the inverted commas will be evident later) characterised by a plurality of belief systems. Only in such a 'society' where truth is relative can liberation through choice amongst diversity of beliefs and lifestyles be more fully realised. This is the postmodern ara.

The postmodern social condition – the end of society

Jean Baudrillard depicts the postmodern condition as one in which high tech mass media promotes a fashion dominated populist consumer culture in post industrial leisure and information societies. Everyday life is characterised by the elevation of consumption over production. In 'societies' where the creation of wealth is no longer a problem to our survival, we are surrounded by consumer products and messages in shops and massive shopping centres which bring together products from many countries. This experience comes to dominate peoples' consciousness. Displays offer meanings to objects such as new lifestyle images and shopping experiences, rather than focussing on their individual utility, and combine objects with the aim of directing purchasing impulses toward networks of products. Objects once purchased for utility become more acquired for the status associated with brand image. This is the cultural dimension of consumerism. The products of consumption are from diverse parts of the world and with heightened obsolescence and rapidly changing fashion become abstracted from context, promote social fluidity, and give the feeling of a 'society' without history.

The sprawling mass media promotes a bewildering diversity of images and information. This brings about brings about what Vattimo calls 'the dissolution of centralized perspectives'. A pluralistic world view undermines any notion of a single reality and a single truth and promotes the recognition of the contingency of all systems of thinking. In the postmodern world, in contrast to modern society, people reach emancipation not through scientific truth but from its single dominance.

For Baudrillard, we are entering a postmodern stage in which a high tech mass media conveys self-referencing signs and images (simulacra). Signs and images which once reflected reality have now taken it over and created a dead culture. They masquerade as reality and encapsulate people in a world where reality and truth are illusive. In this world, the 'real' collapses into electronic images of simulated events because it cannot be distinguished from the latter. This media generated world becomes the realm of experience – the 'hyperreal' – which replaces the reference points of a 'real' world by media produced self-referencing signs. The 'hyperreal' kills the 'real' which it artificially resurrects through self-referencing signs, rather like creating a theme park reality to replace authentic reality. Having no other reference, the 'hyperreal' (illusion) fills the void as the 'real' world is lost to systems of signs and images. When we watch events on the television, they reference other events on the television and in the newspapers, and so on. In this way, emphasises Baudrillard, the Gulf War was experienced, by those not involved, at a clinical distance, rather like a simulated exercise, as a surgical operation of high tech precision bombing! But what really happened?

Baudrillard argues that the phase of modern capitalism described in the economic determinism of Marxist theory, in which power derives from economic production, has been largely transcended. In the postmodern era, power resides in 'hyperreality' – one-way media generated communication to politically passive and privatised consumers.

In such a 'society', cultural production is everything and truth and reality are impossible to substantiate. This spells and end to sociology as an attempt to establish scientific truth about society and as a guide to tackling social issues. People become abandoned to their worlds of personal troubles, unable to meaningfully relate them to broader social structures as authentic society ceases to exist.

Or capitalism in crisis?

Whilst many sociologists believe that profound changes are taking place in society and the world, many do not agree with postmodernist accounts, especially those as radical as Baudrillard's. For example, David Harvey adopts a neo-Marxist interpretation of postmodernity which relates social and cultural changes to the economic base of capitalism in crisis. According to this analysis, during the post second world war decades, capitalism had delivered growth through the application of production line systems. Workers had experienced rising living standards based on systems of mass production of standardised goods. These modern techniques of production are sometimes referred to as 'Fordism', an assembly line approach to production efficiency pioneered by Henry Ford.

However, for Harvey, the oil crisis of 1973 brought a period of crisis to capitalism. The hiking of oil prices by the oil producer nations had a major impact on the economies of modern capitalist societies. Businesses had to be more inventive and dynamic in their quest for profit if they were to compete and survive. New post-Fordist work organisation and production techniques were devised in which businesses became lean, flexible and responsive to specialised markets. Work practices were changed. For many, security of employment diminished, and, assisted by right wing governments in Britain and the USA in the 1980s, the power of trade unions was undermined. According to Harvey, the intensification of time and space and tendencies toward globalisation were the result of an intensification of the work process as capitalist enterprises were driven by the quest for improved efficiency and profit in crisis conditions. Changing fashions were driven by free enterprise to buoy up consumer demand and achieve profitability by businesses showing superior versatility and innovation to that of their competitors. This economic imperative of the quest for profitability under new conditions of capitalist competition was the real dynamic behind a growing diversity of social fashions and interests.

Adopting a neo-Marxist position, Harvey believes that the Enlightenment project of understanding and improving society by means of intelligent intervention remains possible. Indeed, his theory is a theory of the social conditions of emergence of postmodern theory explained from a neo-Marxist perspective rather than a postmodern theory itself.

High modernist theories

The term 'high modernity' is used here as a general umbrella for a group of like terms also including 'liquid modernity' and 'second modernity' that have been identified in a previous section.

1 Liquid modernity and disembedding

In Gane's 'The Future of Social Theory', Zygmunt Bauman explains that his postmodern stance was only a stopgap position. Postmodernism recognised that the world was unlike the grid mapped by modernist theory and it alerted us to new uncertainties. However, Bauman announced that he was now abandoning postmodernism. He signified his change of position thus: 'The 'postmodern' has done its preliminary, site-clearing job: it aroused vigilance and sent the exploration in the right direction. It could not do much more, and so after that it outlived its usefulness; or, rather, it worked itself out of a job.....And we can now say more about the present-day world than it is unlike the old familiar one. We have, so to speak, matured to afford (to risk?) a positive theory of its novelty'. For Bauman, postmodernism was, on the one hand, too negative regarding the prospects of developing a coherent understanding of the contemporary world, and on the other, overly optimistic regarding the individual freedoms of contemporary consumer society.

Bauman now proposed a theory of 'liquid modernity' to explain the contemporary social condition. How does he apply this concept of liquidity? For Bauman, the transition from traditional pre-industrial to modern industrial societies involved the change from one solid social structure, through temporary liquefaction, to another solid structure. In this process, a temporary period of liquefaction disembedded people from the social constraints of a traditional society which had provided a fixed position in a hierarchy of feudal estates. The emergence of modern industrial society re-embedded people into a class system in which position was not so ascribed but where social mobility depended on people learning rules of admission. However, contemporary societies had entered a state of continuous fluidity. In the society of liquid modernity, the structures of the earlier phase of modern society have broken down and life is becoming individualised. People have experienced disembedding from the confines of a class structure, but they have been cut adrift with no clear social rules for re-embedding. This is the new freedom of abandonment and uncertainty, which generates in the individual anxiety in the relentless quest for security and identity.

In the structured modern world of the past, the world of Fordist production methods, top down organisational hierarchies, established career paths and lasting marriages, it was a rational survival strategy to learn the rules and structure of society and adjust one's behaviour accordingly in the expectation that this would serve one's interests in the long term. In the context of liquid modernity, attempting this strategy would be detrimental. Survival in the contemporary situation requires unending trials and errors, learning, unlearning and relearning, and the abandonment of the idea of a single life project.

In structured traditional societies, and to some extent in modern societies, the causes of private troubles were often obvious to the individual as they were experienced directly. For example, the cause of individual hunger was obvious enough – a lack of food – although how to solve the problem may not have been quite so straightforward. In contemporary liquid modernity, new socially generated risks, in particular globalisation leading to the dismantling of social bonds, safety networks, and collective projects, are not so directly seen or easily understood by the individual. The effects of individualisation are those of growing individual uncertainty and anxiety, whilst at the same time an understanding of the processes bringing this about is less easy to recognise through individual experiences. Individualisation in contemporary society increases the rift between private experiences of anxiety and the capacity to understand the broader social causes, promoting the tendency in individuals to retreat into a world of private concerns.

For Bauman, unlike postmodernists, rational sociological analysis and intervention can help remedy the situation. The current time is one of urgent need for a reinvigorated sociological imagination. Detailed sociological understanding of the contemporary condition of liquid modernity is needed to help re-establish the connection between private experiences and their social causes and to guide remedial action. This requires the development of new sociological theories and concepts, not the use of what Beck refers to as 'zombie terms' such as social class and the family which are more applicable to the conditions of the modernist past.

2 Informational society

Manuel Castells argues that the impact of new information technology in the context of globalisation is having a profound effect on society and that time may be running out for our opportunity to shape its effects. For Castells, capitalism remains the social driving force, but the form that it is taking is changing. A key factor in this change is the ever sprawling internet which gives rise to networked communication. According to Castells, such technology is bringing about a new form of capitalism which is far less based on industrial production and more on the maximisation of investment opportunities via instant access and response to the condition of global markets. In the face of such changes, old command economies have had to adapt or fall.

In the informational society, Castells sees social conflict becoming displaced from the class conflict of an earlier era. Under industrial capitalism, organised labour could sometimes check the power of capital as both were locked together and relatively immobile. However, under informational capitalism, capital is global and mobile whereas labour remains more locally rooted. Labour has therefore become relatively powerless and conflict has been displaced from that between classes to that of protest groups, themselves organised through the use of modern technology.

3 Hybrid societies and reconfigured relationships

Sociology emerged historically to reflect a close association between nation states and societies. Founding sociological theory linked the social, society and human, and, even in positivist theory, established clear distinctions between the physical science of objects and the social science of societies. For John Urry, processes of globalisation and technological modernisation require a fundamental rethinking of society and sociology.

Globalisation has weakened the society / nation tie as new networks without centres, in particular based on the internet, have emerged to enhance communication across national borders. As well as a growing separation of the social from nation states, social 'relations' themselves are increasingly made up of a mix of human agency and material objects and technologies. Urry suggests that in this sense we cannot now talk about uniquely human societies but of 'hybrid societies' – networks of connection involving humans and technological objects which change the human experience in ways that we need to understand. Consequently, a change is needed in sociological focus to recognise 'reconfigured' humans – a reconfigured sociology is required to account for the impact of technology and objects on 'relationships' which makes them less authentically social.

What form may a reconstituted sociology take? Urry speculates that what is needed is a move from the study of society based social relationships to the study of high tech globally networked communications as dynamic systems which can be analysed as structures and flows. Theories and methods need to be developed that enable the analysis of connections between human powers and material objects and that track communication flows. As new technologies such as travel, the internet, and the mobile phone have accelerated the experience of time, analysis needs to take account of instantaneous time rather than the traditional exclusive preoccupation with clock time.

As globalisation enhances cosmopolitanism, it is likely that emerging global standards will effect how people think and behave. This will enhance reflective modernisation and sociology will need to reconfigure itself in a global and cosmopolitan way in a post 'societal' era.

4 Society of manufactured risk

In this section will be focussing on theories put forward by Anthony Giddens and Ulrich Beck. Both of these writers adopt a transformationist position on globalisation – they argue that globalisation is bringing about profound changes and new problems and risks, but remain optimistic that these changes can be rationally understood and that positive intervention to improve society is possible. This transformationist stance therefore links closely to their characterisation of contemporary society as 'high modern' or 'second modern' rather than postmodern.

Giddens, in 'Runaway World', periodises history into traditional, modern and high modern phases. Traditional societies were agricultural based. Life for most people was linked to working the land and lived out within small local communities. The tempo of life was dominated by the repetitions and constraints of the seasons and ritual played an important part in peoples' lives. Nature related work tasks at a local level moulded the measurement and perception of distance and time to season and locality.

The dawn of the modern era came in the seventeenth and eighteenth centuries with the Enlightenment. Science and rational thinking were applied to question the superstitions and social constraints of traditional societies. Faith in social progress was invested in the capacity of science to fashion a rationally based social order. Scientific advances included the development of mechanical devices that enabled time to be precisely divided up and universalised. With industrialisation, this standardised time became attached to new routines as work became extracted from the tempo of nature and the countryside and increasingly governed by man made tempo of the factory and the office. The effect of these changes was the experience of the compression of distance and time.

A process linked to the compression of distance and time was the disembedding of social relations. In traditional societies, social relations operated largely at a personal, face-to-face level within the context of small local communities. The development of impersonal institutions accompanied modernisation. These mediated social relationships involving, for example, the exchange of news and money. News could be widely disseminated through printed materials and financial transactions mediated through the institution of banks. These changes allowed such exchanges to become extracted from direct involvement in social encounters between parties.

Giddens argues that the freeing of social relationships from the constraints of traditional society led to life becoming more 'reflexive'. Social relations in traditional societies held certainties in the sense that life was parochial and opportunities were limited. These certainties were upset by the processes of modernisation which brought change and opened up opportunity. Uncertainty encourages reflexivity – the need of people to continuously monitor and interpret their own behaviour and that of others as they make assessments of risks and possibilities that their environment offers. However, if tradition is viewed in terms of behavioural rituals and repetitions which give life form, modern society was also characterised by its own traditions. The need for reflexivity was thus limited.

For Giddens, what has transpired more recently is that change, uncertainty and risk have now reached a new level. The 1970s witnessed an advance in the interconnectedness of the world as advances in technology extended the range and speed of communications and travel. This further compression of distance and time was associated with globalisation and was the hallmark of a new stage in society which Giddens refers to as high modern. Now, accompanying globalisation, change, uncertainty and risk take on new dimensions. In an increasingly interconnected world, unexpected happenings in one part, such as currency fluctuations, can impact globally and heighten instability. For individuals, uncertainty and constant reflexivity are part of high modern globalised life which accompany an extension of individual autonomy.

Globalisation brings with it new risks. Giddens explains the changing nature of risk. Traditional societies were vulnerable to risks of nature such as drought, flood and storm. These dangers Giddens refers to as natural or 'external' risks. The drive and industriousness behind capitalist modernisation saw a leap in the imposition of human action onto nature, creating new problems such as pollution and contagious diseases associated with crowded and unhygienic living conditions in towns and cities. However, because life in modern society was still structured and constrained by traditions and our knowledge of risks could be calculated, some degree of security could be made possible through insurance.

In the high modern global context, our level of intervention into nature has brought about new dangers in the form of 'manufactured' risk. Global warming and its likely consequences is one such manufactured risk and others include the unknown effects of genetic modification of crops and the possibility of economic meltdown. These risks are different from external risks in that there is no experience by which outcomes can be calculated and therefore against which insurance can be provided. We have created through our interventions in nature a fluid and uncertain environment which is at the end of nature and traditions and risks getting out of our control. Given the level of individual autonomy, risk and need for constant reflexivity in contemporary society, there is attraction for some in turning to compulsive behaviour or fundamentalist beliefs (phenomena which are both on the increase) as attempts to close down the uncertainties and anxiety of individual autonomy through retreat to forms of ritual and tradition.

It is to the challenge of this environment of man-made risks that new and enlightened responses and new policies and forms of governmental organisation are required. Reflexivity is necessary at a governmental and global level given the global nature of the risks faced. Difficult as it is, Giddens argues that appropriate new institutions and interventions and can still be rationally guided by a sociology that is up to the mark.

Ulrich Beck places the changing nature of risk at the centre of his analysis and divides modernity into two phases - first modernity and second modernity. Prior to first industrial modernity, risks such as famine were a consequence of nature and largely beyond the control of man. The first phase of modernity was pre-globalised industrialisation. At this stage of development, scientific advances such as in new farming techniques and medical treatments assisted in the control of natural risk. However, the creation of wealth through the growing intervention in nature created new risks such as pollution. Within this first phase of modernisation, risk remained relatively localised and calculable. Uncertainty could be reined in. For Beck, this world was adequately explained in the Parsonian functionalist model in which nation based societies operated as systems which adjusted toward equilibrium and institutions such as the family and the church imposed a degree of certainty into peoples' lives.

The second phase of modernity is marked by globalisation and cosmopolitanism. The latter is a broadening of our experience and imagination fostered by globalisation and evidenced in such phenomena as growing numbers of bi-national couples, more people speaking different languages and the operations of transnational military forces. Globalised second modernity brings a much greater fluidity of life experience. A key feature of this phase of modernity is that uncertainty cannot so readily be reduced to calculated risk. This is because societies have reached the stage where technological advance has led to the creation of new manufactured uncertainties where technological developments attempting to solve manufactured risks introduce their own uncertainties or unanticipated undesirable consequences. Paradoxically, as globalisation has enabled an ever-increasing dominance of nature, the new risks created take on a more challenging global dimension, as in the case of global warming.

Whilst the social structure of first stage modernity constrained individuals, family, class and religion provided a framework of identity and stability to peoples' lives. In second stage modernity, liberation from past constraints leaves individuals vulnerable to new insecurities. For all of the benefits that contemporary society brings, risk becomes so much a feature of life that we can characterise society as 'risk society'. In risk society, individuals are increasingly conscious that they don't readily know or control the consequences of their actions. This can affect the very possibility of predicting or controlling their own biographies in a world of high levels of marital breakdown and flexible labour markets. Actors have to negotiate their life conditions in new social conditions in which risks and uncertainties are transferred to the individual who has no socially handed down playscript to manage relationships but must respond 'reflexively' by continuously weighing up circumstances and available options and adapting response strategies to attempt to promote security. This may include weighing up how behaviour can be changed to reduce global warming, considering whether it is safe at a particular time to travel by plane or considering precautions to avoid contracting sexually transmitted disease.

For Beck, the world has moved on since that explained by Parsonian functionalism. Just as peoples' national experiences and perspectives have been eclipsed by global and cosmopolitan perspectives, so sociology must move on from the methodological nationalism of its founding fathers to methodological cosmopolitanism. It can only do so through engaging in painstaking research across the world and developing theories able to conceptualise contemporary conditions and move beyond what have now become the 'zombie categories' it has inherited from the first modernity, such as the family, social class, career and the nation. By so doing, sociology may be able to assist the process of reflexivity in response to risk at both individual and governmental level.

Recommended Texts

Abercrombie, N. & Warde, A. *et al* (2006) *Contemporary British Society*. Cambridge, Polity

Allan, K. (2005) *Explorations in Classical Sociological Theory*. California: Pine Forge

Alvesson, M. (2002) *Postmodernism and Social Research*. Buckingham: Open University

Berger, P. (1999) *Invitation to Sociology*. New York: Anchor

Bilton, T. *et al* (2002) *Introductory Sociology*. Basingstoke: Palgrave Macmillan

Browne, K. (2005) *An Introduction to Sociology*. Cambridge: Polity

Calhoun, C. *et al* (ed) (2002) *Contemporary Sociological Theory*. Oxford: Blackwell

Cuff, E.C. *et al* (2001) *Perspectives in Sociology.* London: Routledge

Devine, F. & Heath, S. (1999) *Sociological Research Methods in Context*. Basingstoke: Macmillan

Fulcher, J., & Scott, J. (2007) *Sociology*. Oxford: Oxford University Press

Gane, N. (2004) *The Future of Social Theory.* London: Continuum

Giddens, A. (2000) *The Third Way and Its Critics.* Cambridge: Polity

Giddens, A. (2002) *Runaway World.* London: Profile

Giddens, A. (2008) *Sociology*. Cambridge: Polity

Giddens, A. *et al* (ed) (1995) *The Polity Reader in Social Theory.* Cambridge: Polity Press

Hall, S. *et al* (ed) (1993) *Modernity and its Futures*. Cambridge: Polity

Haralambos, M., & Holborn, M. (2008) *Sociology Themes and Perspectives*. London: HarperCollins

Held, D. (ed) (2000) *A Globalizing World?* New York: Routledge

Held, D. (ed) (2003) *The Global Transformations Reader.* Cambridge: Polity

Kirby, M. et al (2000) *Sociology in Perspective*. Oxford: Heinemann

Lloyd, J. (2001) *The Protest Ethic*. London: Demos

Marsh, I. (ed) (2006) *Sociology, Making Sense of Society*. London: Pearson

McIntosh, I., & Punch, S. (2005) *Get Set for Sociology.* Edinburgh: Edinburgh University Press

McNeill, P. & Chapman, S. (2005) *Research Methods*. Abingdon: Routledge

Mills, C. Wright (2000) *The Sociological Imagination*. New York: Oxford University Press Inc.

Monahan, S.C. (ed) (2001) *Sociology of Religion*. New Jersey: Pearson

Punch, K.F. (2005) *Introduction to Social Research*. London: Sage

Ritzer, G. (2007) *Sociological Theory*. Boston: McGraw-Hill

Seldon, A. (ed) (2001) *The Blair Effect*. London: Little, Brown & Co.

Slattery, M. (2003) *Key Ideas in Sociology*. Cheltenham: Nelson Thornes

Swingewood, A. (2000) *A Short History of Sociological Thought*. Basingstoke: Palgrave

Index

Printed in the United Kingdom
by Lightning Source UK Ltd.
133567UK00001B/361-387/P